LOSS *of* FAITH

LOSS *of* FAITH

How the Air-India Bombers

Got Away With Murder

KIM BOLAN

Library and Archives Canada Cataloguing in Publication
Bolan, Kim, 1959–
Loss of faith : how the Air-India bombers got away with murder / Kim Bolan.

ISBN 0-7710-1130-X

1. Air-India Flight 182 Bombing Incident, 1985. 2. Terrorism – Canada.
3. Bombing investigation – British Columbia. 4. Trials (Murder) – British
Columbia – Vancouver. I. Title.

HV6433.C3B64 2005   363.12'465'0916337   C2005-903697-4

We acknowledge the financial support of the Government of Canada through the
Book Publishing Industry Development Program and that of the Government of
Ontario through the Ontario Media Development Corporation's Ontario Book
Initiative. We further acknowledge the support of the Canada Council for the
Arts and the Ontario Arts Council for our publishing program.

Typeset in Bembo by M&S, Toronto
Printed and bound in Canada

This book is printed on acid-free paper that is 100% recycled,
ancient-forest friendly (100% post-consumer recycled).

McClelland & Stewart Ltd.
75 Sherbourne Street
Toronto, Ontario
M5A 2P9
www.mcclelland.com

1 2 3 4 5   09 08 07 06 05

To the families of the victims of the Air-India bombing,
for their twenty-year pursuit of the truth

"Truth is the highest virtue, but higher still is truthful living."
– Guru Nanak

Contents

Prologue

ON JUNE 23, 2005, Prime Minister Paul Martin was in Ahakista, Ireland, where he joined relatives of the victims of the 1985 bombings that thrust Canada into the age of terrorism. He was there in an attempt to correct decades of political inaction. Hundreds of the victims' relatives, rescue workers, locals, and Canadian politicians of all stripes had gathered to commemorate the twentieth anniversary of the death of 329 people aboard Air-India Flight 182 and two baggage handlers at Narita airport in Japan.

"We are not naive. We are not ignorant of the world and its sorrows, but this act of evil defies comprehension," Martin said. "It was an unimaginable loss. It was your loss. It was the nation's loss. Make no mistake. The flight may have been Air-India's, it may have taken place off the coast of Ireland, but in so many ways, this is a Canadian tragedy."

This was the first time since the bombings that a Canadian prime minister had thought to attend the annual service marking the most dastardly act of terror in the country's history. The gesture was appreciated by the victims' relatives, but Martin did little to answer the questions uppermost in their minds: How and why had their country let them down?

Canada failed to stop the bombers as they attempted to take revenge against their birth nation, India, for its perceived persecution of the Sikh minority. Canada failed to recognize that the majority of the 331 victims, while of Indian origin, were Canadians. Canada failed for years to catch those involved and, when charges were finally laid, Canada's justice system showed it could not deal with the complexities of a terrorism plot or with suspects determined not to be exposed, charged, or convicted.

Within three weeks of Martin's acknowledgement that the bombings were "a Canadian tragedy," his deputy prime minister, Anne McLellan, alienated the Air-India victims' families by her comments on the July 7, 2005, terrorist bombings in London. "I do not believe that Canadians are as psychologically prepared for a terrorist attack as I think probably we all should be," McLellan told reporters. "I think we have, perhaps for too long, thought that these were things that happened somewhere else. But Canadians are not immune."

Had McLellan forgotten about the Air-India bombings? Or has she, like many Canadians, underplayed their significance because they primarily affected people who weren't perceived to be our own – brown people with accents whom we didn't accept as Canadians? But they are our own. Our own victims. Our own terrorists. Our own Indo-Canadian community ripped apart and tarnished by the acts of a fanatical few who have manipulated the laws of Canada for twenty years.

Terrorism seemed to enter the North American consciousness only on September 11, 2001, when New York and Washington, D.C., were targeted by religious extremists. Canada developed an anti-terrorism law in response to these attacks, but not in response to the 1985 Air-India bombings. Canada cracked down on terrorist fundraising here only after the 9/11 attacks and not when our own country suffered its worst act of terrorism. Canada waited until June 2003 to ban Sikh extremist groups linked to the Air-India bombing and other crimes on Canadian soil – eighteen years after Air-India Flight 182 was demolished in mid-air by a B.C.–built bomb.

As Canadians, we need to look closely at how we responded to this horrible, unprecedented crime. We need to ask if our own laws and policies, including official multiculturalism, contributed to "this act of evil." We need to know how and why the bombers got away with mass murder.

When I started as a reporter at the *Vancouver Sun* on May 28, 1984, fresh out of journalism school, I had never heard of Sikhism's holiest shrine – the Golden Temple in Amritsar, Punjab. I knew Sikhism was a religion from India, but like most Canadians, I knew little else about it. I certainly knew nothing of the extraordinary history of the Sikh community in Canada, a history of standing up for justice, immigration, and voting rights, and against racism.

Six days after I started at the *Sun*, the Indian Army stormed the Golden Temple to rid it of violent militants who had taken it over under the leadership of the charismatic extremist Jarnail Singh Bhindranwale and were demanding a separate homeland for Sikhs. Bhindranwale and his supporters were killed, but so were hundreds of innocent pilgrims. Canadian journalists were suddenly covering massive street demonstrations by Sikhs in Vancouver, Toronto, Calgary, and Ottawa. I was one of the many sent to find out what was going on.

I found that the Sikhs I spoke with were only too willing to share their culture, religion, and political views with me. They also taught me the basic tenets of their faith – equality for all and the need to fight against discrimination and oppression. They stressed the importance of *sewa*, or service, to the community and the nation.

The reaction of Canadian Sikhs to the storming of the temple brewed for months. There were protests, violent clashes with police, burnings of Indian prime minister Indira Gandhi in effigy, and jubilation when she was assassinated on October 31, 1984. Moderate Sikhs who criticized Bhindranwale were threatened and beaten. And then on June 23, 1985, a bomb blast ripped through Tokyo's Narita Airport, killing two baggage handlers. Less than an hour later, an Air-India flight en route from Toronto to New Delhi via Bombay exploded off the coast of Ireland.

As a young journalist, I was overwhelmed by some of the things I covered that year. I had never before seen people openly express their joy at a political assassination. I had never before listened to violent rhetoric calling for revenge. Like McLellan, I had thought Canada was immune from international terrorism. In June 1985, I believed I lived in a country that would do whatever could be done to right injustices. I believed that the truth about who perpetrated the bombings would be exposed and that the guilty would be punished. I believed that journalists had a vital role to play in uncovering the plot and in ensuring that our political leaders, intelligence service, and police forces spared no effort to catch and convict the cowards who planted those bombs.

Many people have tried to expose or uncover the truth about the twin bombings of June 23, 1985. Dedicated police officers, prosecutors, members of the Sikh community, and journalists, motivated by the enormous losses of the victims' families, have tried to shine the light on the darkest corners of Canada's secret terrorist world. And I have covered related events now for twenty years, becoming, to my chagrin, a character in this convoluted story.

In the intervening years, occasional news reports about the bombings have appeared, my own among them, but they have been just dots, few and sometimes far between. This book has given me a large-enough canvas to connect those dots, to fill in the blanks with what I have learned over the years, both first- and second-hand.

I travelled to India four times to try to understand the root cause of what was happening in Punjab. I met with Sikh separatist leaders there, as well as in Pakistan, England, the United States, and across Canada. Over the years I met with as many family members of the victims as I could, as often as I could. Many members of the Sikh community have taken risks to share information with me, especially the woman I call Rani Kumar, whose true identity I have to protect, Narinder Singh Gill, Kulwarn Singh Parmar, Dr. Jagjit Singh Chohan, and Dave and Rupinder Hayer, who lost their journalist father, Tara Singh Hayer, in 1998. In the early days of this story, I learned a great deal from passionate journalists such as Terry Glavin, Nancy Knickerbocker, and Tom Barrett. In recent years, CBC journalist Terry Milewski has inspired me and provided invaluable assistance in completing this book. I have spent many hours sitting and talking with witnesses and with the suspects themselves. And there are times I have been scared of the consequences of hunting down the truth. Two of my fellow journalists have already died for knowing too much.

I kept at the story because I am more stubborn than afraid. And I have never felt alone in my desire to uncover the truth. I have been helped, encouraged, and at times comforted, not only by other reporters, by the victims' relatives, and by witnesses, but also by those investigators, prosecutors, and court officials who remain as anxious as anyone that the truth finally be told. They have shared with me what they can of their findings and of their own views, and I am immensely grateful to them all. In this account I have also drawn from testimony given at the trial and from documents I have obtained under Access to Information laws.

One of the suspects I talked to several times, the late Hardial Singh Johal, once told me I had the perfect surname for what I was doing. As we sat in the living room of his East Vancouver house in 1998, he explained that in Punjabi Bolan means "to speak a lot." He laughed.

I never imagined that I would still be "speaking a lot" about the Air-India bombing all these years later – not because it wasn't important, but because I assumed it would be over by now, that the perpetrators would have long since been brought to justice.

That hasn't happened. Canada has failed. *Loss of Faith* is an attempt to explain how and why.

CHAPTER I

June 1985

T HE LITTLE BOY was waiting patiently to see inside the
cockpit. He might have been nine-year-old Kuldip Singh
Uppal of Vancouver, who was flying with his widowed mother,
Sukhwinder, and ten-year-old sister, Parminder, to see his grandparents in Punjab. He might have been Deepak Turlapati, aged
eleven, of Toronto, travelling with his teenaged brother, Sanjay,
for a summer holiday at the Delhi home of relatives, where the
boys spent much of their early childhood.

Capt. Narendra Singh Hanse, the pilot of Air-India Flight 182,
didn't know the child's name. But he had agreed to let the boy
peer out over the Atlantic Ocean with the unobstructed vista of
an aviator as the Boeing 747 approached the coast of Ireland,
heading to London's Heathrow Airport for a refuelling stop.

This was June 23, 1985, just before 7:00 a.m. Greenwich Mean
Time.

The purser asked Hanse, a fifty-seven-year-old veteran of Air-
India who was close to retirement, when it would be okay to

bring the excited child forward. Hanse suggested waiting about fifteen minutes more, according to the voice data recorder.

The flight had left Montreal almost two hours late the night before. It had earlier been delayed at Toronto's Pearson Airport, where the flight originated, while technical crews loaded an extra engine for transport back to India. It had malfunctioned during a previous Air-India flight to Canada. It needed to be fixed.

Packed with 307 passengers and a crew of 22, Air-India Flight 182 made up some time during its routine six-hour transatlantic crossing while passengers dined on dishes that are traditional aboard India's national airline – curries and koftas, dal and roti. Chai, the spicy sweet tea, was served throughout the flight. Some passengers attempted to get a little sleep. A Hindi movie entertained those who stayed awake. Small children cuddled their dolls or scribbled away in colouring books as the plane sliced through the dark night sky.

There were six babies and toddlers aboard. There were more women and children than men, as it was the end of the school year: 77 kids aged three to twelve, 59 teenagers, 106 women, and 81 men. Many of the adults were seniors. Many whole families were travelling together. Some of the passengers were Indians returning home after visiting family in Canada. Most were Canadians of Indian origin en route to their native country to visit relatives.

In the morning light, Hanse was thinking about checking in with Irish air traffic controllers, who would give him his route into London. The skies were clear. Hanse's co-pilot, Satwinder Singh Bhinder – a handsome baptized Sikh who had been told he would soon be taking over command of his own plane – was concerned about those passengers who were passing the time with drinks. All alcoholic beverages had to be sealed up before they got to London. It was required by international duty regulations.

"Everybody is having whisky and beer," Bhinder said to Hanse.

"It's a hard-core problem," Hanse replied, before their conversation was interrupted by Shannon Air Traffic Control (ATC), near Limerick, Ireland.

It was now 7:08 a.m. and Flight 182 was headed due east, flying at thirty-one thousand feet – almost six miles above the earth. Its position was fifty degrees north, twelve degrees west.

Bhinder was the first to speak to Irish controller Michael Quinn.

"Air-India 182. Good morning," Bhinder said cheerfully, his voice recorded on a scratchy tape made by Shannon ATC.

"Air-India 182. Good morning." Quinn replied. "Squawk two zero, zero five and go ahead, please."

Bhinder gave the plane's location, and Quinn responded with the designated route into London.

"Right, sir," Bhinder said.

Quinn, a black-haired man with thick eyebrows, continued to monitor the Air-India plane on radar, along with several others that were flying through Irish air space. Air-India was stacked beneath two other planes – a Canadian Pacific (CP) jet was flying two thousand feet above it and a Trans World Airlines (TWA) flight was another two thousand feet higher. For all his experience, Quinn couldn't have imagined what was about to happen overhead.

A suitcase bomb detonated in cargo hold 52 in the rear left side of Flight 182. It was five times more powerful than the bomb that would bring down another Boeing 747 over Lockerbie, Scotland, three years later. It blew a hole in the fuselage, and in a fraction of a second, specks of material escaped from the hole. Before another second had passed, a huge crack raced toward the nose and the tail of the plane. The belly of the aircraft split open. Everyone and everything was thrown out. Some passengers were likely already dead, killed by the impact of the explosion, and most probably lost consciousness or died as they started to plunge toward the ocean. But some people were alive when they hit the water. Autopsies showed that they had drowned.

What was left of the plane, named *Kanishka* after a Buddhist king known for his political and military might, broke up in the air. Vertical cracks travelled upwards from the long one running forward and aft. The front end and the tail of the plane fell off. Before two seconds had passed, major pieces of the plane were disintegrating as they fell.

At 7:13 a.m., the blip representing Air-India Flight 182 disappeared from the radar screen in front of Michael Quinn. There was no distress call from the pilots. Quinn was immediately alarmed, though he had a faint hope that maybe, just maybe, the Air-India blip was obscured by the other planes flying above it. Air traffic controllers attempted to make radio contact more than a dozen times. There was only silence.

Quinn immediately contacted the other pilots in the vicinity and asked if any of them could see *Kanishka*. The TWA pilot reported that he could see a vapour trail where the Air-India flight should have passed. But no plane. On the edge of panic, Quinn asked a British Airways pilot to scan the ocean below for wreckage, but visibility was too poor.

Quinn called the marine rescue co-ordination centre at Shannon Airport and gave them the plane's last known location. He knew there was no hope.

At the same time, on the other side of the globe, at Tokyo's busy Narita Airport, there was also panic. Less than an hour earlier, a suitcase bomb had exploded as workers were unloading CP Air Flight 003 from Vancouver. Baggage handlers Hideharu Koda and Hideo Asano were killed instantly. They may have dropped the bag, which was tagged for Air-India Flight 301 to Bangkok. No one knows for sure.

Four of their co-workers were seriously injured. There was chaos. The explosion shook the entire airport, a major hub and gateway to Asia. Holes were blown in the concrete walkways and metal containers some distance away. The area was strewn with debris from suitcases, luggage containers, and light fixtures. Some of the bags were burned. There was blood on the ground. Mangled carts and metal fragments were everywhere.

Ambulances had already whisked away the wounded, and teams of Japanese investigators in white suits and surgical masks were scouring for clues. Some were wearing gas masks. They sifted through the white powder from fire extinguishers in their search for scraps of evidence.

As the pieces of Air-India Flight 182 began to sink thousands of feet below the Atlantic Ocean, Japanese investigators started to collect the first of the thirty-two hundred fragments they would eventually gather. Among them were pieces of something that looked like a radio or a tuner. There were bits of plastic with AM and FM markings and a volume control knob. There were wires and pieces from a clock. There were tiny particles of green cloth tape, masking tape, and clear tape. One bit of cardboard had a tiny M on it, intact. It proved to be a vital clue later on.

As desperate as the scene at Narita was, the airport authorities realized it could have been much worse. If the bomb had detonated aboard the CP Air flight, or on the Air-India flight about to depart, the death toll would have been hundreds higher.

A week earlier, Nina and Ashok Rao were at their house in a pleasant suburb of New Delhi. The spacious two-storey home was named Sandeep after their two nephews in Canada: fourteen-year-old Sanjay and eleven-year-old Deepak Turlapati. The boys were as dear to them as their own two daughters, and they were eager to welcome them upon their arrival from Toronto for their summer holiday. The Raos had planned to take the boys on a trip to the mountain resort of Shimla.

The boys' mother, Dr. Padmini Turlapati, was completing her residency in Newfoundland, and their father, Narayana, was an accountant working overseas.

Living as they did in the political capital of India, the Raos had heard the militant Sikh talk about boycotting the country's national airline. Some Sikhs were planning a two-week uprising called a *ghallughara* in retaliation for the Indian Army's assault on the Golden Temple, Sikhism's holiest shrine, a year earlier. Nina had suggested to her husband that he warn his sister in Canada to change the boys' tickets from Air-India to another airline. But Ashok didn't see the point of disrupting travel plans that had already been made, especially far away in Canada.

Sanjay and Deepak Turlapati had spent much of their early years with their aunt and uncle and their grandparents while their parents worked in Nigeria. Then, in 1982, the Turlapatis were accepted as immigrants to Canada. The Raos and their two daughters missed the boys terribly and were eager to see them again after three years.

At the same time, some fourteen hundred kilometres from Delhi, Amarjit Kaur Bhinder was happily living in Bombay with her forty-year-old pilot husband, Satwinder, and their two children, Jasleen and Ashamdip. The couple loved to go out dancing and to see movies. Satwinder was always asking his wife to come on little trips with him whenever airline tickets were available. He had wanted her to fly with him to Toronto. It would only take a few days, he said. It was Satwinder's first time on the Canadian route, and his last as co-pilot of the Boeing 747.

But Amarjit was reluctant to go. She was not sure why. There was no good reason. She only knew that she didn't want to leave the children. Two days before the trip, she decided to stay home. Satwinder pleaded with her to join him, right up to the time he left, but she resisted. The couple had never discussed the possibility of a terrorist attack against the airline – no pilot likes to bring up such things. Amarjit didn't want to think about it.

In the United States, Detroit engineer Parkash Bedi was preparing to send his family on an overseas trip without him. He always travelled back to India around American Thanksgiving with his wife, Saroj, nine-year-old son, Jatin, and teenaged daughter, Anu. But in June 1985, the family decided that Saroj and the children should go without him to visit her father, who was in ill health. The family was also contemplating a move back to India to open a factory, and wanted to see whether the children could bear the heat of an Indian summer.

What the children did not know was that their father planned to surprise them a week later by arriving in India for a big party at a five-star hotel to celebrate Anu's fifteenth birthday on July 4.

Bedi had booked his family on a British Airways flight out of Detroit, but the connection to a flight to Delhi was not great. A few weeks before the trip, a friend in Toronto suggested he change the tickets for the direct Air-India flight from Toronto. That way his wife and children would not have to change planes or endure long waits. Bedi agreed, and another friend paid for the tickets with his American Express card.

Many others were also preparing for their trip. For some it would be an annual summer pilgrimage to the homeland to visit relatives. For Sukhwinder Kaur Uppal, a young widow living in

South Vancouver with her two children, it was a trip she had scrimped and saved for, for years. She was so excited to be taking her son, Kuldip, and daughter, Parminder, back home that she changed the original flight to leave a few days earlier. Her sister-in-law, who worked for a travel agent, was able to arrange new tickets for Air-India Flight 182 and the connecting CP Air flight out of Vancouver. Now the family would travel on June 22, 1985.

The Uppals lived in a basement suite near Vancouver's Ross Street temple, and on the morning of the trip, they stopped by, as is the Sikh tradition. They bowed their heads before the Sikh holy book, the Guru Granth Sahib, and prayed for safe passage.

Mohanrani Kachroo was leaving the daycare centre she ran in Saskatoon to return to India for the first time in seven years to see her family and tell them about her exciting new life on the Canadian prairie. The fifty-seven-year-old mother of three was making the trip alone, leaving behind her husband, Nagindra, and her nearly grown children. She loved her life in Canada, where she had finally attained equality as a woman and had been able to open a small business and earn her own living. She was eager to tell her family how well she was doing.

Mukul Paliwal of Ottawa was fifteen when his family decided he should make his first solo trip to India. He was going to see his grandmother in Agra – where the Taj Mahal stands – and to study the tabla, a classical Indian instrument at which he excelled.

In the days leading up to the Air-India flight, some ticket holders were inexplicably feeling ill at ease.

When Amarjit Bhinder put her husband's white pilot uniform into the washing machine, sparks flew and smoke billowed from it. She considered this a terrible premonition on the day her husband was due to return to Bombay on his Air-India flight. Her legs shivered and she felt upset for several hours.

Half a world away, Parkash Bedi and his wife, Saroj, also felt troubled about the trip she would be taking with the children. Two days before their departure, one of Saroj's friends visited their Detroit home to discuss getting a blouse made in India. The three were sitting at the table when Saroj told her friend about a recurring nightmare. She was flying through the air with her children in her arms and was suddenly going down, down in a black hole. Don't worry, the friend assured Saroj, this was only because she would be flying overseas without her husband for the first time. But Parkash also had misgivings about the trip.

It was dreary and rainy as he drove his family from Detroit to Toronto for their flight. He had always got lost on the trip to the airport before, but on June 22 he reached Pearson International without a hitch. As Bedi helped his family check in their baggage, the Air-India clerk mentioned that the X-ray machine was broken but still took the luggage, without explaining how it would be examined. Bedi's son, Jatin, asked about a window seat and was told the only one available was in the smoking section. Jatin said he didn't mind, and the boy's seat was changed.

As Bedi waited in the Air-India lineup to say goodbye to his family, he noticed in the line ahead of them an elderly turbaned Sikh man with a picnic basket. He commented to his friend, who had met them at the airport, that this man might have a bomb and be planning to sacrifice himself and kill everybody. He didn't know why he said this. He had many Sikh friends. He contributed to the Sikh temple in his Detroit suburb of Troy and took his family there and to the Hindu temple.

A short distance away, the British Airways queue was filled with Sikhs. There were hardly any Sikhs in the Air-India line. Bedi asked his friend why all the Sikhs were flying with British Airways. That was when Bedi heard for the first time that the problems in India had been reverberating in Canada, and that extremist Sikhs had warned people not to fly Air-India. Bedi panicked. His wife and children had already entered the restricted area of the airport, so he begged a guard to let him through. But he did not have a ticket and was turned away.

Within an hour of Michael Quinn's call to the marine rescue centre, merchant ships, fishing boats, and naval vessels were racing out to where the airplane went down in a desperate search for survivors.

The merchant vessel *Laurentian Forest* was carrying newsprint from Quebec to Dublin when it received an emergency call about 8:30 a.m. GMT. The ship was already in the area and soon found the nightmarish scene: the ocean was strewn with bodies and debris.

Scottish-born Daniel Brown was just twenty-three. He steered the ship close to the wreckage. Then he and other *Laurentian* crew members agreed to go into the rough sea to search for survivors and gather the bodies of those who had not survived. The men were lowered over the side in a small lifeboat. But the ocean would not co-operate with their rescue efforts. Huge waves repeatedly threw the lifeboat up against the ship's side, and they had to drop some of the bodies they had in their grasp to avoid being crushed against their own ship. At first, the waves were just six or seven feet high. But then a squall forced the swells upwards to fifteen feet. The *Laurentian* was acting as a barrier, trapping the bodies and wreckage against its side.

For the first few hours, the young crew still hoped to find someone alive. But they soon realized that only death surrounded them. Brown looked around and thought that the families of these poor people didn't yet know what had happened. Here he was in the middle of the ocean, looking at absolute devastation, and their families would be thinking they had landed in London.

Brown saw body parts. Some limbs came off when the men tried to pull the bodies into the lifeboat. The horror was unimaginable. But they knew they must not think about it. They knew they must keep working. Hour after hour they struggled to pull the people in. The bodies were slippery, covered with oily fluids from the airplane. Bones were smashed; there was nothing to grip.

Mark Stagg, aged twenty-six, was working hard beside Brown. The first body he pulled into the boat was of a teenaged boy. All his clothes were intact. He looked perfect, except that he was missing one Hush Puppy shoe. Stagg stared at his face, feeling sick that he was not able to save this child.

The seamen knew the window for their work was short. Bodies sink after twenty-four hours when they become waterlogged. Brown and Stagg helped recover seven bodies in all, including a little girl who had barely a mark on her. An older man, probably a Sikh, with long loose hair and a beard, had a look of terror frozen on his face. Brown thought that the man must have known what was happening to him.

There was a stench of jet fuel, and smoke from search aircraft clouded the air. A Royal Air Force (RAF) Nimrod reconnaissance plane dropped flares to guide rescue vessels and helicopters to the wreckage, located about 130 kilometres off the Irish coast.

A Sea King helicopter, also from the RAF, was quick to respond to the calls for help. Squadron commander John Brooks watched bodies popping to the surface. He saw three corpses, then six or seven, then a dozen. His crew zeroed in on the tiny body of what they thought was a baby. As they got closer, they realized it was a doll. They also saw suitcases, seats, trolleys, and bottles. And a violin case that belonged to an Ottawa girl.

The Sea King crew began a dangerous and difficult exercise that continued for hours. Mark Tait, a winch man, was the first to be lowered to the sea from the helicopter by a long cable. He had to work almost telepathically because he couldn't hear the others. Tait had a strap, like a horse collar, that he threw around the nearest victim's torso. He wrapped his legs around the body and pulled with all his might. The body was hard to hold on to because it had no muscle tone and its bones had shattered. Those bodies whose clothes had not been ripped off by the fall were weighed down by garments soaked with oil, hydraulic fluid, blood, and water.

The Irish Navy ship *Aisling*, under the command of thirty-five-year-old Capt. James Robinson, arrived just after noon. En route to the crash site, the forty-eight men aboard the *Aisling* were hopeful they could find survivors and prepared the sick bay. The smoke from the flares made Robinson think the scene resembled a war. When the ship arrived, he was overwhelmed by emotion. Gritting his teeth, Robinson took control of the rescue efforts, as Ireland was the closest country to the scene and therefore had precedence. The British were initially reluctant to relinquish command — even during this crisis, there was a minor power struggle before the British conceded.

Robinson dispatched a Gemini inflatable boat with a crew of three that spent hours picking up bodies – thirty-eight in all. One crew member went into the water to hoist the heavier bodies into the inflatable boat. They had more success recovering victims at water level than the helicopter crew did from the air. The men were soon exhausted. Robinson wanted to spell them off, but they refused.

Eventually, nineteen boats ranging from military vessels to small Spanish fishing boats were on the scene helping.

Sean Murphy was the captain of the *Valentia* Lifeboat Station on the Irish coast. His seven-member crew took six hours to arrive at the crash site. Their vessel was much smaller than the merchant and naval ships and made slower progress through the rough seas. Murphy's men were able to pick up the bodies of three women, a man, and a child of maybe nine or ten years. It was the little girl that bothered Murphy the most. He was the father of four girls, and the horror hit close to home. The *Valentia* had to leave before all the bodies were recovered because the boat was running out of fuel.

The men in the *Laurentian*'s lifeboat were also suffering from the extreme conditions. The crews of the several helicopters that had arrived on the scene left the bodies they had recovered on the *Laurentian*. Brown, back aboard the ship, assisted in moving the bodies to the vessel's bow, where they were placed in bags. A doctor had been flown to the ship, and Brown helped him tag the bodies as either male or female. It was the doctor who first mentioned to Brown that it might have been a bomb that had brought down the plane.

June 23 ended with the exhausted crew so cold and wet that they pulled civilian clothing over their uniforms for warmth. A decision was made to pick up the bodies on Brown's ship by helicopter and take them to Cork. This would get them there much faster. The RAF helicopters could take six bodies at a time. Two areas on the *Aisling* became the morgue for the remaining bodies. The crew wrapped them in sheets as the *Aisling* headed for its home port near Cork, where the Irish police – the Garda – and the international media were waiting for her arrival.

Daniel Brown was so distraught by the events of June 23 that he recorded the day in a diary. He didn't want to remember, but he knew he would never forget. He also thought that he might need to give the police a statement:

9:30:   called to the bridge and informed on our way to a
        position where an aircraft had disappeared from radio.

10:02: I spotted what appeared to be a life raft and I reported
        this to the captain. Then almost immediately I saw
        another. The ship was put into hand steering and I
        steered the ship to the captain's order.

12:00: I was relieved at the wheel and I went down to the
        weather deck to look for survivors. We passed dozens
        of bodies and some pieces of fuselage and parts of the
        undercarriage.

12:30: I was asked if I would be prepared to go into the
        lifeboat to pick up bodies. I said yes and I went for a
        life jacket and stood by, ready to lower the lifeboat.
        Then we lowered the boat into the sea. At this point,
        the sea swell was running at 6–8 feet.

        Once in the water, we cleared the falls and pro-
        ceeded along the ship's side where I grabbed the first
        body, which was that of a young woman. Then I
        picked up a little girl. Then two men and another
        three women. I was involved in the recovery of seven
        bodies. The adults were heavy and needed two of us
        to get them in the boat. The little girl I picked up on
        my own with one hand.

        Most of the bodies were naked with multiple
        injuries. There was hardly a mark on the little girl.

        There was a bit of a squall and the sea was now
        running at 10–12 feet. The lifeboat was taking a bat-
        tering as we were trying to get back.

        We got back on board and I was told that the bodies
        would be left in the lifeboat and covered with blankets.

        Helicopters were arriving and lowering more
        bodies onto the ship. I helped Assistant Steward A.

Thomson to take the body of a young woman from the sling and put it into a dunnage bag. It was then decided to take the bodies from the lifeboat, put them into bags and take them forward beside the others. We did this and proceeded to Cork.

20:00: I was back on the bridge as 8–12 watch keeper. We had a radio call saying that we needn't go to Cork and that the bodies would be taken off in approximately 20 minutes time (the call came at 20:40).

I went downstairs to call the bosun and some other men and told them that we were going forward to shift the bodies to midship where they could be taken off by helicopter.

After we had loaded the bodies onto the helicopter, I hosed away some blood and then I went back to the bridge until midnight.

Ashok Rao was at home in Delhi when the telephone rang in the early evening. It was his sister, Padmini Turlapati, calling from Toronto. Rao immediately began babbling about summer plans and how excited everyone was about the imminent arrival of his nephews, Sanjay and Deepak.

"Shut up," Padmini interrupted. "They are dead. The children are dead."

In shock, Rao handed the phone to his wife, Nina. They both broke down in tears and turned on the television for news of the disaster. They called a brother in Bombay whose neighbour was an Air-India captain, hoping to learn this was all a mistake. He called back an hour later. There was no hope.

Rao decided to go to London to see if he could help. He visited a government minister, a friend, who tried to comfort him.

It was now nine o'clock on a Sunday night, but a new passport and passage to Heathrow were arranged for Rao. At the airport in London, he was met by his sister and brother-in-law, who had arrived from Canada, and together they travelled to Ireland.

"My mind was absolutely numb. I did not know what was happening," Rao said later. "All of the time what was haunting me was: What if they show me the bodies and I don't remember them?"

Amarjit Bhinder, the co-pilot's wife, received a call from a friend in London, asking for details of Satwinder's flight plan. Amarjit sensed something dreadful had happened even before he told her about the crash. Half an hour later, Air-India representatives arrived at her door with official word. Amarjit was so distraught that the officials summoned a doctor, who placed her under medical care. She remained bedridden for seven months.

In Saskatoon, it was early Sunday morning when the phone rang in Nagindra Kachroo's home. His son was on the line from Montreal. "Dad, the plane has crashed and we do not know if anyone survived."

Parkash Bedi of Detroit was asleep at his friend's house in Toronto when the telephone rang about 3:00 or 4:00 a.m. on June 23. The caller, another friend, told him to turn on the television, but did not say why. A nephew from Sarnia, Ontario, who had been studying through the night with the television on, then called with news of the disaster.

As Bedi and his friend watched the images from Ireland on the news, Bedi told his friend not to worry. "They are good swimmers," he said. "We have to go there and see how badly they are hurt."

Just before the bombings, eight-year-old Eddie Madon stopped at a Bombay temple with his aunt and uncle on the way to a party. "Say a quick prayer for your dad," his aunt told him, to ensure his plane arrived safely. Sam Madon was on Air-India Flight 182. He was due to arrive in Bombay to celebrate his forty-first birthday the next day with family and friends. The whole family had not been together since the children and their mother, Perviz, left their home in Burnaby, British Columbia, for Bombay a month earlier to plan a religious ceremony for Eddie. It had been Sam's idea to fly Air-India. Why not give the national airline of their homeland the business, he reasoned.

Eddie left the Zoroastrian temple with his uncle and aunt and his little sister, Natasha, aged four, and went to the party next door. It was there they got word that something terrible had happened to an Air-India plane inbound from Canada. Without explanation, the children were whisked away in a cab. Natasha was confused. Eddie understood the deep concern around him but clung to the hope that it was not his father's plane. When they got back to their uncle and aunt's home, and he saw his distraught mother, he knew his father was dead.

Perviz left her children with her family and caught the next Air-India flight to London. After touching down in England, she learned to her horror that others were saying this flight, too, had been threatened. Even though the Madons lived in British Columbia, they had not known that Air-India had been targeted by Sikh separatists, including some operating out of the suburb where they lived. They had not known there had been a call to boycott the airline, that there had been threats and warnings.

Perviz vowed never to step on another Air-India flight.

On an escalator at the London airport, she saw Jagdish Sharma, the Indian consul general from Vancouver, whom she and Sam knew socially. He had been on leave in India because his father had died. Now he was on his way to Ireland to assist Canadians of Indian origin who were facing the deaths of their loved ones.

He confided to her that he had almost lost his own family, but
that a last-minute illness kept them off the doomed flight.

In Cork, Insp. Joseph Long of the Garda was in charge of dealing
with the influx of bodies. He converted the hospital gymnasium
and recreation hall into a makeshift morgue.

Sheila Wall was just one of the many nurses trying to cope with
the bodies. She was stunned when she saw the first military truck
arrive. Some of the bodies were stacked two metres high. The
women were still wearing their beautiful saris and gold jewellery.

Eighty-eight bodies were taken there the first day aboard rescue
helicopters. Another forty-three arrived by boat the following day.
The final victim to be recovered was found four months later, in
October 1985, in a piece of the plane. Divers brought the body
up as they tried to recover more wreckage for investigators.

The Garda adopted almost a ceremonial procedure to deal with
the unprecedented number of bodies: They lined up stretchers at
the airport and dock, tagged limbs with a unique number, and
placed each victim in a body bag while a priest gave a blessing. Then
they drove the dead in a convoy of army vehicles with a police
escort to the gymnasium. There, each body was fingerprinted and
photographed. The photos were later posted on a display board in
the "incident room" set up at Cork Regional Hospital, and sent
through Interpol to London, Delhi, and Toronto. There, relatives
had the opportunity to look at them before heading to Ireland in
the hope of finding their loved ones' remains.

A team of seven doctors did the autopsies on June 24 and 25.
Most of the people whose bodies were recovered had been sitting
in the back of the plane when it blew up. There were no burn
marks on the bodies, no indication of an explosive substance.

The body of a girl of about ten had a cut on her head, smashed facial bones, and a broken left leg. She was covered in bruises and abrasions. Her brain had been ripped open. Her lungs were damaged, and there had been internal bleeding.

The bones of another girl, aged nine, were completely dislocated. Her spinal column was destroyed and her skull fractured. The coroner believed her injuries came from flailing as she was thrown from the plane. When bodies free fall from such a height, they flutter like leaves and their limbs are thrown about by the force of the descent.

One woman was five months pregnant with a boy. The coroner found frothy liquid in her nostrils and mouth and water in her stomach and uterus. Both the mother and unborn baby had survived the fall, but then had drowned. The baby showed no signs of trauma.

Many of the 132 bodies that were eventually recovered had pelvic injuries. The coroners thought this was because of the force of the blast under them. Many also had fragments of metal and plastic imbedded in the lower parts of their bodies. Some of them had no facial features left.

In Vancouver, news of the Narita bombing and the Air-India crash was first broadcast by CBC Radio in the wee hours of Sunday morning. Soon other news stations also reported that something catastrophic had happened and that there was an apparent link to British Columbia.

I was a twenty-five-year-old reporter with the *Vancouver Sun*, a rookie. I had started work there on May 28, 1984, just one week before the attack by the Indian Army on the Golden Temple in Amritsar, Punjab. In my early days on the job, I had gone with other reporters to cover Sikh demonstrations in Vancouver against the Indian government.

On June 24, I woke up to the news of the Air-India disaster and the Narita bombing – and the fact that there was a Vancouver connection. Like other journalists in the city, I immediately thought the two catastrophes had to be linked to the militant Sikh separatists who had been protesting in the streets and preaching revenge for the Indian Army's bloody attack on the temple a year earlier.

I was supposed to finish wallpapering the small kitchen of my West End apartment, but I got called into work, where I quickly began to phone my contacts. I talked to Ujjal Dosanjh, a moderate Sikh lawyer and activist, who had been trying to get politicians to notice the growing militancy among Sikhs for some time. He had even written to Prime Minister Brian Mulroney to warn him of the problem. For his efforts, he had been brutally beaten, just a few months earlier, by a member of the International Sikh Youth Federation.

I also tried to reach Jagdish Sharma, the Indian consul general in Vancouver, but he was already en route to Ireland. And I called some of the Sikh separatists I knew, such as Manmohan Singh. This fifty-something Vancouver restaurant owner was the colourful spokesman for the International Sikh Youth Federation. He had been cultivating relationships with reporters for a number of months. He was also close to the most militant Sikh separatist leaders in British Columbia. Singh denied knowing anything about a plot to bomb Air-India. Other reporters tried to call Talwinder Singh Parmar, the founder of the extremist Babbar Khalsa group.

It was an unprecedented event for the paper, and the whole newsroom was scrambling. Rick Ouston, usually an investigative reporter, was on the city desk, directing all of us. Anyone who could be reached was called into work. We were also trying to get hold of Terry Glavin, who was on holiday in Ireland. Not only was he one of the *Sun's* best reporters, but he had covered the Sikh separatists more thoroughly than anyone else. He had been in the Golden Temple while the separatists were amassing their arsenal just a month before the Indian government sent in the troops.

He had interviewed Jarnail Singh Bhindranwale, the charismatic leader of the movement who was killed during the temple attack. In fact, Glavin and Bhindranwale had exchanged quips that were still being talked about at the Delhi press club a year later. When Bhindranwale told Glavin that he looked like a woman because he had no beard, Glavin shot back: "In Canada, you would be mistaken for a woman, Mr. Bhindranwale, because you are wearing a dress." Bhindranwale's armed warriors cocked their AK-47s, not amused at the retort to their revered leader.

Glavin was a close friend of mine. He had told me what he witnessed in Punjab and taught me a great deal about the Sikh separatist movement. Over the years, he had talked many times to Talwinder Parmar and knew him better than any other reporter. I called several of Glavin's relatives in County Clare, but I couldn't reach him.

A few reporters were sent to the airport to get the Air-India passenger list. We needed to find out if local people had been killed. We needed to talk to the RCMP. What had happened? Was it really two bombs? Was it really terrorism?

In the late afternoon, Air-India released the list. We were able to identify a number of B.C. families who had relatives aboard the ill-fated flight. The younger reporters, me included, were sent to the homes of victims' families. We were told to knock on their doors and ask for photographs and comments. I had done this grisly job several times before in my short career at the *Sun*. I hated doing it. The families usually slammed the door in our faces, and they sometimes called us names. But it had to be done.

When I arrived at the south Vancouver home of the family of Shinghara Singh Cheema, I expected to be shunned.

"I am a reporter with the *Vancouver Sun*," I explained, waiting for the door to slam. Instead, it was opened, and I was invited into the living room and offered tea. I was told that this was the home of Cheema's brother Surinder, who owned a Beach Drive restaurant called the Mogul Gardens. Shinghara Cheema lived in India with his wife and children and had come to Vancouver in March for another brother's wedding. He loved Vancouver and had left only because his visa had expired.

His mother and another woman were wailing on the couch. Wailing is different than crying. It pierces the air. I had never heard anything like it in my life.

On June 24, some five hundred grief-stricken relatives began to arrive in Ireland. Parkash Bedi joined the stream of devastated family members rushing over there. He was still holding out hope that his children and wife were alive, but his faith was lost when he was handed Jatin's body. His son looked as if he were sleeping. Then he was shown the body of his wife, Saroj, which looked much worse. Her injuries were apparent. His daughter, Anu, was never found. Bedi decided to believe she was still alive.

Nagindra Kachroo went to Ireland but never recovered the body of his wife, Mohanrani, the daycare operator who had so loved her new life in Saskatoon, the woman he had married in India when she was just fourteen and he seventeen. Perviz Madon was one of the luckier ones. She was able to take Sam's body back to Bombay for his funeral rites, not the birthday party that had been planned.

Ashok Rao and his sister and brother-in-law, Padmini and Narayana Turlapati, arrived in Cork to find the boys. Sanjay's body was recovered. But Deepak, the eleven-year-old who was always smiling, was never found.

Sanjay Lazar was just seventeen years old, but he was the last surviving member of his family. His mother, father, and baby sister were all on the plane. His mother was pregnant. All alone in the world, the teenager visited the hospital morgue for twenty-five days in a row to try to get the bodies of his family back. Finally, he got his mother – she was the last one pulled from the sea by divers before they had to quit.

The Irish did whatever they could to comfort the grieving families. One of the relatives taught an Irish hotel worker to cook Indian food. Brenda O'Tighearnaigh of Dublin and her father, both friends of the Indian ambassador to Ireland, had asked him what they could do and were told to get in a car and drive to Cork. There, Brenda helped the families find accommodation. There were barely enough hotel rooms, so some of the Sikhs, including Amarjit Bhinder, the co-pilot's wife, were lodged in hotels out of town. The Irish were worried that the families who were blaming the bombing on Sikh terrorists would be angry even with the Sikhs who shared their loss. This was a country that understands sectarian hatred and violence like few others do.

O'Tighearnaigh spent weeks aiding the families who came from around the world to collect their dead. She met every person who came, saw every body. She became the liaison with the Dublin crematorium, which was newly opened and until then had cremated only two bodies. The crematorium quickly ran out of boxes for ashes and had to use urns. At one point, O'Tighearnaigh raced to the airport to waiting relatives who were booked on a flight that was about to leave. People saw her and cleared a path. They knew the urns she carried contained the ashes of Air-India victims. A hush fell over the airport, and the victims' relatives were alarmed by the silence. "They are just showing respect for your dead," O'Tighearnaigh told them, and the relatives broke down in tears.

As they left, many families gave O'Tighearnaigh a token of their appreciation – a silver bangle like the ones most Indian women wear. The Irish woman received so many of them that they went almost up to her elbow on each arm.

A few of the dead stayed behind in Ireland.

Ankur Seth, a fifteen-month-old baby from Ottawa, died along with his whole family – three siblings, mother, and father. It is against Hindu custom to cremate a child under the age of two, so Seth's aunt decided he should be buried in Ireland. The baby was laid to rest in the historic Glasnevin Cemetery, close to the graves of the Irish independence leaders Eamon De Valera and Michael Collins. Playwright Brendan Behan is buried nearby.

The white marble stone on Seth's grave reads: *In loving memory of Ankur Seth, 18-3-1984, son of Mrs. and Mr. Satish Chandra Seth, Ottawa, Canada. Grandson of Mrs. and Mr. H. K. Seth, Lucknow, India. Victim of Air-India disaster, June 23, 1985.*

At first, O'Tighearnaigh was worried that Seth's extended family would regret their decision to leave the baby behind in Dublin. But the Irish had committed to grieve the child as their own.

And each year since then, on the anniversary of the bombing, the families return to Ireland.

CHAPTER 2

Sowing the Seeds of Terror

THEY CALLED THEMSELVES Babbar Khalsa – Tigers of the True Faith. In their eyes, they were the real defenders of the Sikh religion. The Babbar Khalsa was a terrorist group from its inception in 1978, and in its early years, members in India boasted about the number of kills they had made. In Canada, people started to take notice of the group only after the Babbars killed 331 innocent men, women, and children.

Babbar Khalsa was founded by Talwinder Singh Parmar, a former left-leaning social worker from the Punjabi village of Panshta, who became a baptized Sikh only after moving to British Columbia, cutting his hair, and getting work in a North Vancouver sawmill. Parmar had a magnetism that made people want to listen to him. But he was also feared.

From the Babbar Khalsa's beginnings, Parmar was on a constant quest for cash to fund his objective – the creation of an independent Sikh nation called Khalistan, a nation, Parmar believed, that could be won only by fighting a dirty guerrilla war on at least two continents – in India and in Canada. Parmar turned regularly to his close ally, Ripudaman Singh Malik, a millionaire Vancouver businessman and loyal member of the Babbar Khalsa's sister organization, the Akhand Kirtani Jatha, for financial support.

Parmar's younger brother Kulwarn, who was running the family janitorial business in 1985, witnessed at least three meetings during which Malik pledged tens of thousands of dollars to the extremist organization. Kulwarn does not recall the exact dates or years of the three meetings, but believes they all occurred in the mid-1980s, while Talwinder was living at his palatial six-bedroom, three-bathroom Howard Avenue home in the Vancouver suburb of Burnaby.

"On two occasions, I was with my brother when discussions took place, and my brother was asking $100,000 donation from Malik, and he said he cannot do it because he don't have money, his business is not that good. And then he said, '$50,000 in two instalments: $25,000 each, every six months.' And Talwinder Singh agreed. He said, 'Okay.'"

But Malik was reluctant to make cheques out to or to deposit cash directly into the accounts of Babbar Khalsa's number-one and number-two men, Talwinder Parmar and Ajaib Singh Bagri. Kulwarn told me years later that Malik asked his brother if Babbar Khalsa could provide him with a less recognizable name or account for the transactions. "He said I cannot give to you or Ajaib Singh. You can tell me which name you want, and I can send the money to them or put it in their account or give cash," Kulwarn quoted Malik as saying.

The payments were not continuous, but they were ongoing, Kulwarn told me. "Whenever they needed funds, they'd go ask him," he said of Malik. "Babbar Khalsa didn't have much money except what Malik gave."

After June 23, 1985, Sikhism became unfairly associated with terrorism in the minds of many Canadians. For ninety years, Sikhs had contributed to and succeeded in Canada, but the community had not always received the recognition it deserved. Now it was in the news daily because of a tiny group of violent militants who called themselves Sikhs, but whose ideology ran contrary to all of the religion's teachings.

Devotees of the Sikh faith first came to Canada in 1897. They passed through Vancouver on their way back to India from Queen Victoria's Diamond Jubilee. Struck by the natural beauty and potential prosperity of the West Coast, many settled in British Columbia and found work in farming and logging and in sawmills.

The early Sikhs, mistakenly called Hindus by careless white authorities, for the most part assimilated as they worked hard and began a fifty-year fight for voting rights in their adopted land. They built temples, *gurdwaras*, in Vancouver and Abbotsford, with doors facing north, south, east, and west so that everyone is welcome regardless of caste or religion. But they modified their four-hundred-year-old practices to match the traditions in Canada. Pews replaced floor mats in the temples' main room. Worshippers sat at tables and chairs, not on the floor, to share meals, *langar*, in the communal dining halls. Most of them did not cover their heads inside the temple.

Sikhism is a young religion by world standards. It was founded in 1499 by a Hindu man named Nanak, who travelled the countryside of what is now northern India and Pakistan preaching a gospel of universal tolerance. He incorporated the teachings of Hinduism, Buddhism, and Sufism. He favoured equality for women and rejected the Hindu caste system and its multiplicity of gods.

"Truth is the highest virtue," Nanak said. "But higher still is truthful living."

Nanak, who stressed the need to do community service, or
sewa, became the first Guru of Sikhism, followed by nine others.
Gobind Singh, the proud warrior and last guru, began the tradition in 1699 of baptizing Sikhs into the Khalsa, the pure faith. Men
were given the name Singh, or lion; women were called Kaur, or
princess. To rally the faithful against their Mogul oppressors,
Gobind Singh introduced the physical symbols of the religion
known as the five Ks: *Kara*, a steel wrist bangle that originally
fended off Mogul swords. *Kirpan*, the dagger or sword to be drawn
to defend one's faith. *Kaesh*, the refusal to cut hair or beard, creating a distinguished physical image. *Kangha*, the comb that
represents cleanliness. And *Kachaira*, a cotton undergarment that
is drawn tight against the lower leg.

Gobind Singh decreed there would be no gurus after he died,
except for the Sikh holy book, the Guru Granth Sahib. It is considered the living guru and contains the words of all ten holy
men of Sikhism, as well as writings from Hinduism, Islam, and
other faiths.

With such a distinct linguistic, cultural, and religious identity,
it is no wonder that Sikhs also wanted an autonomous region in
India. As renowned Sikh writer Khushwant Singh writes in his
book *A History of the Sikhs*, "The ideal of a sovereign Sikh state
has never been very far from the Sikh mind." But the calls for
an independent Sikh nation grew much louder after the partition of India in 1947 and the bloody riots between Muslims and
Sikhs that ensued. Partition granted Muslims their own country,
Pakistan, whose borders took in the western half of the state of
Punjab, where most Sikhs lived. Many Sikhs felt betrayed by partition and demanded that they should also have their own nation.

Aspirations for a separate country diminished as the Sikh community prospered in an independent India, and Punjab was soon
the wealthiest state in the country. Sikhs were just 2 per cent of

the Indian population but held a much-higher percentage of military, police, and government jobs.

They also began to look abroad to improve their fortunes. They emigrated not only to Canada, but to the United States, Malaysia, Thailand, and Australia, as well as to Great Britain, Germany, and Holland. It was the Sikhs abroad who were disproportionately drawn into the struggle for Khalistan in the late 1970s and early 1980s. Especially those in British Columbia.

The Sikh population remained low in Canada for decades because of discriminatory immigration laws, but quickly grew after an October 1967 policy change allowed visitors to apply for immigration status while in Canada. By the 1980s, there were tens of thousands of Sikhs living in British Columbia. They also began to form large communities in other parts of Canada for the first time.

It was in this period that a few intriguing Sikhs arrived in British Columbia, men who would make an indelible mark on the country.

First, in 1969, came Surjan Singh Gill, a refined Malaysian-born businessman with impeccable manners who had been living in England. Talwinder Parmar, who worked with Punjab's poor, emigrated from India on May 29, 1970. Another former political activist in Punjab, Ajaib Bagri, came in 1971 from his native Punjabi village of Chak Kalan to meet his fiancée in Kamloops. With his short blond hair and blue eyes, he was often mistaken for a white man, or *gora*, at the mill where he found work. Hardial Singh Johal, who worked for the committee that runs Sikh temples in India, arrived in 1972, as did Ripudaman Malik, who would find great success in Canada, but started out living in an East Vancouver basement suite. Inderjit Singh Reyat came from England in the mid-1970s and settled in the Vancouver Island town of Duncan. All six men got to know each other at religious gatherings in homes and temples, at which they would sing hymns and discuss Sikhism.

Parmar, who had already made a tidy profit from the sale of his first home, was the first to be baptized into the Sikh faith – during a 1975 trip to Nankana Sahib, the birthplace of Guru Nanak in Pakistan. It was a huge moment for the immigrant to Canada, who had cut his hair and shaved his beard when he first arrived in his new land. Now, after the drinking *amrit* – sweet nectar – the central act of baptism, he was committed to follow all the tenets of the faith, including the five Ks. He would soon start calling himself a high priest of Sikhism.

Parmar's friends snapped photographs of the ceremony, for which the millworker wore a beige suit, a tie, and light blue turban, crossed in front in the style of most Sikh Canadians. His beard was neatly tied up. He had not yet begun to dress like a seventeenth-century Nihang warrior, the traditional guardian of the Sikh faith, whom he would come to emulate.

When Parmar returned to Canada, he persuaded many of his supporters – including Bagri – to drink the nectar in baptism ceremonies held around the province. Bagri had assimilated into Canadian society quite quickly after he arrived in British Columbia, but he turned back to the tenets of his faith when a critical illness nearly killed his nephew and left Bagri emotionally devastated. "He went to the *gurdwara* and said prayers and then our nephew was all right," his brother Piara told me years later. "After that he became *amritari* [baptized]. It increased his belief in God."

Parmar and Bagri were adamant that their version of Sikhism was the one that should be followed by all other Sikhs, and they both tried to force their newfound beliefs onto their community. Parmar tried to exercise his religious authority even before he founded the Babbar Khalsa in the last few months of 1978.

He took to the stage at Vancouver's Ross Street Sikh temple in front of hundreds of worshippers on January 15, 1978. The temple was run by the Khalsa Diwan Society, the oldest Sikh group outside India. As the congregation listened, Parmar pleaded with the temple's executive committee, asking them to become baptized, as he had. "If you can't be good Sikhs, then why do you remain on the executive?" Parmar asked them.

Parmar didn't stop his campaign there. On April 25, he got a lawyer to send a letter to the executive committee members declaring that they had two weeks to change their sinful ways and take *amrit* as he demanded, or resign their positions for leaders that suited him. No one took up Parmar's offer to follow his form of Sikhism, and a lawsuit he served on them was eventually thrown out by the B.C. Supreme Court.

Meanwhile, a critical event in Punjab changed Parmar's political and religious path. On April 13, 1978, as Sikhs in the holy city of Amritsar were preparing for Vaisakhi Day celebrations, members of a sect known as Nirankaris assembled in one part of the city. They were viewed as heretics by the fervently religious Sikh group – the Akhand Kirtani Jatha. AKJ supporters raced to the spot where the Nirankaris had gathered. A violent clash ensued that left thirteen AKJ men dead.

Talwinder Parmar was close to the AKJ. On a trip back to India shortly after the Vaisakhi murders, he, along with others within the organization, founded the Babbar Khalsa. It saw itself as a militant army that would defend the Sikh religion when necessary, and would remain closely affiliated with the AKJ. It would also become the most feared terrorist group in India and Canada.

The late 1970s were turbulent times in India, especially in Punjab, where the Sikh political party, the Akali Dal, was pushing for more autonomy and was being pushed back by the Indian government. Increasingly violent clashes were becoming the norm. And Sikhs around the world began to listen to the separatists' message with more sympathy, if not outright support.

A young adherent to the AKJ named Ranjit Singh, from the carpenter class within Sikhism, plotted to take revenge for the 1978 Nirankari murders. He managed to get work at the sect's compound in Delhi, but it was just a ruse to exact retribution for the thirteen deaths of AKJ members. On April 24, 1980, Singh machine-gunned the Nirankari leader to death. He was eventually rewarded with an appointment to the highest post of Sikhism – *jathedar* – of the Akal Takhat, the central ruling body in Amritsar's Golden Temple complex. As *jathedar* he would later dramatically impact the lives of many Sikhs on the other side of the world in Canada.

Another key AKJ leader who would have great influence over B.C. Sikhs was a small man with a white beard and a seemingly gentle spirit called Bhai Jiwan Singh. Some viewed him as a saint, others as their spiritual leader. He travelled frequently to Canada and had regular contact with Parmar, Bagri, Malik, Reyat, Johal, and Gill.

Parmar was not the only one in Canada flexing his muscles to get others to adhere to his strict version of Sikhism. In the late 1970s, Inderjit Reyat, who was employed as an auto and marine mechanic in Duncan, would stand outside the historic Sikh temple there, urging everyone going inside to cover his or her head. Once when a private wedding was being held at the temple, Reyat stood at the door and prevented the groom's father, Rajinder Singh Mayo, from entering the temple he had attended for years until he tied a scarf around his head. Two others came to Mayo's aid and got Reyat to leave the temple entrance.

"He was not going to let me go in for my own son's wedding," Mayo told me years later.

In the summer of 1981, Wally Oppal, a successful Crown prosecutor who was proud of his Sikh pioneer roots in British Columbia, was invited to speak about his life at the founding convention of the Federation of Sikh Societies of Canada. He travelled to Calgary for the meeting in the first week of August. But before Oppal could take the stage, a group of Babbar Khalsa members from Kamloops, led by Bagri, objected to his presence. They said he wasn't a real Sikh, with his clipped hair and beardless face. The organizers caved into the bullying and Oppal – the future judge and B.C. Attorney General – was axed from the program.

Hardial Johal, a custodian for the Vancouver School Board, was active at the Ross Street temple and assumed the leadership of it on several occasions after Parmar's 1978 stunt to sack the executive. Ripudaman Malik was lower profile than the other leaders, but he would regularly host religious programs at his house or attend them at the homes of others in the Babbar Khalsa and AKJ. Bhai Jiwan Singh eventually baptized the Vancouver entrepreneur, who founded a thriving women's clothing company called Papillon Eastern Imports. The diminutive religious leader from India would also spend long stretches at Malik's Vancouver mansion.

Another man who would often travel from Punjab to Vancouver was Dr. Jagjit Singh Chohan. A medical doctor by profession, the tall, gentle Chohan had entered the political arena in India and held a number of state and federal posts. He was also the first post-independence Sikh leader to declare publicly that the religion needed its own homeland, Khalistan, to be carved from India's Punjab state. Chohan brought his separatist views to small gatherings in Vancouver in the early 1970s.

Chohan later told me that on one such trip in 1980 or 1981, he was introduced to Surjan Gill by a mutual friend, lawyer Iqbal

Singh Sara. Sara told Chohan that Gill could run the separatist movement in Canada. Chohan agreed. The separatist doctor was also introduced to Ajaib Bagri by Gill at a religious function in a Vancouver home. But the influential Chohan did not meet Parmar on this trip. In late 1981, Parmar was hiding in the jungles of Uttar Pradesh in northern India after being accused of killing two police officers in his native Punjabi village.

During his time underground, Parmar had an interesting visitor from Canada. Ripudaman Malik visited India and made his way to the state where Parmar was hiding. There, Malik approached a relative of Parmar's wife, Surinder. The relative knew the location of Parmar's secret jungle hideout but would not disclose it – not even to a committed supporter like Malik. Instead, he agreed to make the trek to see Parmar and seek permission to return with Malik. The separatists had their own code of conduct. If an ally arrived unannounced and accompanied by another person, it would be assumed the stranger was a police officer and both would be shot.

Malik waited for a day before being taken to see Parmar by the fugitive's relative. Only the two men knew the topic of their conversation. Shortly afterwards, on November 19, 1981, Parmar was helped out of India by Surjan Gill and Chohan, who was by then exiled in Britain and living in a large brick home in Reading, near London.

Chohan did not yet know who Parmar was, but he agreed to help on the basis of Gill's recommendation. More than twenty years later, Chohan said, "Surjan Singh told me [Parmar] is a very good man, very close to him and very religious. He said, 'Can you help me bring him out of India?' He took a letter from me for somebody in Nepal. That man brought Talwinder [Parmar] to Nepal, got him into the plane along with Surjan [Gill]."

On their way back to Canada, Parmar and Gill touched down in England, where Chohan met the charismatic Babbar Khalsa leader whom he would both aid and clash with over the coming years. The growing network of separatists in the Sikh diaspora was also lobbying on behalf of a group of militants who had hijacked an Indian Airlines flight in 1981. The B.C.–based Babbar Khalsa and Malik's AKJ would later aid the hijackers in jail in Pakistan.

Back in Canada, Gill opened what he called the first consulate for Khalistan on Kingsway Avenue in East Vancouver. Next door was the office of the *Indo-Canadian Times*, the first Punjabi language weekly in the country, run by publisher Tara Singh Hayer.

All the men were close and visited each other often and had lively discussions on Sikhism and the future of Punjab. From his bogus diplomatic office, Gill distributed colour postcards of Parmar, now sporting the regalia of a Nihang warrior – a tall saffron turban rounded at the front, a long blue tunic, and shoes with curled-up toes. A sword was also visible. Gill handed out maps of his hoped-for land, which included far more territory than the state of Punjab, and issued passports and currency that became souvenirs for the curious.

In 1982, Gill bought Parmar's Union Street home, and the Babbar Khalsa chief moved into the larger, lavish residence on Howard Avenue that was later frequently photographed by members of Canada's fledgling spy agency, the Canadian Security Intelligence Service. By this time, Parmar had abandoned daily work in favour of full-time preaching and real-estate deals. Money was also coming in from a growing number of supporters.

There was an allure and charisma to Parmar that is hard to explain. Those who were devoted to him would do almost anything for him. On one international trip in 1983, Parmar was picked up in Germany on an Interpol warrant related to the

outstanding 1981 murder charges in India. His supporters immediately lobbied the German government for his release, but it
was months before they were successful. In the meantime, his
financially strapped family turned to Malik for support. Malik,
who viewed the Babbar Khalsa leader as a political prisoner,
made monthly payments into the Parmar family account to cover
the mortgage. Gill, meanwhile, looked after getting the legal
team together to aid Parmar, and he again turned to Chohan. But
the separatist struggle did not wait for Parmar.

Punjab has always been a key state in India and one that every
central government has wanted to control. When the Sikhs of
Punjab, who were slightly more than half the population, were
united, they usually voted with the Akali Party. When they
were divided, it was much easier for the Congress Party to take
the state. In that context, Indian prime minister Indira Gandhi
came up with a clever plan to keep Punjab under her Congress
Party's control. She encouraged a magnetic Sikh preacher named
Jarnail Singh Bhindranwale to rise to the political forefront with
fiery speeches demanding independence and assailing the Hindu
threat to the Sikh faith. Her Congress Party officials manipulated
Punjab's media to get Bhindranwale's speeches covered. Orthodox
Sikhs began shifting away from the Akalis and to Bhindranwale,
despite the violence of many of his followers.

The plan worked until Bhindranwale and his armed supporters took over the sacred precincts of the Golden Temple
complex in Amritsar, Punjab, on December 15, 1983. Gandhi
had not anticipated the move. The optics were terrible. The
holiest shrine of the Sikhs was being occupied by armed
militants demanding independence and harassing pilgrims by controlling access to the temple. One of those pilgrims was Rattan
Singh Kalsi, who lived in southern Ontario. When he tried to
enter the temple complex, he was stopped by Bhindranwale's

gun-toting gang, who objected to his leather camera case. They were not real Sikhs, Kalsi thought. Eighteen months later, his daughter would die in the Air-India bombing.

The Golden Temple standoff became increasingly tense in early 1984. Leaders of the other militant groups – the Babbar Khalsa, the Akhand Kirtani Jatha, and the All India Sikh Student Federation – were backing Bhindranwale. Some of Parmar's comrades in the Babbar Khalsa were holed up with the rebels, while others were agitating outside India for a separate Sikh state. In March 1984, Malik, Bagri, and Parmar's teenaged children were among dozens of demonstrators who burned an effigy of Indira Gandhi outside the Indian consulate in Vancouver. They chanted and carried signs calling for greater autonomy for Punjab.

As fascinating as the story was becoming in both India and Canada, few western journalists were covering it. Maybe their editors thought it was just an internal dispute in an ethnic community and not relevant to the majority of readers. One reporter who was committed to covering the strife was Terry Glavin. He had already interviewed Parmar in Canada and covered his German arrest. When a labour dispute closed the *Sun* for three months in the spring of 1984, Glavin took the opportunity to travel to Punjab, where he wrote several stories about the escalating conflict for the *Globe and Mail*. He did one of the last known interviews with Bhindranwale before the leader was killed a month later at the temple. Glavin also spoke to Parmar associate Sukhdev Singh Babbar, who was among the militants in the Golden Temple. Babbar, whose widow and children would one day come to Canada, pledged his allegiance to Parmar as a "pure Sikh" and told Glavin that all the radical Sikh groups worked together across international boundaries. He said that the Babbar Khalsa would continue to kill "the enemies of Sikhs" and fight for the establishment of Khalistan. "It will start in Punjab, then it will end up in the whole world. The Khalsa will rule, all over the world," he predicted.

By June 1984, Punjab was almost in a state of anarchy, with constant separatist and paramilitary killings. Gandhi and her military advisers ordered the Indian Army to regain control of the Golden Temple complex in a mission dubbed Operation Blue Star. Tanks and soldiers attacked Sikhism's holiest shrine in a mighty show of force on June 4. Hundreds were killed, including Bhindranwale, then just thirty-eight, and most of his inner circle. But many innocents also died, and Sikhs around the world – even those who had been opposed to separatism – were outraged at the attack on the heart of their religion. There were international protests, some of them violent. Indian diplomats were threatened. There were vitriolic calls for revenge, many of them at Canadian Sikh temples and street rallies.

Vancouver saw many of the protests. On June 4 – the day the Indian Army opened fire on the Golden Temple – Sodhi Singh Sodhi and Jasbir Singh Sandhu stormed the Indian consulate at 325 Howe Street, smashing glass doors and pictures of Gandhi. Protesters returned the next day and again on June 6. As police stood by, a small group of men, two carrying swords, burned Gandhi's effigy, set an Indian flag ablaze, and chanted anti-India slogans.

Thousands of Sikhs protested next outside the Vancouver Art Gallery a few blocks away. Surjan Gill was there, wearing a black T-shirt proclaiming in English, "DEATH TO INDIRA GANDHI" in large, white capital letters. He was standing beside Inderjit Reyat, who was brandishing a metre-long sword. Ajaib Bagri stirred the angry crowd with a passionate anti-India speech.

As the Indian Army pored through the documents they found in the Golden Temple complex, they came across Hardial Johal's business card, listing his East Vancouver address and a phone number that would soon be part of the largest criminal investigation in Canadian history. Lying right beside Johal's card was a notebook that contained instructions on the preparation of improvised explosive devices. The suspicious find could never be concretely linked to the B.C. resident.

That summer Parmar won his release in Germany and returned a hero to his Canadian admirers, enraged by the temple attack and searching for a fitting response. Parmar never hesitated to preach violence when he was speaking to his diehard supporters, but he adopted a more measured approach when he spoke to Canadian journalists, including me. "I just preach . . . I do not believe in killing," he told my newspaper in July 1984. Then he proclaimed, "Every Sikh – every man, woman, and child – is a member of the Babbar Khalsa. If he isn't, he is a traitor!"

In that summer of angry rhetoric, Parmar, with the help of his Babbar Khalsa soldiers, set in motion a chain of events that led to hundreds of murders within months. He spent just a few days with his family in British Columbia before he was off again, preaching his gospel to militants in Ontario.

It was a bizarre scene that greeted Parmar when he flew into Toronto's Pearson International Airport on July 21, 1984. With police and airport security close by, Parmar supporters raised their swords above their heads and shouted frenzied slogans, calling Indira Gandhi a bitch and condemning her to die. Parmar walked under the swords, with his loyal Babbar Khalsa lieutenants, Ajaib Bagri and Surjan Gill, at his side. Parmar was then whisked away in a car and driven to a temple on the outskirts of Hamilton, where he made a speech condemning a number of Sikh political leaders. "Until we have the heads of those sinners on the tips of our swords, we will not rest," Parmar declared. "Now the iron is hot, no power in the world can defeat us."

The Babbar Khalsa chief had planned to cross into the United States to continue his speaking tour at the founding convention of the World Sikh Organization in New York that July, but Parmar was already on a U.S. watch list and was denied entry. Bagri went instead and spoke for Parmar to a crowd of thousands at Madison Square Gardens on July 28, 1984. He proved to be even more fierce than his boss.

"They say Hindus are our brothers. Many have said that. But I give you my most solemn assurance – until we kill fifty thousand Hindus, we will not rest," Bagri pledged.

As several New York police officers helped conference organizers with security, and with video cameras rolling, Bagri publicly threatened to punish traitors by crushing their children to pulp. His emotional oratory gripped the crowd, who stood, fists in the air, shouting the Sikh war cry – *Bole So Nihal* – and yelling, "Indira bitch! Death to her." Of all those in attendance, no one publicly criticized Bagri for his provocative rant.

In August, Parmar's supporters rushed the home of Indian consul general Jagdish Sharma in the British Properties, an affluent West Vancouver neighbourhood. About three hundred militants invaded the grounds to stop Sharma from raising the Indian flag at a party to mark his country's Independence Day. I had been on the job for just three months and was one of several reporters sent to the scene. It was frightening and volatile. Even police didn't know what would happen. Sharma and his family were given twenty-four-hour police protection because of the threats.

Sikhs and Hindus who spoke against the militants' violent rhetoric were also threatened. There was talk of hit lists circulating, and anonymous leaflets were printed in Vancouver warning all Hindus to leave Canada or face death. The tensions were so high that on August 16, External Affairs Minister Jean Chrétien apologized to the Indian government for threats being made to its diplomats in Canada. He also warned that Sikh extremists who threatened anyone could land in jail. "This type of action by groups or individuals against diplomatic or consular facilities in Canada must not be tolerated," Chrétien said.

In this frightening climate, Inderjit Reyat began to ask around the tightly knit community of Duncan about getting dynamite. Just thirty-two, the devout Sikh tried to explain to his white friends and co-workers that revenge against India was necessary. He approached Lake Cowichan contractor Edward Wayne Robertson more than once to ask for explosives. Reyat said he needed two or three cases and was willing to pay three times the regular cost. At first, he said the dynamite was to blast stumps on his property, but eventually the truth emerged. "There is trouble in the old country," Reyat said. "I would like to have explosives to help my countrymen." Robertson never gave Reyat the dynamite, but at another time he did provide him with a four-hundred-page blasting manual with technical information on mining techniques and the use of explosives.

The Babbar Khalsa's speeches and trips continued, and the militant separatists became a blip on CSIS's radar screen. Bagri and Parmar spent most of their time in Ontario, particularly in the Hamilton area, where the Babbars ruled. Both men urged Sikhs there to get their weapons ready "so we can take revenge from the Indian government." Bagri told followers that they needed to raise an army, with rifles and ammunition to fight the Indian government.

Certainly there were plenty of warnings about what was happening, both in policing and intelligence circles and at the street level among Indo-Canadians. In September 1984, Vancouver liquor store employee Harmail Singh Grewal tried to bargain down his sentence on theft and fraud charges by giving information to CSIS and the RCMP about a plot to put a bomb aboard an Air-India flight out of Montreal. But the deal fell through after Grewal was dismissed as "unreliable." A Toronto resident, Paul Besso, also claimed he told the RCMP about the bomb attack two weeks before it happened. A British Babbar Khalsa leader was quoted in a newspaper saying anyone who flew Air-India would be killed either in Britain or in India.

Indian government officials warned repeatedly in the months after Operation Blue Star that Canadian Sikh separatists were planning to target Indian diplomats and Air-India flights as part of a campaign of terror. Rumours of imminent attacks swirled around the Indo-Canadian community and word was circulated quietly among Sikhs to boycott Air-India. Some understood this to mean that the airline would be physically attacked. Others thought the boycott was simply an economic protest against a legitimate target – the national airline of India.

CSIS was by then collecting a great deal of information. In the eleven months before the bombing, the spy agency issued fifteen threat assessments to the RCMP that specifically mentioned, or were devoted entirely to, Air-India. CSIS would later claim that none mentioned Air-India Flight 182 leaving Toronto on June 23, 1985. But, since there was only one Air-India flight a week leaving Canada, how hard would it have been to protect?

The agency had many other targets as well, including Cold War spies and supporters of the Irish Republican Army. Sixty-one threat assessments were issued in the same period for other marks operating in Canada.

For those of us following the story of the new Sikh militancy, it was sometimes hard to figure out if events in Canada were mirroring those in India or vice versa. As the violence and rhetoric increased in Punjab, it also escalated in British Columbia. Anyone in Canada who dared to suggest that retaliation was not a solution to the treatment of Sikhs in India was threatened or beaten or both. In October 1984, a respected Punjabi poet named Gurcharan Rampuri was beaten by three turbaned men after taking a stance against Sikh separatism in several articles published by a Punjabi-language newspaper in Vancouver. No one was ever charged. Surrey community activist Charan Gill was also assaulted.

From their Canadian base, Parmar, Bagri, Surjan Gill, and others repeatedly called for the assassination of Indira Gandhi. When she was gunned down by her two Sikh bodyguards on October 31, 1984, Sikh separatists danced on the plaza in front of the Ross Street temple in Vancouver. Temple president Daljit Singh Sandhu, who would later deny under oath that he supported violence, told reporters he wished he had killed her himself. Moderate Sikh lawyer Ujjal Dosanjh was so concerned with the violent rhetoric that he spoke publicly, warning that the large Vancouver temple was a "hotbed for fanatics, an organization place for separatists."

But the popularity of Parmar, Bagri, and the other separatist leaders only increased. They were invited to speak all over Canada. At one meeting in Calgary in early 1985, Parmar pledged that Air-India planes would "fall from the sky." An AKJ member and Babbar sympathizer named Balwant Singh Bhandher was there. So was Amrit Singh Rai, who later became the national spokesman for the International Sikh Youth Federation – the spinoff group from the All India Sikh Student Federation that was banned in India for terrorist activities. Narinder Singh Gill, then the treasurer at the Calgary temple, also heard Parmar's speech.

Hundreds packed into the temple that day to hear Parmar preach, but his more ominous message was delivered privately to a group of about twenty men who gathered in an upstairs room. Parmar insisted that the Indian government had to be punished for its attack on the Golden Temple. One attendee suggested a boycott of Air-India so the airline would stop flying to Canada, but the

conversation soon turned to a more violent strategy. One pro-
posal was for militants in the Babbar Khalsa and the International
Sikh Youth Federation to get missiles and try to hit the weekly
Air-India flight as it left Toronto or Montreal. Parmar said neither
suggestion was right. "We'll think of something. We will make
a plan," he pledged.

You might think that someone plotting a major act of terrorism would tell his cohorts to cool it for a while, to lie low,
to back off the threatening, intimidating, and bullying of opponents. But the Canadian militants didn't see the need to worry.
They continued with assaults and beatings. And without fear
of prosecution.

One of the highest-profile attacks came in February 1985
against Ujjal Dosanjh, the lawyer and community activist who
would go on to make Canadian history as the first Indo-Canadian
premier. Dosanjh was leaving his Victoria Drive law office when
a bearded man jumped out of the dark and hit him on the head,
again and again, with an iron bar pierced by a bolt.

Dosanjh's law partner chased off the attacker, then helped
Dosanjh into a nearby doctor's office. Then he called Dosanjh's
wife, Raminder, who was unpacking groceries – the couple was
expecting Vancouver mayor Mike Harcourt and Judge Wally
Oppal for dinner. Dosanjh was taken to hospital, where doctors
put eighty stitches into his skull and set the bones in his broken
right hand, injured as he tried to ward off the blows.

Few activists were as committed as Dosanjh was in those days.
Outside the hospital, reporters were waiting. He was so determined to talk to them he asked Raminder to wheel him to them
before all the stitches were in. "There is nothing that will stop
me until I achieve my goal of seeing peace and harmony in our
community," Dosanjh vowed, blaming the attack on "fascist

fundamentalist beasts in the community who are trying to stifle freedom of speech."

Angered by the assaults on himself and other moderates, Dosanjh fired off a letter to Prime Minister Brian Mulroney, pleading for help to free the Indo-Canadian community from the violence and intimidation of Sikh separatists.

"We were all worried there was going to be violence, and there was violence," Dosanjh later explained. "I was attacked. Charan Gill was attacked. Gurcharan Rampuri was attacked. Shushma [Datt] was threatened. People's windows were smashed. Threatening messages were left on people's answering machines, including mine. Threats were made to kidnap children and firebomb your homes, things of that nature. And if you add that together with the hit lists that were going around – that is why I wrote the letter and made the kind of statements I made."

Dosanjh's pleas didn't stop the Sikh extremists. The violence was about to get much worse than anyone, even Dosanjh, had imagined. The terrorists were so brazen and felt so free in Canada that they did not work clandestinely in plotting the worst mass murder in the country's history.

Parmar and Bagri's Babbar Khalsa already had one account in Scotia Bank, in North Vancouver, the same branch that handled the accounts of workers at the sawmill where Parmar worked. He would get short-term loans for the extremist organization and pay them off with help from friends like Malik. In February 1985, Malik introduced Parmar and Bagri to the manager of the Bank of Credit and Commerce Canada, resulting in the pair, as well as other members of the Babbar Khalsa, opening an account there. Though Parmar's group had admitted to dozens of murders in

India, in Canada it enjoyed the status of any non-profit organization, such as the Canadian Cancer Society or the United Way. The Babbar Khalsa would later apply for and receive charitable status, meaning tax breaks for donors.

Not only was Malik supporting the Canadian wing of the Babbar Khalsa, he donated to operatives in Punjab as well, Kulwarn Parmar later recalled.

On one of his visits to his brother's home in the mid-1980s, Kulwarn witnessed Talwinder ask Malik for money for some of the Babbars in the Indian state. Kulwarn said that Malik told Talwinder that the diminutive, white-bearded AKJ leader, Bhai Jiwan Singh, had enough of Malik's money at his Amritsar base to help out the Babbars. The two groups were indelibly linked, after all.

"Malik said he can phone [Bhai Jiwan Singh] and they can go collect from him," Kulwarn recalled years later in an interview. "To me that was support for Babbar Khalsa. What else was Talwinder Singh asking for?"

The younger Parmar, who went on to be a director of the Babbar Khalsa after his brother's death, said Talwinder told him that Malik was the moneyman for the group. "They had no other supporter," Kulwarn said.

Sometime between 1985 and June 1988, Malik was asked by police about his financial contributions to the Babbar Khalsa. At first the millionaire denied making any, which frustrated Talwinder Parmar. "Talwinder told him, 'You are stupid because if they have a cheque from the bank then how you can say you didn't give? They can't do anything if you tell them you give. Why don't you tell them yes, you gave the money to me? The simple question and it is over,'" Kulwarn quoted his brother as telling Malik.

When police asked Malik a second time about his contributions to the militant separatist leader, he admitted he had given money, but said it was just to support Talwinder Parmar's preaching. But Kulwarn said his brother never took a cent from anyone for his preaching or to support his family except while he was a political prisoner in Germany. His wife and three children worked. Any fundraising the Babbar Khalsa leader did was for the cause, his devoted younger brother said.

Kulwarn said he believes Malik made some deposits directly into the Babbar Khalsa account at the Bank of Credit and Commerce because the financial institution was downtown near Malik's office. "When Khalsa Credit Union was opened, they asked Talwinder to transfer that money from that account to Khalsa Credit Union," Kulwarn said.

Three months before the deadliest act of aviation terrorism to date, CSIS had collected enough intelligence to get authorization for a wiretap on Parmar's telephone. Finally he had been identified as a threat to national security. What the agents didn't know was that Parmar was already well into planning twin bombings designed to bring down two jumbo jets and kill more than six hundred people.

Parmar knew he was being followed. He assumed his telephone was bugged. But he brazenly continued his plan – meeting with his supporters, doing test explosions in the woods, and flying several times to Toronto and Hamilton to meet with other conspirators. He chatted candidly on his phone about a plot to kill the new Indian prime minister, Rajiv Gandhi, and about financial support for the jailed hijackers in Pakistan. He referred affectionately to them as "the boys." But Parmar was more guarded when it came to discussing details about the Air-India plot with other co-conspirators. He would often arrange to call them from pay phones or meet them in person. His calls should have raised red flags for the CSIS agents monitoring the Babbar Khalsa chief, but the agents did not speak the language in which Parmar most often talked, Punjabi. No one in the Vancouver office did. They had to wait for a translator to provide them with notes.

Parmar was right not to worry. The agents sitting outside his house often confused him with other members of his group. Their tall orange turbans, long blue tunics, and black beards seemed to leave the Anglo-Canadian agents struggling to figure out who was who. "Trying to identify these people while they are in a vehicle is very difficult," a CSIS agent wrote in one surveillance report. "Anyone in the back seat of a car wearing a beard and turban looks like the next guy." Their surveillance was so obvious that some of Parmar's neighbours reported the strange men in cars to the RCMP, who came by to investigate the CSIS agents.

Parmar was on the phone to his close friend Amarjit Singh Pawa, owner of Friendly Travels, almost every day, booking international and domestic airline tickets, always in the name of Singh, even when the tickets were for himself, Bagri, or Surjan Gill. It was better to remain anonymous and hide the real identity of travellers.

There were dozens of cryptic calls and regular meetings between Parmar and the men who would later become the suspects – Surjan Gill, Malik, Bagri, Johal, Avtar Singh Narwal, and other Babbar Khalsa members from Kamloops. The agents carefully marked down who was visiting and who was calling. But the "what" of the equation clearly eluded them.

One of the most disturbing calls was one Parmar received from a contact in Germany named Jang Singh, who offered to assassinate Rajiv Gandhi during his U.S. tour in June of that year. Parmar expressed frustration at the naive exuberance of the would-be killer. He repeatedly warned the man to "keep quiet" and "shut up." U.S. officials were not alerted to the threat for more than a month, and only days before Gandhi's U.S. trip.

Parmar was not only dismissive of the threat posed to him by CSIS spies, but he also chatted freely with journalists who called his house regularly looking for comments or reaction to international events. Some suggested he was holding military training camps in the B.C. interior. Others told Parmar a deal was in the works to extradite him to India on the 1981 murder charges.

Parmar was the central figure without a doubt. His bugged telephone line showed that. Calls came in from around the world. Meetings and visitors were constant. He would hear gripes from some followers about other Babbar Khalsa members and he would mediate if necessary.

He patiently listened in April 1985 when Babbar Khalsa member Satnam Singh Khun Khun complained to him that Bagri was ruining the reputation of all of them by having an extra-marital affair with a Vancouver woman, Premika (whose real name cannot be published by court order). Parmar appeared to humour Khun Khun during the call, without actually agreeing to the suggestion that Bagri should be kicked out of the group. Parmar, despite his brand of Sikh supremacism, did not judge Bagri's relationship with Premika. He sometimes called Bagri at the woman's house and even dropped him off there late one night a few weeks after Khun Khun's call.

Was Parmar brazen or foolish? Or did he understand the weaknesses of Canadian police agencies and the spies watching him constantly? He may not have admitted to planning a terrorist act on the phone, but he did not hesitate to set up meetings that appeared to be related to the unfolding plot. He called Inderjit Reyat and said he was sending Surjan Gill in early April to the ferry terminal in Nanaimo to meet with the Duncan electrical

whiz. Gill spoke about "delivering bows and arrows" from Reyat
to Parmar.

Twenty years later a judge suggested that high-profile Sikh
leaders could not have been involved in openly collecting
materials needed for the murderous plot. But Reyat, despite his
leadership in the Duncan Sikh community, was doing just that.
He again went searching for dynamite. He talked to his contractor friend about the sacrilege at Amritsar and the need for revenge.
"He was almost talking like Hitler," a man who overheard the
conversation later commented. Throughout May 1985 he assembled everything he needed for his role in the bombings. He was
stupid, really, walking into stores in the town where he was well
known to ask for advice on how to rewire clocks and timers and
buzzers. His car had a vanity licence plate that said IREYAT.

Reyat also visited an acquaintance at a television repair shop
in Duncan. He brought a partially disassembled car clock with a
lantern battery attached. Reyat wanted help to change the wiring
of the device to get a continuous, rather than an intermittent,
alarm. He claimed he wanted to install the device in his camper
so that it would turn on a light to wake him up. He also bought
a portable stereo with a twelve-hour timing device that activated
the radio. He asked a co-worker at Duncan Auto Marine Electric
to help him fix the timer, telling the man it was for a friend. The
two worked on the unit but were unable to make it work the way
Reyat wanted. He returned the stereo the next day.

Finally, after months of trying, Reyat got his hands on some
dynamite. A Duncan well driller, Ken Slade, offered him a few
sticks after Reyat fixed the man's truck at his home one Sunday
afternoon. A few days later, Slade also gave Reyat two or three
blasting caps. It was fairly common at the time in rural British
Columbia for people to use dynamite to blast stumps.

CSIS again displayed its incompetence in mid-May, when agents tried to tail Parmar on his five-hour drive to Kamloops for a Babbar Khalsa meeting that was likely related to the bombings. The agents noted that Parmar drove with a shorthaired man in a car owned by Avtar Narwal, a member of Parmar's group. They arrived at Narwal's Kamloops home shortly after four, then they drove to another house owned by Babbar Gurmit Singh Gill, where Bagri and others joined them. That evening they went back to Narwal's house, apparently for another meeting, before Parmar was driven to Gurmit Gill's to spend the night.

CSIS agents began their surveillance on May 16 at Gurmit Gill's house. They thought they saw Parmar in the yard shortly after 8:00 a.m. Several cars came and went throughout the morning. A number of vehicles were followed by CSIS, but the agents soon realized Parmar was not in any of them. They could not tell the Babbars apart. They had lost their target. They searched for him for twenty-four hours without success before giving up and returning to Vancouver.

After Kamloops, Reyat wanted Parmar to arrange a meeting on Vancouver Island. It was now May 19 – five weeks before the day. The countdown was on.

On May 20, Parmar told Malik that he needed to see him "within a day or so." CSIS watched the financier arrive at Parmar's house about 8:20 p.m. on May 21. Malik also had distinctive vanity plates on his beige Volvo, reflecting his company's name – PAPION, albeit misspelled. Malik's brother from India was also there, along with several other Sikhs who were seen on Parmar's deck. While the meeting continued, Bagri called from Kamloops.

Throughout early June, CSIS agents followed Parmar, Surjan Gill, and other Babbars as they drove around to various Burnaby pay phones to make calls, clearly assuming that Parmar's phone was tapped. But, tragically, none of the CSIS agents assigned to Parmar and his associates figured out what was going on right under their noses, despite months of telephone taps, weeks of surveillance, suspicious behaviour, and test explosions. CSIS followed Parmar for seventeen consecutive days beginning June 1, 1985. Then the agency reassessed and scaled back its team as the worst terrorists in Canadian history put the finishing touches on their murderous plot.

Where CSIS misjudged was in assessing the duration of the threat to Air-India. Agents assumed there would be greater risk of something happening on the first anniversary of Operation Blue Star: June 4 to 6, 1985. They also were worried something might happen during Rajiv Gandhi's U.S. visit from June 11 to June 16. Once Gandhi left the continent, CSIS let its guard down.

An RCMP memo from early June 1985 discloses the kind of intelligence about threats to Air-India that was coming in to police: "On June 6, 1985, the RCMP headquarters in Ottawa asked CSIS for a threat assessment as a result of correspondence the RCMP received from Air-India concerning the likelihood of their aircraft being sabotaged. This threat is believed to be worldwide. CSIS replied on the same date that the threat potential to all Indian missions in Canada was high and this was intended to include Air-India. CSIS, however, was not aware of any specific threat to the airlines and further advised that should they learn of any specific threat to Air-India, the [RCMP] would be advised immediately."

On June 3, Jaswinder Parmar checked the arrival time for a flight from Toronto. A mystery man later dubbed Mr. X, who was to participate in bomb testing a day later, likely arrived on the flight, which got in just before 9:00 p.m.

Surjan Gill picked up Parmar and Mr. X on June 4 and drove the pair to Horseshoe Bay, where they caught a ferry to Nanaimo.

From there, they were driven to Reyat's house in Duncan by a local man named Joginder Singh Gill. He didn't know the pair but had been asked by a friend to help out. He would later be asked by both Parmar and Malik to deny to police giving the Babbar Khalsa leader a ride that day.

Reyat had collected almost all the requisite parts for the bombs: batteries, relays, dynamite, and other components. At the local Radio Shack he had bought a Micronta car clock and two Archer electrical relays. Neither of the relays would have been useful in his day job, they were deemed too flimsy for cars. Then Reyat, Parmar, and Mr. X drove to the woods on the outskirts of town and played with the explosives, all the while being tailed by two CSIS agents who were unaware of what was going on. They heard a loud blast, which they thought was either a gunshot or exploding dynamite. They later reported the incident to the RCMP, but neither agent actually saw what had happened.

On June 5, Reyat made more suspicious purchases. He went to Woolworth's in Duncan, where he bought a Sanyo tuner. He exchanged one of the relays for another that could be activated at a lower voltage. And he also bought some smokeless gunpowder at Buckey's Sports Shop.

There was a flurry of calls over the next few days between Parmar, Pawa (the travel agent), Hardial Johal, and Surjan Gill. Parmar travelled to Toronto with Bagri late on June 7, but CSIS agents watching Parmar's house mistakenly reported he was home. The person they saw was actually Avtar Narwal, the Kamloops man who wore the same traditional clothing as Parmar. The agents tailed Narwal when he left and eventually realized they had made yet another mistake.

Parmar and Bagri returned from Ontario, arriving at the airport just before 11:00 p.m. Parmar's wife picked them up, dropping Bagri a few minutes later at Premika's Vancouver basement apartment. Parmar did not seem preoccupied with the propriety of a married and baptized Sikh man staying the night at the home of a single mother.

The plotters did not rest. They met again at Parmar's house late the next afternoon as CSIS watched from a safe distance.

On June 11, Parmar called Annie, an employee at Scotia Bank, who told him there was still $5,309 owing on the current Babbar Khalsa loan. She confirmed that a $4,000 cheque from Malik had been applied to it. Parmar asked whether the Babbar Khalsa would be able to get another $20,000 for four months once the current loan was paid off.

That same day, Surjan Gill was visited by the RCMP, who had received word from the U.S. Secret Service that B.C. Sikhs might have been harbouring two extremists wanted in connection with the plot to kill Rajiv Gandhi on his American trip. Gill, who clearly raised no suspicions with the investigators, looked at a few photos and politely sent the police away.

Malik called Parmar to ask for a meeting and also suggested a $50,000 deposit should be invested with him. Parmar said he would have to talk to others in the organization.

On June 18, CSIS observed Malik, Johal, and others arrive at Parmar's house for an evening meeting. Jaswinder Parmar called Surjan Gill's home to get him to attend, but Gill's daughter Pamela claimed he was too ill to come to the phone or leave the house. Gill appeared to be pulling out of the plot.

Those meeting at Parmar's that night would later claim it was a gathering to discuss a lawsuit they had all joined in against *Indo-Canadian Times* publisher Tara Singh Hayer. Their former ally had been writing critically against them, suggesting they had misused donations. But one of the claimants in that suit was the anti-separatist poet Rampuri, who had been beaten months earlier. He was never invited to the meeting at Parmar's, which suggests it may have had a more sinister purpose. CSIS agents knocked off shift at 9:50 p.m. as the meeting continued inside Parmar's house.

Talwinder Parmar was very busy on the phone on June 19, 1985, with coded calls likely related to last-minute details of his terrorist plot. He called Malik at 8:30 that morning. He called his travel agent ally, Amarjit Pawa. Then at 5:17 p.m. he placed a cryptic call to Johal. "Have you written the story yet?" Parmar asked the school janitor, who replied no.

Thirty-five minutes later, just before 6:00 p.m., CP Air ticket agent Martine Donahue took a call from a Mr. Singh. She said later that he had an "East Indian" accent and booked tickets for two travellers, one who was travelling east and one who was going west. She suggested a few flights, but the caller insisted that whatever airlines were booked out of Vancouver would have to connect later with Air-India flights. She booked one ticket to Tokyo, where it would connect with an Air-India flight to Bangkok, in the name of Mohinderbel Singh.

There was a glitch in the other booking. The passenger, who was identified as Jaswant Singh by the caller, was booked for the Vancouver-Toronto flight but could not be confirmed on the Air-India flight from Toronto. Donahue had to book him to Montreal, where he would have to pick up his luggage and switch airports to get on the plane to India. The caller provided the same phone number for both ticket files: 604-427-3216. It was Johal's old home phone number.

Seven minutes later, at 6:02 p.m., Johal called Parmar. Now the story was completed, Johal said. He invited Parmar over to read it. CSIS watched Parmar leave his house at 6:39 p.m. Surveillance was discontinued before Parmar arrived home.

People were coming and going from Parmar's house throughout June 20. At about 10:00 a.m., three Sikhs arrived from
Toronto on tickets that had been arranged by Parmar's friends in
Ontario. Two hours later, a turbaned man of average stature, with
his beard tied up in a net, arrived at CP Air's ticket office at
Georgia and Burrard Streets in downtown Vancouver. He handed
agent Gerald Duncan a piece of white paper. On it were details
of the two CP Air/Air-India flights booked a day earlier. The man
wanted the names on the tickets changed from Mohinderbel
Singh to L. Singh and from Jaswant Singh to M. Singh. When
Duncan printed out a return ticket to Bangkok, the man objected,
saying he just needed one way. The turbaned man handed Duncan
a stack of bills, folded in the middle. It was $3,005 in cash.

Later that day, Surjan Gill was captured by surveillance talking
to Parmar on his front steps for ten minutes.

At the crack of dawn on June 21, Gill arrived at Parmar's and
handed him a manila envelope. It was his resignation from the
Babbar Khalsa, a copy of which would be found by police a few
months later during a raid on a Kamloops house. Parmar seemed
to be trying to negotiate with Gill. Gill went to Parmar's house
again at 5:25 p.m.

CSIS agents watched as Bagri's vehicle arrived at Parmar's at
9:20 p.m. Their report said they did not believe it was Bagri
driving the car. The driver was wearing the traditional Nihang
garb and was with a woman and small child. But given the
number of errors CSIS had made misidentifying Babbars in the
previous month, their observation about the man in Bagri's car,
made as the sun was going down, was also suspect.

On June 22 – arguably the most important day for the Air-
India conspirators – CSIS agents were told to call off their
surveillance of Parmar. The observation post they had been using

was no longer available. Some of the agents had to check out a Soviet spy who had arrived in the area.

If they had stayed, they might have seen Inderjit Reyat at Parmar's house. Reyat was in the vicinity at about 10:00 a.m. that day. He stopped by Auto Marine Electric's Burnaby store, where he bought a twelve-volt battery like the one later found in the debris at Tokyo's Narita Airport. He showed the clerk a rectangular metal bracket with dangling wires into which he wanted the battery to fit. The clerk later told police Reyat seemed nervous and in a hurry. But he still asked for his employee discount and foolishly told the store staff he worked at the Duncan branch of the same chain. Less than an hour later, a minute-long call was made from Johal's house to Reyat's Duncan residence. Johal's house on East 30th in Vancouver was midway between Parmar's Burnaby residence and the Vancouver International Airport.

The cryptic phone calls between Parmar and other suspects continued. He asked Johal, "Did you mail the letter?" Johal said he had. Johal was seen at Vancouver Airport that morning. He even had a chat with Daljit Singh Grewal, an acquaintance who was flying to Toronto to board the targeted Air-India flight. There was a second call around 4:00 p.m. between Johal's home and Reyat's residence. Was he checking in with his family, having successfully placed two bombs on two planes? Later, Parmar's brother Kulwarn called him and asked, "Has that work been done?" "Not yet," Parmar replied.

Jeanne Bakermans was called in to work an early shift on June 22. It was supposed to be her day off, and she would soon wish that she had stayed home. Bakermans was alone at the CP Air check-in counter at Vancouver International Airport as dozens of

Toronto-bound passengers lined up to pass her their bags and get their boarding passes. One of them was a clean-shaven man of Indian origin who wanted to check his suitcase all the way to New Delhi even though he was only wait-listed on the Air-India flight out of Toronto.

He had a round face and distinctive, sparkly black eyes. He was probably in his mid-thirties and of medium build. He spoke English well and without a heavy accent. Identified only as M. Singh on the ticket, the man kept insisting that he had called Air-India that day and been told that his ticket was now confirmed all the way through. He badgered Bakermans, telling her he had paid business-class fare in order to get a confirmed reservation on the flight. "He was arguing with me. He started to move away from my counter and he said, 'My brother knows I'm confirmed. I'll go get my brother,'" Bakermans later said.

Eventually, Bakermans relented and switched the orange tag she had placed on the bag to a pink one, signalling that it had to be transferred in Toronto to the Air-India flight. It was about 8:00 a.m. Mr. Singh, whom Bakermans checked into seat 10-B for the connecting CP Air flight to Toronto, never boarded the plane.

In the early afternoon, Bakermans dealt with another man, identified as L. Singh, with a ticket for a CP Air flight to Tokyo and an Air-India flight from there to Bangkok. Bakermans checked in his suitcase without incident.

Two bombs were now headed in opposite directions around the globe.

Later that evening, more than a dozen of Parmar's supporters gathered at his home where they sat in the living room decorated with pictures of Sikh gurus and photos of bloodied bodies – "martyrs" – from the Indian Army raid on the Golden Temple. The group held a ghoulish tea party, drinking chai and eating sweets as they awaited the news.

On June 23, the world awoke to reports of the terrorist bomb-ings that had killed 331 people. Parmar spent most of that day at home, with people coming and going throughout the day.

Malik had left his three young sons the day before at the Tsawwassen home of close family friends Jagdev and Brajinder Dhillon. His wife, Raminder, was in India. He picked the boys up about 10:00 a.m. on June 23, telling a startled Mrs. Dhillon that an Air-India plane had been bombed. Later, Malik got a call at home from Mrs. Parmar, inviting him to come over to their house. He said he would be over about 6:00 p.m.

In Parmar's last intercepted call that day, he asked a woman, "Which channel is [the] report coming?" She told the terrorist to turn on the CBC on Channel 3. It was broadcasting news of his lethal handiwork.

CHAPTER 3

The Struggle to Understand

I N THE SPRING OF 1985, Ray Kobzey and his partner, David Ayre, were responsible for investigating Sikh extremists in British Columbia for the new Canadian Security Intelligence Service. Kobzey had prepared the affidavit to get a wiretap starting in March 1985 on the home of suspected terrorist Talwinder Singh Parmar, whom CSIS believed might have been involved in a plot to kill Indian prime minister Rajiv Gandhi.

Kobzey, who like many of the new CSIS agents, had been a long-time RCMP officer, was on holiday from June 8 to 22, 1985. He called Ayre's house about 9:30 a.m. on June 23 to let his partner know he was back in town. He had not been listening to the news. Ayre's wife answered and told him that Ayre was at work.

"As it was a Sunday morning, I recall asking her why he was working overtime," Kobzey told the RCMP years later. "I recall his wife saying to me, 'Raymond, didn't you hear?'"

"Hear what?" Kobzey replied, a little confused.

"The plane's gone down . . . an Air-India plane."

Kobzey's first thought was, Parmar did it. He may have even muttered something to that effect to Ayre's wife. He raced to the office to join his colleagues already deep into the work related to their extremist targets and their link to the Air-India bombing.

Kobzey had always had a feeling that Parmar was "up to something no good." He just wasn't sure what until the bombings. That sense of urgency on the part of CSIS agents would soon be undermined by one of the most outrageous and devastating bureaucratic bungles of any government agency ever.

CSIS had been in operation for just eleven months on June 23, 1985, and it was already facing the most severe threat to national security in the country's history. The fledgling agency was not prepared. Most of the operatives had come over to CSIS from the old national security section of the RCMP, which had faced regular political attacks for its choice of targets and for sometimes blurring the lines between policing and intelligence gathering. Some who remained in the RCMP were resentful at losing their spy function. Those who went over to CSIS were seen as disloyal by some who stayed behind. Many of the agents, including Kobzey, would later admit that, at the time of the bombings, they didn't even know all of CSIS's policies, especially regarding the sensitive area of information-sharing with the RCMP.

Talwinder Parmar, now the key suspect in Canada's worst mass murder, would not have known of the growing pains of the new spy agency. But he was nevertheless confident that no one could touch him. How could he have been so sure that the agents he suspected were watching him were so ineffective? Was it the June 4 test blast that had led to no charges? Was it the fact that the RCMP had responded to neighbours' complaints about the strange men sitting in cars and had not actually bothered Parmar? Was it his stubborn arrogance that made him feel invincible? Maybe he thought it was because he had God on his side.

Reporters called Parmar's house constantly in the days after the bombing. Salim Jiwa of the *Vancouver Province* asked Parmar if the Babbar Khalsa were responsible for the bombings. Parmar adamantly denied any involvement. Terry Glavin was also captured on CSIS wiretaps talking to Parmar. Parmar confirmed to Glavin that CSIS had talked to him and had shown him some photos.

The *Sun* kept a team of journalists working on the biggest story in the country's history. I was assigned to call Surjan Gill and other separatists with whom I had spoken over the past year. Gill admitted to me that he had been visited on June 11 by the RCMP and two U.S. Secret Service agents, who showed him photos of several suspected Sikh extremists believed to have been hiding in Vancouver and linked to the plot to kill Gandhi on his U.S. visit. Gill hinted that the men, who he said he had not recognized but were from Eastern Canada, could have been involved in Air-India. "I'd never seen these people," he said of the Sikhs in the photographs he was shown. "There are sixty-thousand [Sikh] people here. I wouldn't know if I passed these people on the street."

The majority of Sikhs in British Columbia and Canada were outraged at the Air-India and Narita bombings. About two dozen of the doomed passengers were Sikh, but a disproportionate number were Hindu, as many Sikhs had heeded the warning to boycott Air-India, not wanting to face the wrath of the militants. Sikh separatist groups – including some of the suspects themselves – immediately pointed the finger at the government of India, suggesting that it had blown up its own plane to discredit the Khalistani movement.

But most of the Sikhs on the streets of Vancouver suspected Sikh separatists were to blame, if not specifically the Babbar Khalsa and Parmar. A young Sikh named Pritam Singh, who was in the Punjabi market of Vancouver on the day of the bombings, summed up the feeling of most Sikhs when he said the attacks were horrible, devastating. He was too nervous to have his picture taken for my paper, "because," he said, "those guys will come after you if you say something bad about them," adding, "They are really crazy. People are very afraid of them."

Some Sikh moderates, such as Ujjal Dosanjh, not only condemned the bombings, but also the Canadian government for not having done more to stop the militants. "We have been alerting the government of Canada – the various ministers, MPs, the Attorney General – that there is a very real kind of terror and tension spread through the community by the minority of the terrorist element," Dosanjh told me. "I'm really angry. If Sikhs have done this, the responsibility must be shared with the government of Canada because they knew this was happening." Dosanjh said he and others specifically warned the federal government "things were going to mushroom into something that couldn't be controlled."

Politicians right, left, and centre were condemning the apparent acts of terrorism, but even they were confused about who were the aggressors and who were the victims. Prime Minister Brian Mulroney announced that he had called Indian prime minister Rajiv Gandhi to offer his condolences.

But India had lost an aircraft, its twenty-two-person crew, and some of the passengers. The vast majority of the victims – 278 – were either Canadian nationals or Canadian residents. Mulroney had missed the point. This was a Canadian tragedy. This was an unprecedented Canadian act of terrorism.

Although police were already regarding Parmar as a suspect, he did not curtail his association with Ajaib Bagri, Ripudaman Malik, Surjan Gill, Daljit Sandhu, and other suspects. The day after the bombings, Sandhu, a leader of Vancouver's Ross Street temple, was seen going to Parmar's house just after 4:00 p.m. Sandhu was also caught on wiretap two days later chatting with Bagri.

Parmar went to Kamloops to see Bagri within a week of the terrorist blasts. Bagri was captured by a CSIS camera arriving at Parmar's house with other Babbar Khalsa members on the weekend of July 7 and 8. He also went to Ontario with Parmar a week later. While Bagri was at the Burnaby house, Parmar's teenaged son Narinder pointed a pellet gun out the window. Several neighbours called police, who responded immediately.

Parmar was worried enough about the RCMP's July 8 visit to call Malik. He asked Malik to help him find a lawyer who could find out the real reason police had gone to his house. He also called Satwant Singh Sandhu, an electronics expert, to find someone capable of sweeping Parmar's home for listening devices. Satwant Sandhu would go on to be a close associate of Malik's and, thirteen years later, someone who would openly threaten me on radio.

With news of the bombings less than a day old, CSIS pledged to do everything it could to aid the RCMP investigation of the twin terrorist attacks. On June 24, Randy Claxton, the regional director of CSIS since it began the previous July, met with the top RCMP officers in the region at their headquarters on Heather Street in Vancouver. Claxton, a twenty-eight-year RCMP man when he took over his new job, told RCMP deputy commissioner Tom Venner and assistant commissioner Don Wilson that they had "the fullest cooperation of the CSIS."

Claxton had specialized in counter-terrorism with the Mounties, following the sympathizers of radical leftist groups like Japan's Red Army and Germany's Bader-Meinhof Gang. He had investigated Soviet KGB agents in Montreal and Ottawa, and many years earlier he had worked on the case of Soviet defector Igor Gouzenko.

Claxton's agency was concerned enough about Parmar and militant Sikh separatists to be watching and listening to them but did not understand how dangerous the Canadian Sikh terrorist leader was. Claxton later testified in a pre-trial hearing that Parmar was merely "an individual who was involved in the politicization of a community in the Lower Mainland." Yet he also later described the bombing of Air-India Flight 182 as "the most diabolical incident that I had encountered in my service."

Claxton told his RCMP counterparts in that first post-bombing meeting that CSIS had some vital information from "an installation" – code for a wiretap source. He did not name Parmar as the subject of the intercepted phone calls, but he thought it would be clear to these experienced RCMP officers.

RCMP Insp. John Hoadley headed the Air-India investigation in its early days. He knew there would be some debate about what could be provided by CSIS, as its mandate was to collect intelligence and not to gather evidence for criminal cases. But he was sure after talking to Claxton several times in the days following the bombings that they could work this out under existing legislation.

On June 26, Hoadley wrote a memo about a meeting with Claxton in which he indicated that he understood the spy agency had been intercepting someone's calls and that this "may yield evidence" in the Air-India probe.

A day later he captured another conversation with Claxton in his notes, which would become critical evidence of CSIS misconduct years after Hoadley died: "Any incriminating evidence of CSIS installation will immediately be isolated and retained for continuity with advice to ourselves. If they are asked to tender evidence, Randy will seek ministerial approval," he wrote.

Hoadley later told one of his superiors that he believed he had arranged with CSIS "to preserve all wiretap information that CSIS came into possession of."

It made sense. A February 18, 1985, memo to the regional chiefs from J.J.L. Jodoin, CSIS director general of communications, intelligence, and warrants, said any "incriminating passages" or "vague passages from which we are trying to draw an incriminating conclusion" should be kept for one year. The top-secret memo could have been written to preserve the cryptic coded messages in the soon-to-be-taped Parmar calls.

But many CSIS field agents and their bosses never read Jodoin's memo. And despite Claxton's reassurances of total cooperation with the RCMP, in the weeks after the bombings, his CSIS colleagues in both Vancouver and Ottawa would seriously undermine his promise.

When the Parmar intercepts began, the B.C. office of the spy agency did not have a Punjabi translator on staff, even though the Sikh community in the Lower Mainland was the largest in Canada. Claxton later explained that it was hard to find suitable Punjabi-speaking workers whom CSIS trusted – "You had a dimension first and foremost, of someone who is prepared to do it knowing full well that, should they be exposed, there would be a horrendous reprisal within the community and their homeland. And secondly, we were not about to make a risk that the person we would hire had been an agent of the Indian Intelligence Service."

A decision was made to send the tapes off to Ottawa, where there was a Punjabi-speaking staff member, while they searched for a suitable translator.

Even though Parmar was designated a threat to the nation's security, there didn't seem to be any sense of urgency in the B.C. CSIS office to find out what he was discussing in his many calls to and from associates. The B.C. office would wait until it had fifteen or so reels of tape before shipping them off as a package to Ottawa. Sometimes it took five days for the box to reach the capital, where the CSIS translator would then spend a couple of weeks creating logs of the conversations. No verbatim transcripts were produced.

By the time the logs were returned to the B.C. investigators, as much as six weeks had passed from the time the calls were made. If Parmar had openly discussed upcoming plans to bomb or assassinate targets, no one in Canada's spy agency would have known until well after the attack had taken place.

The Ottawa translator was told to look for "time sensitive information" and submit a report immediately when something was discovered. But even that process had a lag time of several weeks. By the time the translator made a report on Parmar's discussing his travel plans on April 1, 1985, eleven days had passed. Even when the translator listened to a suspicious conversation between Parmar and his German ally about an assassination plot against Rajiv Gandhi, the report of the April 8 call was not issued until May 31, 1985.

There was a space shortage in the Ottawa office as well. The large reel-to-reel tapes were kept in a locked cabinet until the translator got to them. After the notes were made, an X was marked through the tape's label, signalling to special agent James Laking that the tape could be erased. After thirty days, either Laking or his colleague Gene Pokoj took the tapes to a machine for erasure.

The Ottawa translator got so bogged down with the tedious process of documenting Parmar's calls that just thirty-three of the eighty-three tapes sent to Ottawa for the period March 27 to April 25 were processed. Those thirty-three were erased in Ottawa and the rest, which had still not been processed, were shipped back to British Columbia in July – after the bombings – so that the newly hired B.C. translator could tackle the backlog.

Things didn't go much better on the West Coast. The translator, who began work on June 7, was listening to Parmar's calls daily and reporting to Ayre in a general way what had been said. The logs were eventually made up, but there wasn't the staff to make verbatim transcripts, despite Claxton's repeated requests for personnel who could speak Punjabi.

What Claxton didn't realize at the time was that as soon as the logs were made and the required thirty-day retention period had expired, a bit of masking tape was placed on each Parmar reel, giving technicians the licence to erase them. David Ayre, who was assigned the task of writing up intelligence reports based on translator's logs of Parmar's calls, later admitted that he didn't read all the translators' notes of the Parmar intercept. He also said he did not know the tapes were being erased throughout the summer and fall of 1985.

Kobzey, his partner, didn't do much better. Though he was the agent in charge of monitoring Sikh extremists, Kobzey later told the RCMP that he did not know what the rules were about tape retention.

"As regards written policy concerning tape retention in both the [RCMP] Security Service and CSIS from 1981 to August 1985 I was never provided any opportunity to familiarize myself with formal written policy concerning this issue," Kobzey told the RCMP in 1991.

Throughout the summer of 1985, Claxton continued to argue with his superiors in Ottawa about giving the RCMP access to Ayre's intelligence reports, if not the translator's actual notes and tapes. But there was resistance from CSIS officials in Ottawa, who were worried about maintaining the separation between the agency's intelligence-gathering role and a live police investigation.

A CSIS analyst in Ottawa named Charlie Koghlin appeared to understand the significance of the exchanges between Parmar and other suspects captured on the wiretaps in the weeks before the bombings. He outlined in an August 1985 memo all the suspicious calls about delivering papers, mailing letters, and writing stories made in the days before the bombing.

"If the RCMP have not been provided with the information on the June 21st and June 22nd items, I suggest we provide the same as the dates and substance of the conversation between Parmar and Gill and Parmar and Johal may be significant vis-à-vis Reyat, Johal, Parmar['s] direct involvement in Narita bombing. In addition, if the RCMP are going to apply for technical coverage, it may be useful for them to have the preceding information re: discussion about papers by targets over the phone likely refer to weapons or explosives," the memo read.

In September, memos were flying back and forth between the RCMP and CSIS and between the regional CSIS office and its Ottawa headquarters about how and when the RCMP could have access to the CSIS wiretap material. Finally – three months after the Air-India and Narita bombings – an arrangement was worked out for Sandy Sandhu, a Punjabi-speaking RCMP constable, to be seconded to CSIS so he could listen to some of the tapes made after the bombings. There would be no policy violation because he would be a CSIS employee.

By the end of September, Sandhu had gone through the fifty tapes he was given. He asked CSIS for more. He was especially eager to review the tapes from early June, just before the bombings, when so many cryptic comments had been made by Parmar and others. Sandhu was casually told that the rest of the tapes had been destroyed.

Later Claxton had to concede that in months of negotiations over access to notes, transcriptions, and the critical tapes, no one at CSIS had bothered to make a retention order. But he also claimed that the reason the tapes weren't saved was because the

RCMP never asked the agency to preserve all or any of them. "Had I received one," he said, "it would have been incumbent on me to communicate with my headquarters immediately."

Perhaps the most critical evidence in the deadliest murder plot in Canadian history had been destroyed.

For all the criticism that can and has been made of CSIS and the RCMP for their handling of the Air-India case, some superb investigative work was done. The Japanese police, working closely with the RCMP, were able to link bits of debris found amid the wreckage at Tokyo's Narita Airport to purchases made by Inderjit Reyat in British Columbia in the weeks and months before the bombings. The small M, stencilled on a tiny scrap of cardboard found among the bomb rubble at the airport, was examined and linked forensically to the box of a Sanyo tuner he bought in June 1985.

The RCMP worked with British and Indian officials, repeatedly diving at the crash site to recover parts of the Air-India wreckage. The work was dangerous and difficult. In the end, just 5 per cent of the plane was recovered. But it was enough to determine that a bomb had destroyed it.

CSIS had been on the ball enough to report the June 4 blast in the woods near Duncan to the RCMP, and Cpl. Doug Henderson had been assigned to investigate. When Reyat's name came up, he realized that he had met the electrical wizard when Reyat had been referred to the veteran Mountie as someone who could help him with a '51 Fargo truck he was restoring.

In early June, at the request of CSIS, Henderson completed his report on Reyat's political activities in the Duncan area. Henderson was called upon again after June 23, when investigators from the RCMP's Air-India Task Force needed someone local to show them around the Vancouver Island town as they traced purchases linked to the forensic evidence in Japan. The RCMP was also hunting for witnesses.

The case was moving forward with great speed through the summer and fall of 1985. At one point, Henderson was sent to Reyat's home with the story he was setting up a liaison position between the local Sikh temple and police. He was really there to see if he could spot the Sanyo tuner or anything else suspicious in the house Reyat shared with his wife, Satnam, and his four young children. He made it into the basement where the family room was and then the upstairs living area, but he didn't see a tuner.

Investigators were talking to some of the suspects. They visited Bagri at his Kamloops home on October 10 to ask him about the bombings. He claimed to know nothing. A short time later he left for England en route to Pakistan.

At Heathrow Airport, Bagri was stopped by Scotland Yard Chief Supt. Keith Weston, who had been tipped to the Babbar Khalsa leader's arrival. Bagri admitted to Weston that the Babbar Khalsa might engage in acts others would see as terrorist, but only in India. He said he was in England to try to unite the British Babbar Khalsa faction with Parmar's group, under the Canadian's leadership. Bagri also told Weston that the Babbar Khalsa and the Akhand Kirtani Jatha, Malik's group, were connected.

Bagri not only visited the British Babbar Khalsa leader, Gurmej Singh Gill, and others from his group, he also stopped by to see Dr. Chohan, the Khalistani leader in exile, and he visited the Southall office of the Punjabi-language *Des Pardes* newspaper and its publisher, Tarsem Singh Purewal, who was a strong supporter of the Babbar Khalsa. Bagri did not know it at the time, but he was not the only Canadian in the *Des Pardes* office that day. Tara Singh Hayer was also there, out of sight behind a padded partition. Hayer had turned into a vocal opponent of Bagri and

Parmar; he believed they had been discrediting the separatist
movement by advocating violence.

By November, RCMP investigators felt ready to move in on
their suspects. They planned in advance who would interrogate
Reyat. Henderson was picked as one of the officers because of
his connection with the devout Sikh electrician-turned-terrorist.

Early in the evening of November 6, 1985, RCMP officers,
bolstered by the Vancouver police, moved in on Reyat, Parmar,
Hardial Johal, Surjan Gill, and two members of the International
Sikh Youth Federation – national spokesman Manmohan Singh
and Sodhi Singh Sodhi, who had been arrested for trashing the
Indian consulate in Vancouver a year earlier.

The sweep was dramatic. Singh called me at the *Sun* from his
popular Main Street restaurant, the Punjab.

"Kim, what can I do?" he said. "The RCMP is surrounding
my place. The customers are very unhappy."

"Manmohan," I replied. "They think you have something to
do with the bombing."

Ripudaman Malik, known to be one of Parmar's financial
backers, was the first over to Parmar's Burnaby house after the
Babbar Khalsa leader was picked up by police. He also called
Reyat's home the following day from his business.

Only Reyat and Parmar were charged. At first Reyat was
charged with offences that looked as if they were linked to the
Air-India bombing – intent to endanger life or cause serious
injury to property between June 3 and 24 in or near Duncan,
unlawfully making an explosive substance with intent to enable
another person to endanger life or to cause serious damage to
property between June 3 and 24 in or near Duncan, and possession of a restricted weapon – a Ruger .357-calibre revolver –
without a registration certificate.

Both Reyat and Parmar faced one joint charge: possession of an explosive substance for which they did not have a lawful purpose.

Over the objections of their lawyer, David Gibbons, search warrants were issued the day of the arrest that also linked the pair to the Narita bombing. The warrant said police were searching for a receipt for the Sanyo stereo component in which the Narita bomb had been concealed. They were also looking for other electronic components, timing devices, black explosives powder, an automotive starting fluid known as Liquid Fire, and rolls of adhesive tape.

Reporters from across the country descended on Duncan for the first court appearances of the accused. Sikh leaders from both the ISYF and the Babbar Khalsa condemned the Canadian government for doing India's bidding by persecuting their leaders. Air-India victims' families expressed optimism about this development in the case.

Henderson and RCMP Cpl. Glen Rockwell spent hours with Reyat at Duncan police headquarters after his arrest.

Reyat admitted that he and Parmar had done test explosions, and said that they weren't to Parmar's satisfaction. He admitted he bought the tuner and claimed that he had given it to a person who had stayed at his house. He admitted borrowing a book on how to use dynamite. He admitted buying gunpowder at Buckey's Sports Shop and relays at Radio Shack. He admitted Parmar had asked him to build bombs, but only to blow up objects in India.

Reyat's November 1985 statement to Henderson and Rockwell would become one of the most important pieces of evidence in the ensuing, twenty-year investigation.

When both Reyat and Parmar were released on bail, there were suggestions that the RCMP had jumped the gun and had moved in on the Air-India suspects before building the case against them. Those criticisms would soon be proven accurate.

Tensions in the Sikh community were even higher in 1986. There were more threats, demonstrations, and attacks. In January, a bomb was placed against the front door of Tara Hayer's newspaper office. Five sticks of dynamite connected to a ticking clock had been placed inside a McDonald's bag. The RCMP bomb squad managed to defuse it before it exploded. Still a diehard separatist, despite his split with the Babbar Khalsa and the ISYF, Hayer blamed the Indian government.

But police soon picked up several members of the ISYF, including Lakhbir Singh Brar (nephew of Bhindranwale, the man who had led the occupation of the Golden Temple in Amritsar), ISYF founder Harpal Singh Nagra, and Harjit Singh Atwal. They were questioned for several hours and released.

By March, it was apparent that the RCMP had been overly confident when it claimed that Parmar and Reyat were facing justice in the Air-India bombing. The explosives charges against Parmar were dropped for lack of evidence, and Reyat was convicted only on two minor charges. He was fined $2,000.

No wonder Sikh separatists felt secure in continuing their violence in Canada. Just three days after Reyat paid his fine, Vancouver Island was the scene of another act of terrorism. A Punjabi politician, visiting British Columbia for his nephew's wedding, was gunned down on an isolated logging road near Gold River. Amazingly, Malkiat Singh Sidhu survived the three gunshot wounds to his chest and arm. The spot where he was ambushed was so remote that the gunmen had only one route of escape. Alert RCMP officers closed the road and nabbed four ISYF members as they fled toward Campbell River.

I was one of many reporters who flocked to the Vancouver Island town when the men made their first court appearance.

David Gibbons sat next to me on the small plane over to the island from Vancouver. Fresh from his victory in defending Reyat and Parmar, he had been hired to represent some of the new defendants.

The Sikh community, for the most part, widely condemned the violence and worried about being linked to terrorism by the media. Both Tara Hayer and Ujjal Dosanjh were always at the forefront with their concerns.

"I can foresee racial violence if people keep seeing us as not being fit to stay in Canadian society because of these things. I can only pray that people will see fit to see us as living peacefully in Canada," Hayer said in response to the Sidhu shooting.

Dosanjh added, "I would say that the local Sikh people themselves are pretty mad and some of that anger is directed against the Canadian government. The people are angry because there have been so many incidents over the past couple of years and we have been crying out for help. The police seem to think sometimes that this is just a political problem. I know they are trying to do their job, but this is a police problem."

It only got worse. Five days after the assassination attempt, five of Parmar's followers in the Babbar Khalsa, all based in Montreal, were arrested and charged with conspiracy to blow up a second Air-India jet, which was due to leave New York on May 31 with an Air-India cabinet minister aboard.

On May 31, CSIS wiretaps picked up a conversation between Parmar and his Ontario lieutenant in the Babbar Khalsa, Tejinder Singh Kaloe. Kaloe was describing the Montreal arrests to his leader. Clearly annoyed that members of his group were being arrested again, Parmar said he had warned the Montrealers: "We told those bastards to stop it."

As if the Sikh community wasn't reeling enough from nine terrorism charges in a matter of days, two weeks later, Parmar, Kaloe,

Bagri, and four Babbar Khalsa members from the Hamilton area
in Ontario were picked up and charged with conspiring to blow
up the Indian parliament buildings in New Delhi, as well as several
trains and an oil refinery. Wiretaps indicated they also wanted to
kidnap the child of an Indian MP.

Canadians linked to the ISYF in other parts of the world were
also implicated. On June 15, 1986, six federation members,
including the Canadian leader, Satinderpal Singh Gill, were
charged in Lahore, Pakistan, with attacking some Indian diplomats with their swords.

Law enforcement agents may well have congratulated themselves on finally getting the upper hand on Sikh terrorism in
Canada. In September, five more B.C. ISYF members, including
Harjit Atwal and Piara Singh Natt, were charged with conspiracy to commit murder in the Sidhu case. The four men already
facing attempted murder charges were also charged with conspiracy. CSIS had captured conversations on tape that police
believed implicated a wider group in the assassination plot.

From Montreal to Hamilton to Vancouver Island, the Sikh terrorist cases, including the Air-India bombing, had common
threads that tied them together. But the cases would be the first
sign that Canada's laws were inadequate in dealing with suspected terrorists like those in the Babbar Khalsa and the ISYF.
Their members would be arrested on serious criminal charges;
they would hire prominent defence lawyers like David Gibbons
of Vancouver and Michael Code of Toronto; their prosecution
relied on information from confidential informants or on wire-
tapped calls intercepted by CSIS; and they would eventually get off
on technicalities, primarily evidence that the wiretap warrants were
improperly obtained or because the RCMP refused to reveal the
identity of informants. Upon their release, they would claim they
were being persecuted in Canada, just like the Sikhs of Punjab.

Despite the escalating violence, CSIS was less concerned with helping the RCMP than with its own image, as a memo to a CSIS lawyer, dated July 16, 1986, indicates. Signed by Jim Warren, director-general of counter-terrorism, it said that, during litigation over the Air-India bombing, "certain claims were being made by the RCMP that implied, if not directly alleged, a lack of cooperation by CSIS with respect to the Air India criminal investigation.

"To the best of my knowledge, the RCMP has made no formal charge to [CSIS] of failure to pass on relevant intelligence, prior to or subsequent to, the Air India disaster. The agency has, however, suffered a certain amount of innuendo to flow around."

In less than a year, four terrorist plots related to a political struggle in India had been hatched in Canada. As few Canadians really understood that struggle, I decided to go to India to learn more about the Khalistan movement and its links to home. I arranged to go in September 1986, despite travel restrictions on foreigners because of the conflict there.

In New Delhi, I found numerous academics, activists, and political leaders eager to tell me who and what was responsible for the conflict in the rich northern state with its Sikh majority population. Supporters of the separatists and human-rights activists alike blamed the federal government for authorizing the attack on the Golden Temple and for doing nothing to stop the massacre of Sikhs following the assassination of Indira Gandhi. Others blamed Sikhs in Canada for financing the separatist cause, and the Canadian government for doing little to prevent it.

I had not truly understood the intense bond between Sikhs in India and those in Canada until that trip. I met Harji Malik, the daughter of India's first ambassador to Canada, in her gorgeous south Delhi home, where she leafed through an old photo album of a huge parade down Vancouver's Main Street in 1947 to welcome her father. He had played a big role in India's independence movement, and as Malik explained, "My father was a hero to the Sikhs there."

The connections to Canada were even stronger in the villages of Punjab, where everyone had a cousin, brother, or friend living somewhere in Canada. The rural farmers rattled off the names of suburbs of Vancouver and Toronto to me with surprising familiarity.

There was another surprising element in the views I heard in Punjabi villages – people were angered by both sides in the political dispute. Most felt caught between the separatist groups, who resorted to terrorism and would bully the villagers for support, and the Indian government forces, who were equally brutal in their crackdown, often jailing or shooting innocent parties.

Intellectuals like the famous playwright Gursharan Singh were being threatened and attacked by separatist groups who were upset that they had been exposing the violence of their movement, while also condemning the government's ineffective response.

I was not yet used to the instant intimacy that is so Punjabi. People would do anything for you and treat you like family after just a brief visit with them. Their warmth and generosity seemed such a contradiction to the extremists' hatred of Hindus or less-orthodox Sikhs.

Because of the conflict, there were virtually no tourists in Amritsar. I had never seen anything like the Golden Temple, its white walls and gleaming dome surrounded by sacred waters and marble pathways.

A former MP from the Women's Akali Dal party, Dr. Rajinder Kaur, offered to take me on a fact-finding trip to the villages. We rode with seven others, jammed into a Jeep for the two-hour journey. It was more than forty degrees, and the kirpan of one old woman standing next to me kept jabbing my face with every bump in the road.

We passed roadside tea stalls – *dhabas* – where dozens of people crowded around, each sipping a Campa-Cola, Thums Up, or Oranogola. The country was very flat, green, and lush. Huge deciduous trees arched over the bumpy road, and every kilometre or two we crossed canals and passed waterholes where water buffaloes wallowed to avoid the heat.

After an hour or so, we arrived at the small green farmhouse where, two months earlier, the Indian border police had murdered a pregnant woman and her brother and shot three bullets into their elderly mother. The dead woman's sister welcomed us while her filthy children grabbed her leg in shyness and stared intently at the first white person they had likely ever seen. Their huge brown eyes looked almost fierce as their mother pointed to the chipped plaster where the bullets had hit and demonstrated how the rest of the family escaped slaughter by crouching behind a stack of bricks and inside a small porch. Earlier, the border police had mistakenly been involved in a shootout with the central police on the old farmer's property, the former thinking the latter were terrorists. One border policeman was killed in the exchange. When the border police leader realized the tragic error, he staged a shootout at the farmers' house, killing a couple of people to make the earlier fight look legitimate. Police eventually admitted their mistake in targeting the family.

"They said someone at this house must die when they came in, and my brother was pushing up against the wall like this," the sister said, demonstrating her brother's position when they pumped the first bullets into his stomach. As he screamed at them, his sister pleaded with the attackers to stop. They shot her too. "Some bullets went right into her stomach and the baby started coming out," the sister said.

The dead woman was also shot in the face, as was shown in the black-and-white photos the family produced of the carnage. The elderly mother was hit under her right armpit and twice in her face. Amazingly, she survived, though most of her face was gone, half her nose and tongue missing. She lifted her loose cotton smock to show me the bullet hole, her daughter gently lifting her arm as the old woman cried in pain, her sagging breasts unashamedly exposed, tears streaming down her face.

By the time we left, most of the cousins and other relatives had arrived from the fields to see the strangers. Ox and cows stood in the driveway staring as the grey-haired father of the clan, his thick glasses masking his eyes, said he had served in the Indian Army and should not have been treated that way. He said he had showed the police his veteran's card.

The old man then climbed into the Jeep and escorted us to the spot where the Border Security Force had shot ten boys a week earlier. We bounced down a pathway through the fields and stopped about five hundred metres from the Pakistan border, where the Border Security Force had blocked the road. They stood there, their rifles aimed at us. I was more than a little nervous because I had no idea what my escorts intended to do.

The men got out of the Jeep and walked toward the police. They talked awhile, but obviously weren't getting anywhere. Kaur's daughter told me to get out my press card and join the men. "They are all wearing blue and black turbans – the Akali colours – so the police don't think they are a press group. You'll be able to make it more legitimate," she said.

I hesitated, not really wanting to argue with men pointing guns, but I felt obliged to do what my hosts requested of me. I flashed my press card at the policeman in his undershirt and rolled-up pants. Farm workers labouring nearby put down their loads to watch the exchange.

"We want to go to the spot where the boys were shot. Press," I said, but the man kept shaking his head and pointing his gun. I was ready to give up, but my crew kept pestering the policeman until he gave us a definitive no. About four hundred metres away we could see the riverbank where the bodies were found, but there was no way we were going to get to the spot.

So off we went again, ten of us sweating and sneezing at the dust that blew from under the Jeep's wheels. We blinded every wagon driver we passed as we drove another five kilometres or so to the village of the man on whose land the bodies were found. He said all the boys had been seen in their villages before they were shot and had not come from Pakistan, as the police claimed. It was a powerful lesson about the climate in which the average Punjabi was living.

Back at the Golden Temple complex, Sukhwant Singh Akkanwali strutted around like a construction-site foreman, watching carefully as each brick was laid in an effort to repair the damage. One of the few leaders of the All India Sikh Student Federation not killed in the temple attack, Akkanwali told me how Sikhs were rebuilding part of the complex by hand more than two years after the army attack. He said his organization, labelled terrorist by the government of India, had 300,000 members there and another 20,000 in Canada, all members of the Vancouver-based International Sikh Youth Federation. He said the Indian group got its financing from compatriots in Canada.

"We may kill, but we don't want to live as slaves," Akkanwali said. "The terrorism is there. If my father is burned and my brothers and sister raped in front of the people, what will I do? I will kill the Hindus who have killed my father and raped my sister."

There were no subtleties in his message. It was clear and direct, and it was reiterated when I travelled to Lahore, Pakistan, a couple of days later. I was there in search of his Canadian colleagues in the ISYF, who were living in the city's historic Dera Sahib temple.

There I met Satinderpal Gill for the first time. A member of the Panthic Committee and leader of the International Sikh Youth Federation, he had come from the Vancouver suburb of Surrey. He denied that he was leading the Sikh insurgency in India, and claimed that he and the other Canadians were stuck in Lahore only because they had been unfairly charged a few months earlier with attacking some visiting Indian diplomats.

He told me that they were under house arrest at the temple, and I did see a number of Pakistani police guards there. But then the Canadian Sikhs ordered the guards to get us tea and later ordered them to give me a tour of the historic sites of Lahore. If they were prisoners, it was not custody as I understood it.

The Canadians slept on simple cots inside the temple. They were young, good-looking men, who bragged about their willingness to kill, terrorize, and bomb to get Khalistan. One boy had just turned eighteen and had missed two years of his schooling back in Ontario to be there. A picture of Jarnail Bhindranwale, their martyr, was taped to the wall beside others of the carnage after the temple attack. *Blood, blood, blood*, was scrawled underneath in red ink.

The Canadians said they wanted to go to northern Pakistan to get better weapons for their battle. "The ISYF doesn't like to break the laws in Canada, but sometimes we have to," Pritam Singh of Surrey told me.

Two of the young men I met that day would eventually be killed in gun battles in Punjab. Another would be arrested on terrorism charges.

The final stop on my journey was the disputed Punjabi capital, Chandigarh, with its world-renown architecture and gardens. There, I met Malkiat Sidhu, the Punjabi politician who had been shot on Vancouver Island a few months earlier by members of Satinderpal Gill's ISYF.

Sidhu told me he had never imagined he would be at risk in Canada and said the Sikh separatists in British Columbia were misled. "Sikhs here don't want Khalistan. Where do the Canadians want it to be – in Vancouver? They wouldn't come back here."

Sidhu was assassinated a few years later by a separatist who finished the job started on the other side of the globe.

Life went more smoothly for some of the Air-India suspects than it did for others after the bombing. While Talwinder Parmar and Ajaib Bagri fought criminal charges, Ripudaman Malik obtained additional properties, expanded his companies, incorporated non-profit societies, and applied for charitable status for them. He also founded the Khalsa Credit Union and the Khalsa School. He hired Ujjal Dosanjh to do the paperwork for the societies he created. The Satnam Education Society of B.C., which Malik founded to run the Khalsa School, easily got federal charity status. He already headed another group with charitable status: the Satnam Trust, which would later be linked to a dead terrorist in Punjab named Gurbax Kaur.

By September 1986, Malik had opened the first Khalsa School in Vancouver. It had 185 students and almost $200,000 of government funding. He told a reporter at the time that the school was necessary in order to isolate Sikh children from Canadian society because it was so corrupt.

"We are isolating them from sex at ten, from smoking and from drugs. In this society, the family structure is pretty weird. I want to separate my children from that and teach them to respect themselves and their own parents." He went on to say, "We can be successful and be isolated. We don't need to learn the bad things from your society. We can mix sometimes, though, and learn the good things."

The Khalsa Credit Union opened the same year near the school on Fraser Street in Vancouver. It was duly incorporated as a legal financial institution, with Malik heading the board, even though its founding members were linked to terrorist groups that CSIS had been tracking for years. Both the Babbar Khalsa and the International Sikh Youth Federation opened accounts at the credit union.

Canadian jurors seemed convinced of the guilt of both the Babbar Khalsa and ISYF members. Two Montreal Babbar Khalsa members, Santokh Singh Khela and Kashmir Singh Dhillon, went to trial in December 1986 in connection with the plot to blow up an Air-India jet out of New York. The charges against three others were dropped. A jury convicted Khela and Dhillon, and they were sentenced to life in prison in January 1987. A month later, a Vancouver jury convicted the four ISYF members of attempted murder in the Sidhu shooting. They were each sentenced to twenty years. They were still supposed to face a second trial in the Sidhu case for conspiracy, based on the CSIS wiretaps.

No wonder Solicitor General James Kelleher was feeling confident enough to congratulate the director of CSIS for progress made in the Air-India case. In a January 28, 1987, memo, Kelleher expressed what would turn out to be premature concern about developing "a fully coordinated ministry approach to the handling of media and other public inquiries when arrests are eventually made in this case."

In February, as police dug for more evidence in the twin 1985 bombings, key suspect Inderjit Reyat, his wife, Satnam, and their four children quietly left for the United Kingdom, where Reyat got a job at the Jaguar factory in Coventry.

In April, the Hamilton case against Parmar, Kaloe, and their associates unravelled because the Crown said it could not identify an informant without crippling a police investigation in Vancouver. All the charges were dropped. After his release, Parmar attended a religious service with his associates.

"What we have gone through in this trial has been hectic for our families, our friends, our congregations and whole communities of Canada. This should not happen in the justice of this country," Parmar complained.

Bagri had earlier been freed for lack of evidence. He told me he was pleased the rest of his group would soon be joining him. "They never did anything. All they did was just talking, like we're talking. That's all they did," he claimed.

Parmar granted me his first media interview when he returned to British Columbia. It was the first time I had been inside his luxurious Howard Avenue home, although I had interviewed him several times on the phone and outside various temples and demonstrations over the past three years. I was made to cover my head upon entering because, his wife told me, it was a holy place. Parmar refused to talk to me in English even though I had heard him speak it many times before. I had to hire a translator for the day.

We spoke in a room decorated with large framed photographs of bloodied bodies of Sikh warriors strewn across the Golden Temple courtyard taken the day the Indian soldiers hit. As he talked, his head was tilted slightly backwards, his hands punctuated his points, and a blue-swathed sword lay across his lap. I felt the force of his charisma.

He was full of the usual bluster, claiming that India was pressing Canada to frame his members and supporters. He denied involvement in the Air-India bombing and the other crimes in which he was a suspect. With all the surveillance on him by police and spies, how could he possibly do anything, he reasoned. "I'm happy if the RCMP are following me. If I am not followed, Indian government agents might kill me."

A few weeks later, Parmar flew to Halifax to greet 174 Indian boat people who had been dropped by a freighter off the coast of Nova Scotia. Most were Sikhs with links to the separatist movement. They all claimed refugee status, most of them successfully. Politicians who dared to suggest the men were queue-jumping were chastised in the press by refugee groups and Sikh associations. B.C. premier Bill Vander Zalm accused the migrants of slipping through the back door and said they should be sent back to India to apply through the regular channels. That comment prompted a public tongue-lashing from Parmar.

A number of Sikhs offered cash to aid forty-seven of the refugees to come to British Columbia, among them Air-India suspects Daljit Sandhu and Hardial Johal supported the campaign. Malik donated $7,000. "These people are assets, not burdens, to the community," he said, adding that he felt the Canadian government had not treated the Sikh refugees well.

Right before the second Sidhu trial was set to begin in September 1987, Canada's spy agency was once again haunted by problems with its wiretaps on suspected Sikh terrorists. CSIS was forced to admit that the information used to get the wiretap of ISYF member Harjit Atwal was "inaccurate and unsubstantiated." Charges were consequently dropped against all nine men accused of conspiring to kill the visiting cabinet minister. Just the original four arrested near the scene would face any jail time.

But that was not all. It was also revealed by MP Svend Robinson that Atwal had talked on his bugged phone about Sidhu's pending visit and a beating the cabinet minister would receive. This information had never been passed on to the RCMP. If it had, perhaps Sidhu's shooting could have been prevented. In the resulting political furor, CSIS director Ted Finn was forced to resign. Atwal and Natt were let out of a Vancouver jail and were met by a grinning Parmar, shouting, "Khalistan, Khalistan."

Because of this bungling, many Sikhs and non-Sikhs in Canada were a little skeptical when the RCMP announced on February 5, 1988, that Inderjit Reyat had been arrested in England in connection with the Narita bombing. His arrest left important questions unanswered: If there was a real case to be made – finally – why wasn't he being charged in the Air-India massacre? Why was he facing only a manslaughter charge for the slayings of the two Japanese baggage handlers?

But the arrest was enough to put the other Air-India suspects on edge, especially when police visited Bagri, Parmar, and a number of other Babbars who had gathered in Kamloops for a weekend prayer meeting the day after Reyat was nabbed.

"I don't know what they wanted to ask me. They've asked me all these questions a hundred times," an agitated Bagri told me. "Everyone is thinking there will be more arrests, this whole thing is political. I think the Indian government is putting pressure on the Canadians."

B.C. Sikh temples began collecting money for Reyat's defence. Bagri contacted Reyat's British lawyer, Harjit Singh, within a day of the arrest but, when I asked, refused to say why he would be talking to Reyat's lawyer. From London, the dual British-Canadian citizen pledged to fight his extradition to Canada, no matter what.

Tara Hayer was worried that the police may have jumped the gun again. "If they arrest prematurely, they might spoil their case, and the Sikh community will be harassed again," he said. Dosanjh referred nervously to the other bungled Sikh terrorist cases: "It would be a sad thing to have the events of the last year or two repeated."

Their comments served to point out how rare it was to see politicians condemning Sikh terrorism in Canada. None stood at news conferences behind the battered victims of assaults. Instead, they lined up behind Parmar on such issues as granting refugee status to the Nova Scotia boat people. They attended Sikh religious parades. They visited the newly opened Khalsa School in Vancouver. They learned to recite the Sikh religious greeting – "WaheGuru Ji Ka Khalsa, WaheGuru Ji Ki Fateh" – in perfect Punjabi to impress crowds at temple functions. The words sounded odd in the mouths of politicians, considering they mean the Khalsa belongs to God, victory belongs to God. I often wondered if they even knew what they were saying.

So it was a surprise when Conservative External Affairs Minister Joe Clark issued a written warning in February 1988 to the country's premiers. In it, he asked them to stay away from Sikh separatist groups, specifically the International Sikh Youth Federation, Parmar's Babbar Khalsa, and the World Sikh Organization. He said that members of these groups had used violence to agitate for the separate state of Khalistan, and that "the activities of these organizations have been a significant irritant in our relations with India."

After the letter was publicized, Clark faced blistering attacks from some of the same MPs who were lobbying for a public inquiry into the Air-India bombing. Both Liberal John Nunziata and New Democrat Svend Robinson spoke out on behalf of the groups. Presumably, neither of them knew about their terrorist links.

Nunziata then took it a step further. He joined eight other Liberal MPs and MPPs at an ISYF convention on March 20 in Mississauga, Ontario. At the convention, while 150 delegates, some with terrorist links, surrounded him, Nunziata called Clark "a patsy of the Indian government." He went on, "If he has evidence that any member of these organizations is involved in criminal activity, it's his responsibility to prosecute."

After the news conference ended and the politicians left, a bizarre scene erupted on the convention floor. As Bagri took the microphone to tell the congregation about Parmar's achievements, Ontario Babbar Khalsa leader Tejinder Kaloe stood up and accused his B.C. counterparts of misappropriating donations. He then pulled out a handgun, prompting B.C. ISYF leader Amrit Rai to lunge at him, sending the gun flying through the air. Bagri was hustled out the back door and whisked away to safety. Kaloe was calmed down by his associates, though no one told police what had happened. If the politicians had stayed awhile longer, they would have witnessed all the action.

Sikh-Hindu relations became volatile in India again in the spring of 1988 when Sikh militants began to amass arms inside the Golden Temple complex once more. A limited military exercise, dubbed Operation Black Thunder, was carried out in May by the Indian Army. The Indian government claimed to find letters during the operation that substantiated links between Canadian and Indian Sikh separatist groups. There was some fear it would bring reprisals in Canada, as Operation Blue Star had done. But there were few civilian casualties and limited reaction around the world.

In Canada, Sikh separatists were much quieter than they had been in a long time. So quiet that CSIS and the RCMP did not notice when Parmar and Bagri – two suspects in one of the deadliest terrorist attacks in history – slipped out of the country for Pakistan. Sikh moderates, including Ujjal Dosanjh, asked how it could have happened. The RCMP, Dosanjh said, "have egg all over their face. It's a shame. If they are out of the country, it's rather shocking and surprising. It's sad."

Most observers concluded that the pair was trying to avoid the same fate that Reyat was facing – years of court battles in an attempt to avoid prosecution in the June 1985 terrorist attacks. The families of both men were cryptic when asked where the two men were. Jaswinder Parmar told me that no one knew where his father had gone. Bagri's wife said he had left the country, but she didn't know his destination. She claimed he was travelling with Parmar.

I managed to reach Parmar by phone at a Pakistan temple where he was staying. Hayer had given me the contact number. When he came to the phone and I identified myself, Parmar slammed down the receiver. But I was not deterred. That August I travelled to India for a second time to try to find him.

I had been told that Parmar was holed up at the sacred shrine in Pakistan where he had been baptized ten years earlier – Nankana Sahib – so I headed there first. When I asked, a worker at the shrine confirmed that Parmar was there. But he came back minutes later and said he was mistaken. It was frustrating.

I did find my ISYF contacts at the other historic Sikh temple – Dera Sahib. Satinderpal Gill was still claiming that he was under house arrest, despite building himself a fully equipped apartment in the temple since my visit two years earlier. He now had a Persian carpet and a queen-sized bed. Gill refused to say if he had seen Parmar, but several British Babbar Khalsa members there told me that Parmar had recently visited. They said they didn't know where he had gone afterwards.

Parmar's frail parents, Jamiat Singh and Surjit Kaur, were surprised when I visited them in their small plaster house in the Punjabi village of Panshta. They said they did not know that their son had fled Canada, and they begged for help in getting visas to Canada, saying they were in ill health and had no one in India to care for them. I doubted they would ever be allowed to enter a country that wanted to put their separatist son in jail for mass murder. But I told them I would write an article about their plight.

The Punjab of 1988 had even more connections to Canadian Sikh separatists than on my 1986 visit. Three Canadian ISYF members had been convicted and jailed in the previous year on charges of murder, gun smuggling, and supplying cash to aid terrorism. And farmers across the Punjabi countryside still felt caught in the middle.

After I returned to Canada, one of the first calls I got was from Tara Hayer. He was eager to hear about my trip, and I was eager to ask him about rumours I'd heard about a contract on his life. We tentatively agreed to have lunch on Friday, August 26. I called him a day before and said I might have to postpone because of a deadline I was facing.

But by 1 p.m. that day, I was racing to Hayer's Surrey office, not for lunch, but to cover a shooting that had left him paralyzed and near death.

CHAPTER 4

Silencing the Lions

I QUICKLY LEARNED THAT, after shooting Tara Hayer, a
teenager had raced out the front door of the newspaper office,
his weapon still in his hand. While frantic office employees dialed
911, one of them, Surjit Singh Madhopuri, chased after the young
man. Madhopuri ran for several blocks after the shooter, who frequently looked over his shoulder. Finally Madhopuri caught up
and wrestled the lithe youth to the ground. It was a daring act
for the faithful Hayer employee. The young man could have
killed him.

Police quickly arrived on the scene and arrested the hit man,
who told them he was just seventeen years old. His said his name
was Harkirat Singh Bagga, a native of Punjab, who had been
living in England before moving to Ontario to be near his
parents. But the RCMP already knew who he was. They had followed him around a few months earlier when he first came to
British Columbia and met with militants from the International
Sikh Youth Federation and other supporters of the Khalistan
movement.

Hayer had actually spoken to Bagga a couple of weeks before the shooting. The young man had been staying with a mutual friend in Ontario, Darshan Singh Saini, who had urged Bagga to call Hayer and demand space in the newspaper to respond to an article Hayer had written criticizing his father.

The attempt on Hayer's life made headlines across the country. It was the first time a Canadian journalist had been shot in this country, and there was worldwide condemnation. Reporters like me who had covered the Sikh community for years knew the shooting was political. Hayer had been relentless in his weekly attacks on the Babbar Khalsa and the ISYF. He attacked Bagri and Parmar personally for what he claimed was the misappropriation of hundreds of thousands of dollars in donated money.

He had linked their group to the Air-India bombing, and he had even alleged in Punjabi-language articles that Bagri had confessed to several people about playing a role in it. The problem was that Canadian law enforcement agencies were not monitoring Punjabi newspapers. And Hayer did not tell his many white colleagues, including me, the specifics of the allegations he had made against Bagri. It would be years before the RCMP figured out just how brazen Hayer had been in his stories about Bagri before the 1988 shooting.

Hayer was a controversial and colourful man who enjoyed attacking his opponents on both a personal and political level. That opened the door for some Sikh extremists to claim that the shooting was not related to militant separatists, but was the act of a teenager distraught over published personal attacks on his father.

Bagga helped to settle the debate when he told police he had been aided by both the ISYF and the Babbar Khalsa. He claimed that Bagri had given him the gun to shoot Hayer – a gun that was later traced to the same California man who had owned the gun with a filed-off serial number found in Reyat's house during the November 1985 Air-India police raid. Bagga claimed ISYF members had provided him with financial support and assistance as well. He also claimed to be sorry for what he had done, and refused the government-appointed lawyer offered to him. He said he would represent himself at trial.

Hayer, meanwhile, was struggling to come to grips with his devastating injuries. He spent weeks in the Royal Columbian Hospital in the Vancouver suburb of New Westminster under police guard. I visited him there in early October once he was well enough to see people other than devoted family members who had spent hours with him each day since the shooting.

I was shocked by how grey he looked, and he admitted that he was in excruciating pain, adding unrealistically that he hoped to regain the use of his legs. I could see the purplish marks on his arm where one of the bullets had entered.

In true Hayer style, he pledged to continue with his journalism. Attempts on his life would not stop him from printing the truth, he said. He also told me the shooting was without a doubt politically motivated – linked to the groups that he had exposed so many times in his newspaper – the ISYF and the Babbar Khalsa.

But Hayer did not tell me the full story behind the shooting – that he held a dangerous secret about who was involved in the Air-India bombing, a secret that he had stated in several articles he wrote just before his attempted murder, a secret that would eventually cost two men their lives.

Shortly after my interview with Hayer, I drove to Kamloops to meet with members of the Sikh community there. Ajaib Bagri welcomed me into his home, plying me with tea and snacks as we chatted for two hours about Sikh politics. He made the usual claims – that Sikhs in India were being persecuted and needed a homeland – and that Sikhs in Canada were now facing the same prejudice and were being harassed by CSIS and the RCMP although they had done nothing. He defended the Hayer shooting, but claimed not to know anything about it. He also defended Parmar, but would not say where he was or when he might return.

On the eve of the 1988 federal election that November, several candidates were invited to Vancouver's Ross Street temple to speak to the congregation. None of them knew that the temple leaders, Air-India suspects Hardial Johal and Daljit Sandhu, had advertised the event as a prayer service for the assassins of Indira Gandhi.

It was a common tactic of the separatists to invite politicians to the temple under one guise and advertise it in Punjabi as something else. They would then claim that the politicians were supportive of the Sikh cause. Two parallel worlds – one English and one Punjabi – would cross paths but never connect.

A Sikh cab driver gave me a copy of the Punjabi leaflet advertising the memorial for Beant Singh and Satwant Singh – the Sikh bodyguards who had turned on Gandhi. I called a number of the politicians for a story about their being used without their knowledge. Several cancelled their engagement once they knew the real purpose of the service to which they had been invited. A few others decided to go anyway.

For journalists, the arrest of Harkirat Bagga, the young Hayer shooter, gave us hope that there might finally be a criminal trial that would delve into the violent extremism that we had been covering for four years. We had found it hard to explain to the broader community about the threats Sikhs had hanging over them constantly. Until Hayer was shot, even the police did not seem to understand the danger faced by anyone in a position to expose the militants or who dared speak again them. The broader Canadian community, including politicians, and most journalists and editors, did not understand that what some moderates in the Sikh community were facing was just as repressive as what was going on in totalitarian regimes. They were threatened and attacked for writing or speaking their mind on issues of extremism, but police did not treat the crimes against them as real crimes. There was no widespread support for them or outrage for what they faced. I think their plight was perceived as part of an internal problem within a minority community, one that mainstream Canadians did not identify with. These were Canadians facing death threats, persecution, and assaults for trying to get others to pay attention to the extremism hijacking their community. Yet they were ignored.

Despite his tender age, Bagga seemed to understand what would be at stake in his trial. Without the advice of a lawyer, he completely changed his story and his plea. He claimed that he had been distressed over Hayer's attacks on his father and went to shoot the fifty-two-year-old publisher as an act of personal revenge. Crown prosecutors and police did not buy the story, but in the end it didn't matter. His guilty plea meant all the evidence against him – some of which would have implicated the Air-India suspects – would now not come out in court. In December 1988, the teenaged assassin was sentenced to fourteen years.

Many RCMP investigators, as well as close associates of Hayer, believe that the real organizers of the conspiracy to kill the publisher persuaded Bagga to take the rap alone and keep a lid on their involvement. It would not be the only time that someone linked to the Air-India bombing suspects would agree to plead guilty to prevent damaging testimony against others from being heard.

The Hayer family and the Sikh community were understandably upset that the truth did not come out at Bagga's trial. So many of the criminal cases involving the Sikh separatists never materialized as promised. The November 1985 arrests of Parmar and Reyat – for crimes that appeared to be linked to the Air-India bombing – had ended up in a $2,000 fine for Reyat and nothing for Parmar. The ISYF suspect charged in the 1985 beating of Ujjal

Dosanjh was acquitted. Most of the Babbar Khalsa suspects in the 1986 conspiracy to blow up an Air-India jet in New York were let go. The Hamilton case against seven Babbar Khalsa members, including Parmar and Bagri, fizzled. Five of the alleged conspirators in the Malkiat Sidhu shooting had been let go because of a tainted wiretap application.

A certain level of cynicism was building in the Sikh community. Many people wondered if the Canadian authorities were being completely inept in dealing with criminals and terrorist thugs just because they were from a minority, non-English-speaking community? Some also thought that race and culture played a factor. They asked themselves whether white Canadians would tolerate the same lawlessness in their community if threats, beatings, and shootings were going unpunished.

The silent majority in the Sikh community abhorred the violence, the communalism of the Khalistanis, and the transplantation of Punjabi village politics to Canada. So many in the community were succeeding in business, in politics, in the judiciary, and in other facets of Canadian society. But the violent separatist minority was getting all the attention.

Secular Punjabi literary organizations continued to write against extremism. Some of the pioneer founders of the Ross Street temple decided to build a new *gurdwara* in the neighbouring suburb of Richmond rather than continue to battle the separatists. But some, like moderate Bikkar Singh Dhillon, did try to oppose the extremists. When Dhillon took on ISYF leader Ranjit Dosanjh for control of the Ross Street temple, Dhillon, then age sixty-seven, was shot several times. Amazingly, he survived.

Ranjit Dosanjh, who was financing the Khalistan movement by trafficking in cocaine, was gunned down years later by a rival drug dealer. Even within Dosanjh's ISYF, some members were moving away from the group's extreme militancy. A young man

named Jag Singh, who had been an active ISYF member but now
had doubts about its tactics, was shoved up against a wall by
Dosanjh at the temple and threatened one day. He told me he quit
the group right after that.

Inderjit Reyat was pulling out all the stops to avoid extradition
to Canada to face manslaughter charges in the Narita bombing.
His first extradition hearing began in July, adjourned for a while,
then ended in August 1988 with an order of extradition against
him. But the dual Canadian-British citizen didn't stop there.
With the financial backing of Sikh separatists in both Canada
and England, he fought on in the British courts. His lawyer
announced in October 1988 that he would appeal and the
hearing began January 16, 1989. I covered the appeal, which took
place at the famous Old Bailey in London. Reyat's barrister,
Harjit Singh, was a diminutive baptized Sikh who wore a white
turban instead of the white wigs the judges and other lawyers
wore in court. He was passionate in his defence, suggesting Reyat
would not get a fair trial in Canada, that the evidence against
him was weak, and that while he was being sought for extradition on the Narita charges, he would be charged instead in the
Air-India case.

    But he was spinning the facts. When he said that Reyat had been
seen in Burnaby buying batteries about three hours before the
Narita-bound bomb was checked in at Vancouver International
Airport, he claimed the distance between Burnaby and the
Richmond airport was so great that Reyat could not possibly
have driven to the airport in time. Neither the judges nor the
lawyer representing the Canadian government were familiar
with the geography of the Vancouver area, so they looked my
way for help. "It is about a twenty-minute drive between

Burnaby and Richmond," I piped up, completely shooting down Singh's argument, if not flouting the protocol of the high court.

The three judges hearing the appeal did not seem moved by anything Reyat's lawyer said. They dismissed his arguments in a somewhat rude and abrupt manner. I actually started feeling sorry for him. Their attitude was in stark contrast to how they treated Clive Nicholls, the distinguished barrister hired by Canada to argue its case in the court. Nicholls and his barrister twin brother were among the most well regarded in their profession. He went on to represent Chilean dictator Augusto Pinochet in another high-profile extradition case.

The panel of judges seemed to lap up Nicholls's every word. One even went so far as to comment that he did not understand why Reyat was not being charged with first-degree murder. The judges made little comments that indicated they knew Nicholls socially. Harjit Singh was clearly up against more than clever legal arguments.

The historic Old Bailey is full of carved woodwork, impressive stone etchings, and stained-glass windows. The gallery, where just a handful of us sat through the proceedings, is at a higher level than the court, so we looked down on the judges and lawyers. Reyat did not attend his appeal, nor did his wife, Satnam. But a handful of cousins and other relatives were there on and off during the two-week court hearing. Many of them were westernized, with short hair and clean-shaven faces. They said they were there to support a family member and not out of solidarity with a political movement that supported violence.

Sikh separatist leaders in England stayed away from the courtroom. I believe it was a deliberate strategy of Harjit Singh to make the judges see Reyat as a simple individual – a family man – and not part of a foreign political movement that had used violence for its cause.

I met with British leaders of the Babbar Khalsa and the ISYF. And for the first time I met Dr. Jagjit Chohan. I interviewed him in his comfortable home, named Khalistan House, in Reading, northwest of London. He was a soft-spoken and gentle man, with a plastic right hand that he held out for me to take. His long white beard, traditional white clothes, and white turban made him seem ageless and otherworldly.

He spoke of Parmar and Reyat and the Canadians that he knew, but he did not reveal as much as he would one day tell me about his relationships with those linked to terrorism in Canada, including the teenaged assassin, Bagga. Chohan criticized the violence, but defended the separatist movement as a legitimate political struggle for an independent nation. He claimed that he had nothing to do with the violence linked to the ISYF and Babbar Khalsa, but admitted he maintained ties with them and other extremist groups within the movement.

He introduced me to some of his supporters, Ajit Singh Khera and Iqbal Singh, his nephew, who ran a Khalistan government-in-exile office in London. Educated and reasonable, both men presented a softer, more moderate image of a Sikh separatist than I had ever encountered in Canada.

I made my first trip to Southall, in the London borough of Ealing, described as the largest Punjabi community outside India. Everywhere, the streets were crowded with Sikh families. Orange Khalsa flags flew in front of some of the ubiquitous brick row-houses. Punjabi signs hung outside businesses and at the local train station. It was also the dominant language on Southall's streets.

In the middle of the borough, across from a large Sikh temple and beside a train station, was the office of *Des Pardes*, the leading British Punjabi newspaper, run by Tarsem Purewal. Purewal was an old friend of Hayer, and it was Hayer who gave me the contact information for the British publisher. The two men had worked together and had been close friends when Hayer lived in England before emigrating to Canada. I learned that Purewal had been a close friend to many Sikhs who moved on to live in British Columbia. He called leaders on both sides of the separatist debate friends.

Hayer had told me that Purewal was close to Parmar and his Babbar Khalsa members, as well as to the ISYF. That's how Purewal was able to get into separatist training camps in Pakistan. At one camp he had taken a widely circulated photograph of Parmar with a rocket launcher perched on his right shoulder.

I met with Purewal on the second floor of his newspaper office in a large open room divided into the various work areas related to the production of the newspaper. Little did I know at the time that I was standing in the same room in which Hayer claimed to have overheard the information about Air-India — information that may well have led to the attempt on his life.

Purewal knew his old friend had condemned the two groups to which he was still loyal. But he asked after Hayer's health with genuine concern. Old friendships were more important than political differences.

I told Purewal I was on my way to India and Pakistan to look for Parmar and for evidence of the complicity of Pakistani government officials in supporting the Sikh militants. I explained my credentials: the two trips to Punjab I had made in the last two years, during which I had met separatist leaders from several groups. Purewal was polite with me, but coy. He wasn't about to tell me the addresses of training camps or Parmar's whereabouts. To him, I was still a rookie reporter, despite my five years covering the Sikh community. And I was a *gori* — a white woman — and therefore someone who could not be trusted with secrets.

Before I left for India, Reyat was ordered extradited for a second time. Moderate leader Piara Singh Khabra, who would go on to become the first Sikh MP in Britain, had been fighting the same battle as moderates in Canada who were opposed to militant separatists. He had also been threatened. But many separatists who demonstrated in the streets of London when I was there chanted their support for Reyat and against the Indian government. Reyat would continue with his legal challenges, but he was soon to be returned to Canada for prosecution.

Chohan's supporters insisted on taking me out to dinner on the eve of my trip to New Delhi so they could try to convince me of why Sikhs needed a separate state. They were bright, educated men who wanted to debate Punjab's future with someone interested in, if not sympathetic to, their cause. We went to an expensive Indian restaurant in Covent Garden and spent several hours drinking and talking Punjabi politics. They were furious when they learned I was flying Air-India to New Delhi because it was the best-priced ticket available.

"You should switch your ticket," they said.

"Why? Do you know something I don't know?" I asked.

They didn't disclose a thing, but still the next morning I felt a little nervous waiting to board the flight at Heathrow Airport. I was handed a newspaper by a flight attendant as I took my seat. I surveyed the other passengers – no one was wearing a turban. Most appeared to be Hindus or tourists like myself.

I started reading the newspaper. My eye was immediately drawn to a small item in the briefs column. It was datelined Dublin and said an Air-India flight had been forced to make an emergency landing there the day before after a bomb threat had been telephoned in. This must have been why my Khalistani friends had warned me, I thought.

The airplane left on schedule and proceeded smoothly until an hour into the flight, the pilot made a strange announcement:

"Due to a security issue with the plane, we will be making a landing in Frankfurt, Germany," he said.

Not everyone on the flight interpreted the message the way I did: that a bomb threat had been made against the plane. There was no real panic at first. But then the announcement did not use the word *bomb*, nor had the other passengers just sat through two weeks of evidence on how a bomb had made its way onto a flight with little difficulty.

The pilot's cryptic announcement came more than thirty minutes before we would be able to land in Germany. My heart started racing. I thought that this would be the definition of irony – a reporter determined to investigate the 1985 Air-India bombing killed aboard another Air-India flight by a terrorist bomb.

I thought I should write a note to my family – but then I figured it would be destroyed in the crash. So I and a young Toronto man next to me decided to order drinks. It seemed to make sense. I was a little surprised when the flight attendant insisted we pay U.S.$4 a beer.

Passengers began asking flight attendants what was going on. Their reluctance to answer made people more nervous. Tension on the flight mounted as the minutes ticked slowly by. Finally we began our descent to Frankfurt. We could see the fluorescent pink and green emergency vehicles on the runway below, lights flashing, far away from the terminal building.

There was some relief when we touched down, but it was soon countered by the slow process of disembarking. The Air-India staff did not want to open the emergency doors and let us slide down the chutes, so just the usual front exit was opened, and people began to push and shove at the back of the plane. "Hurry up or we are going to blow up," one passenger yelled.

After fourteen hours at the Frankfurt airport, investigators determined that there was no bomb aboard the plane. I filed a rather embarrassing and beer-induced story about the scare back to my newspaper in Vancouver. I was not exactly excited about the prospect of flying in the same plane to Delhi. But I was persuaded by other passengers who pointed out that ours was probably the most thoroughly inspected plane in the entire airport. I cursed the men in London I had met the night before. Had they known what I was about to go through?

The rest of the flight was uneventful.

In Delhi, I met with several political leaders and academics to get an update on events in Punjab. I learned that the state was still under central rule. It was still heavily militarized and it residents were still being terrorized by the violence of Sikh separatists and of the Indian security forces.

Once I got into Punjab, most of the Sikh separatists I met were eager to get news of their brethren in England and Canada. This was a pre-Internet world, where news travelled slowly and separatists feared their phone calls were tapped. They wanted to hear about Reyat's case. They claimed not to know where Parmar was hiding.

I took the now-familiar train trip from Amritsar in India to Lahore in Pakistan. It was just a fifty-kilometre journey, but it took hours because of heavy security along the border. As a foreigner who was in Punjab only by special permission, the guards scrutinized me even more than they did the locals. I was the only white person on the train.

In Lahore, I went straight to Dera Sahib, the Sikh temple where the Canadians had now been holed up for three years.

Satinderpal Gill was still there and still under "house arrest," with his police servants satisfying his every need. I told him I wanted to find Parmar, but he claimed not to know where he was.

Next, I tried the other Sikh shrine about thirty kilometres outside Lahore, Nankana Sahib, where Parmar had hidden and where he had first taken *amrit*, or sweet nectar, in his baptism ceremony in 1975. He was not there.

It was the middle of February and the historic withdrawal of Soviet troops from Afghanistan was to be completed within days. My editors in Canada suggested that I go to northern Pakistan to cover a special meeting of the various mujahedeen factions, called a *shura*, to determine the new form of government for the wartorn country.

The time I spent in Islamabad, Peshawar, and the refugee camps dotting the Afghan/Pakistan border was a fascinating detour from Sikh politics. I got into Afghanistan along a rutted gravel road through the Khyber Pass in the back of a truck filled with guns, ammunition, missiles, and rocket launchers. We passed enormous walled fortresses containing lavish mansions and guest houses of the region's drug lords. I was told not to take pictures.

Back on the Pakistan side of the border, the mujahedeen showed me the weapons factories where any gun from anywhere in the world could be duplicated cheaply and quickly. I would later learn that the same factories were making weapons for Sikh militants eager to increase their armed power in Punjab. I also learned later that at the time I was in the region, Parmar was there too, as the guest of his arms supplier, a factory owner involved in the mass reproduction of everything from AK-47s to rocket launchers. The B.C. Babbar Khalsa lord was put up at the luxurious home of his weapons dealer, a close relative of his confirmed years later. Parmar had been told by Pakistani Intelligence officers to make himself scarce around Lahore, where Indian diplomats were keeping an eye on Sikh separatists organizing against the nation of their birth.

I got back to Canada just before Satinderpal Gill returned to Vancouver from his three-year exile in Pakistan. He was greeted at the airport by dozens of ISYF supporters who claimed he had been forced to stay away for so long because of Indian government pressure on Pakistan to hold him. But I knew he had never been under detention. On my three visits there I had seen the freedom he had enjoyed in Pakistan.

I was starting to become dangerous to the separatists. What I had learned on my trips to India, Pakistan, and England was enough to allow me to expose their lies, contradict their claims of persecution.

Purewal, the British *Des Pardes* editor, had made one of his many trips to Pakistan just before Gill left the country. He had visited a training camp and saw Parmar there. He wrote a controversial article quoting the Air-India suspect, saying anyone who dared to fly on Air-India was suicidal. Air-India planes are going to fall from the sky, Parmar said.

The story was picked up around the world, making it into my newspaper and others in Canada just as Gill's ISYF was about to hold an international convention in March 1989 at Vancouver's Ross Street temple. Bagri was one of the designated speakers and many Babbar Khalsa members were in attendance. In all at least four Air-India suspects attended the convention. The presence of so many with suspected links to terrorism did not stop Liberal leader Gordon Wilson from attending the event. He addressed the crowd, prompting criticism from community moderates angered by the ongoing pandering to extremists by Canadian politicians of all persuasions and levels.

After I quoted the critics of Wilson and the ISYF in my article on the convention, the neophyte politician called me up and asked to go to lunch. He admitted he did not know much about the Sikh community and the different factions within it.

Reyat was finally returned to Canada in December 1989 and his family soon followed. The Jaguar factory worker had mustered enough cash to spend two years in unsuccessful legal challenges to his extradition.

His trial for manslaughter in the deaths of the two Japanese baggage handlers began on September 18, 1990. There was a great deal of local media interest, but it was not seen as an international terrorism trial. The lack of world interest came, in part, by the fact that the trial did not officially link to the Air-India bombing. But there had to be more to it. I thought there was a subtle, perhaps unconscious, discrimination against the mostly non-white victims. After all, the 1988 Pan Am bombing over Lockerbie, Scotland, which had claimed 270 lives, had been much more prominent in the news. Its victims were predominantly white Americans. Those aboard Air-India were mainly Canadians of Indian origin.

The case against Reyat unfolded over six months – sixty-two court days in all – and evidence was given by two hundred Crown witnesses. It was a trial by judge, not jury, and was heavily dependent on forensic research done both in British Columbia and Japan.

Doug Henderson of the RCMP testified about his November 1985 interview with Reyat. At first Reyat had denied even knowing Parmar, but when confronted with CSIS surveillance reports, Reyat had admitted he not only knew the Babbar Khalsa leader, but had been asked by him to build an explosive device capable of taking out a bridge in India.

Reyat had told police that he was incapable of carrying out Parmar's wishes. But the forensic evidence told a different story. Lead prosecutor Jim Jardine worked closely with senior RCMP investigators Ed Drodza and Ken Schmidt and with an explosives expert, Dr. Alexander Beveridge. The B.C. team had visited Japan five times for meetings with Japanese authorities in advance of the trial. With the help of Japanese scientists, they were able to determine the components of the bomb and prove that Reyat had acquired similar items.

The first break in the Tokyo case came when a lab worker identified a metal fragment from the face-plate of a Sanyo tuner. Other tests showed that other fragments were from a cardboard box in which the tuner had been housed, as well as from foam packing. The analysis of other debris at the airport proved the bomb contained dynamite for a high-explosive charge, a blasting cap as igniter, smokeless gunpowder, Liquid Fire starting fluid, an Eveready twelve-volt battery as a power source, an electrical relay as a switch, and a Micronta clock as the timing device.

The Japanese scientists determined the bomb had been concealed in a piece of soft-sided Jetstream luggage. Neither the starting fluid nor gunpowder had been needed to make the device work. But their inclusion had made it easier for experts to link the bomb to Reyat.

The RCMP had rounded up a number of witnesses in Duncan who testified that Reyat had purchased a Sanyo tuner, model FMT 611K, the clock, the relays, and the gunpowder. They also described his relentless efforts over several months to get his hands on some dynamite.

Reyat's defence team claimed his rights had been violated by the erasure of the CSIS wiretaps of Parmar's calls. But B.C. Supreme Court Justice Raymond Paris dismissed the claim, saying that it did not affect the strength of the Crown's case at all. In

May 1991, five weeks after the trial ended, Paris found Reyat guilty of two counts of manslaughter. In his verdict, he said that Reyat had "either fabricated or at the very least aided others" to build the bomb that killed Hideo Asano and Hideharu Koda — the two baggage handlers.

Reyat was eventually sentenced to just ten years in jail.

While there was little mention of the Air-India bombing at Reyat's trial, Perviz Madon, whose husband, Sam, was a victim of the other bombing, was there throughout the trial. She knew it might be the only justice she would get for her husband's sense-less murder. But the short sentence and lack of a link to the bigger terrorist attack made the verdict unsatisfying to the Air-India victims' families and their political allies. Reyat's conviction renewed their calls for a public inquiry into the bombing, which still ranked as the world's worst single act of aviation terrorism.

They were even more frustrated that Talwinder Parmar, the terrorist leader even by Reyat's account, had managed to slip out of the country to places unknown and might never face justice for the lives he had taken and the thousands of others he had ruined. There were many people in the ISYF, the Babbar Khalsa, the Akhand Kirtani Jatha, and the general Sikh community who knew where Parmar was. Indian and Canadian intelligence sources believed he had flown to Pakistan.

Later, I learned from people close to Parmar exactly how he had got out of the country. The Sikh with the best-known face in Canada tied up his loose beard, changed the style of his turban, and crossed into the United States from British Columbia on a friend's passport. It was June 1988 — three years after he had plotted and executed from his Canadian base the slaughter of 331 innocent people.

Parmar then travelled to New York where he met with some of his most trusted supporters. He was given a ticket to Pakistan

in the name of Balwant Singh Bhandher, another Air-India
suspect who was a close associate of Ripudaman Malik and who
had hosted Parmar whenever the Babbar Khalsa leader visited
Calgary. Bhandher had moved his family to the Vancouver area
after the bombings and settled in Surrey in a house across the street
from where Malik later built his second Khalsa School.

Bhandher travelled to New York three days after Parmar
arrived there. A sympathizer drove him to John F. Kennedy
Airport, not knowing Parmar was awaiting Bhandher. On the
way, the driver raved to Bhandher about what a great and holy
man Parmar was. When Bhandher asked him if he would like
to meet Parmar, he panicked and kicked Bhandher out of his car
short of their destination.

At the Pakistan International Airlines counter, Bhandher got
a boarding pass and checked in a suitcase belonging to Parmar.
He then handed his documents to his leader, said goodbye, and
sent Parmar through to the restricted area. There was little
scrutiny of the passport. The two men were different heights and
had different colouring, but their turbans and beards made them
look the same to western eyes. It was a simple and effective ruse.

Pakistani government officials knew Parmar was back in their
country. So were many other leaders of the ISYF, the Khalistan
Commando Force, the Khalistan Liberation Front, and other
Sikh separatist groups deemed terrorist by India. They were
allowed to live openly, to run businesses, to purchase arms, and
to meet and plot and organize.

At first, in the summer of 1988, Parmar was based alternately
at the two main Sikh shrines in the Pakistan portion of Punjab:
Dera Sahib and Nankana Sahib. Many Sikh pilgrims visited both
shrines and not all were sympathetic to the separatist movement.
So Pakistani officials asked Parmar to move north to the Wild

West-like region along the border between Pakistan and Afghanistan. Once there, he was helped by Satinderpal Gill, the ISYF leader who spent years there, and Wadhawa Singh, a leader of the Babbar Khalsa faction headed by Sukhdev Singh Babbar.

By late 1988, Parmar began to criss-cross the border between Pakistan and India clandestinely, his brother Kulwarn told me years later. The man who had maintained such a distinct appearance throughout his last few years in Canada became a master of disguise, posing as a businessman or a farm worker – even wearing the doti cloth made famous by Mahatma Gandhi – or whatever would allow him to travel freely. Whenever he arrived in a village, two armed men on motorcycles would arrive first to secure the site and make sure Parmar would be safe. He even returned to his native village, Panshta, several times undercover to see his mother, Surjit, and father, Jamiat. When his father was near death, Parmar visited him in the hospital. He also attended his father's *bhog*, or memorial service, when Jamiat died.

A devoted family man even when he was living the life of a revolutionary leader, Parmar made sure his wife and children back home always knew his whereabouts. He couldn't call them, for obvious reasons, but they would get messages containing the telephone number of where he was staying. They could call him every two or three weeks.

Devoted family man, terrorist, Sikh separatist, racist – Parmar wore a lot of hats. He always put on a tough-guy demeanour publicly, but once suffered severe chest pains when reporters suggested he was about to be extradited to India. He claimed he hated Hindus, but secretly dealt with Hindu real-estate agent Ved Sharma for years as he bought and sold properties. He was once captured on wiretap warning Sharma not to tell people they did business together. His first concern was that Sikhs would be disturbed that he had a Hindu agent. His second concern, according to a police report of the recorded conversation, was that "Mr. Parmar also did not want other people to know that he was investing money here and there when he was not working."

For all his violent rhetoric, Parmar did something that few other Canadian Sikh separatists did – he went back to India to wage the war on that country's soil.

His main contacts in Canada continued to be Malik, from the AKJ, and Bagri, the de facto leader of the Babbar Khalsa in Parmar's absence. And his stay abroad was funded by supporters in Canada, particularly Sikh separatist leaders in British Columbia. Especially generous were the others suspected of being involved in the Air-India bombing plot. Some had business dealings with India and would send money to Parmar under the guise of payments for goods shipped to Canada. Parmar would then arrange to visit the Punjabi recipients of the cash, or send an agent to collect it. The financiers back in Canada would actually get receipts for their donations to Canada's number-one terrorist, receipts they could use for income tax purposes.

In the four years he was operating in Punjab, Parmar was behind several insurgent attacks and successfully eluded police throughout his stay. He had good relations with Muslim militants fighting in nearby areas. He had met mujahedeen when he was based in northern Pakistan. He had met Kashmiri independence leaders when he later spent time in that region. And he was known across Punjab by the leaders of the major Khalistani groups.

Back home in Canada, Parmar's right-hand man, Ajaib Bagri, confirmed publicly that Parmar was in India and not Pakistan, as police claimed. It was a sign of strength that the Babbar Khalsa leader could travel to and from Punjab state without being discovered by Indian forces.

In the spring of 1992, Parmar's Babbar Khalsa devotees in Montreal, who had been convicted in the 1986 plot to bomb an Air-India jet in New York, won their release after a successful appeal. The two men, Santokh Khela and Kashmir Dhillon, who had served six years, got out because police refused to disclose the true identity of an informant codenamed Billy-Joe, with whom the pair had planned the terrorist attack. Without the right to hear from Billy-Joe in a trial, the Charter rights of the two men had been violated, a Quebec judge ruled. Both men visited British Columbia after their release. Dhillon spent time doing construction work for a new Khalsa School being built in Surrey.

Clearly not worried about being the number-one suspect in the world's deadliest aviation terrorist attack at the time, Parmar secretly left India in the spring of 1992 on a worldwide fundraising tour, with stops in Germany, Holland, the United Kingdom, and Canada. He was wise enough to know that he should not speak in temples or public places on the trip. Instead, he met supporters in private and demanded that they donate to the cause. Chohan met him on the U.K. leg of the trip and witnessed one Southall man give Parmar a significant donation of a few hundred pounds, saying it was all he could afford. Parmar angrily threw the money on the floor, shouting that it was not worth taking. Chohan was not impressed.

It is hard not to be impressed by Parmar's brashness. In April 1992, he once again tied up his beard and returned to British Columbia, where his family was living in the even more impressive house he had built on Worthington Place in Vancouver. His brother Kulwarn received a call telling him to come to the house for a special event. He was not told that Talwinder had slipped

into the country, undetected by CSIS or the RCMP. It was quite
a surprise for Kulwarn to see his brother there after so many years.
Parmar was dressed in a business suit and was driving a rental car.
With him at his Vancouver house that day were Ajaib Bagri and
other Babbar members from Kamloops, including Gurmit Gill
and Avtar Singh Toor. He did not stay long. He did not say how
or why he had come. Parmar also saw Malik on the trip, and
visited Toronto and Montreal – again without CSIS or the RCMP
catching on that he was in the country. It would be the last time
his followers and family would see Parmar alive. As mysteriously
as he had arrived in Canada, he slipped away again – never to be
brought to justice in the Air-India and Narita bombings.

Within a month, Parmar's eldest son, Jaswinder, and Bagri's
eldest daughter, Dipinderaj, wed in an arranged marriage that was
brokered before Parmar left in 1988. The ceremony took place in
Kamloops on May 2. Two weeks later at the Vancouver Ross Street
temple, Parmar's daughter, Rajinder, married a young man from
India named Sartaj Singh Chima in a double wedding. Parmar's
only other child, son Narinder, married Sandeep Kaur Parhar at
the same time. Hundreds of hard-core separatists from their father's
group attended. Parmar sent a taped message to be played at the
service that proclaimed, "Khalistan will be free one day."

The Babbar Khalsa founder and number-one Air-India
bombing suspect would not live to see that day. At age forty-seven,
in his native Punjab, he was arrested and brutally slain after endur-
ing days of torture and interrogation. His death was announced
by Punjab police chief Karam Pal Singh Gill on October 15, 1992,
who, it later turned out, stuck to the official story when he stated
that Parmar and five other Sikh militants had been killed in a gun
battle in Kang Arwanian village near Jalandhar. Two of the dead
men were Pakistanis. Police claimed the men had been driving in
a car filled with U.S. currency, Pakistani rupees, guns, ammunition,

and a rocket launcher. When the car was stopped at a roadblock by police, the terrorists fled into a field, where the two-hour gun battle occurred. There were no police casualties.

The statement that no police officer was hurt was not believable. The police had complained to me on each of my three trips to Punjab that the Sikh separatists were always better armed, that the police force's Second World War Sten guns could not compete with modern Pakistani-made AK-47s.

From the moment they got the awful news, Parmar's family disbelieved the official story. They had their own sources: supporters in Punjab who told them he had been arrested, kept in custody for several days, and then killed. Bagri told me the same thing when I called him after the reports from India began to come in.

I also called some of my journalist friends in Punjab. Darshan Makkar, of the Chandigarh-based *Tribune*, had been to the site and told me that most people in the area doubted the official story and believed Parmar and the others had been arrested crossing the border and turned over to the police for interrogation. There had been no witnesses to the purported shootout.

The way the Indian police dealt with the body also cast doubt on their story. Parmar was cremated even before the Canadian government had been notified that one of its citizens had been killed. His family was not allowed to take his ashes away for testing. Punjab police just pointed his elderly mother, Surjit, to six piles of dust, claiming that these were the cremated remains of the Babbar Khalsa supporters who died that day. They told her to go to pile number five. The ashes lay exactly where the body had been burned. They could have been donkey ashes for all they knew, one relative told me.

His mother and sister were then escorted by police to a nearby river to perform the ritual of emptying the ashes into the water.

Only when his sister was knee-deep in the river was she given the container allegedly containing Parmar's remains.

The circumstances of the death and cremation were so suspicious that the family immediately suspected the police story was a lie and asked for the Canadian government's help to find out the truth. But the government refused, saying it did not want to upset India by making accusations.

When I wrote stories raising questions about the circumstances of Parmar's death, I was given a hard time by several Canadian bureaucrats in External Affairs, as well as by some of my contacts in the Indian diplomatic service based in Canada. They didn't understand why I was writing about how Parmar was treated when he was obviously a terrorist without regard for the lives of others. I tried to explain that nothing justified a country turning a blind eye to extrajudicial executions and that Parmar should have been returned to Canada to face trial for the Air-India bombings.

MP Svend Robinson also took up the case for the family, who lived in his riding. He later told me he was also privately chastised by his Parliamentary colleagues about standing up for the principle that state-sanctioned executions were wrong.

The reality is that Parmar's in-custody murder not only ruined the chances that the families would one day see him brought to justice for the Air-India and Narita bombings, it also allowed his supporters to suggest that his death was proof that India was behind the Air-India bombing and had murdered Parmar because he would have exposed the truth. Still other militants now had a new *shaheed*, or martyr, to inspire them.

Parmar was not the only victim of K.P.S. Gill's brutal, but successful, crackdown on Sikh separatists. Forces under the command of the Punjab police chief killed dozens of suspected leaders like Parmar and Sukhdev Singh Babbar in 1992, though he would claim the deaths were in shootouts or encounters. Other leaders, including Gurdeep Singh Sivia, a British Babbar Khalsa leader who did not get along with Parmar, were arrested and interrogated and used to lure other leaders to locations where they were captured. Sivia, along with many other detainees, claimed he was tortured by Gill's police force.

Gill saw it as a war. In a war, human rights just don't factor into it, he later told me. He was frustrated that the United States and the United Kingdom constantly complained of his tactics. As Gill sipped Scotch and watched cricket in his Jalandhar headquarters I confronted him with new information I had about Parmar's death. He repeated his original story and claimed he had gone to the site where Parmar was gunned down.

"It looked like a real encounter to me," Gill said, but unconvincingly.

When he was arrested, Parmar had been travelling from Punjab to Kashmir. En route, he stayed with a contact known as Prof. Manjit Singh. Some of Parmar's supporters believe either Singh or a Canadian supporter who knew Parmar's whereabouts tipped off the Indian police so he could be arrested.

Parmar was due to receive a $200,000 payment from a Canadian supporter when he was killed. The money had already been sent through an Ontario foreign exchange company. After Parmar's death, the person who sent the cash quickly arranged for its return. That wasn't the only suspicious occurrence. Manjit Singh ended up coming to British Columbia and making a refugee claim. He got a job working for Malik in his Khalsa School in Surrey. When a supporter of Parmar's confronted him there one afternoon in the summer of 1999, Singh claimed he had not turned Parmar in. Later that day, he disappeared.

The Canadian government did little to get to the bottom of the murder of one of its most controversial citizens. Documents

I obtained under Access to Information legislation paint a picture of a government unwilling to break diplomatic protocol and challenge the Indian government's official version of events.

The ninety-five pages of documents reveal that bureaucrats at External Affairs, while claiming publicly in 1992 to be "vigorously" pursuing the facts of Parmar's death, simply wrote several polite letters requesting information from India, later abandoning the inquiry before they even received a full response.

On October 16, 1992, a confidential memo, with the author's name blanked out, from the Canadian High Commission in Delhi to External Affairs in Ottawa said: "India authorities have confirmed the basic elements of story of Parmar death. He, with five others, including two identified as Pakistanis and three other unidentified persons were killed in 'two hour encounter' with Indian police in the village of Kang Arwanian, district of Jalandhar, in Punjab state. All six, in two cars, were stopped at a roadblock, fled to an open field where shoot-out took place. There were apparently no police casualties."

That same day, the High Commission wrote to the India government: "The High Commission wishes to inform the ministry that the family of Mr. Parmar has requested the return of his remains to Canada. The High Commission would appreciate the assistance of the ministry in facilitating this."

The note is not signed, but a copy of it was sent to External Affairs in Ottawa by Acting High Commissioner D. Gordon Longmuir.

Four days later, the High Commission sent another note asking for a death certificate and saying Canada "would be grateful to receive a full report regarding the circumstances surrounding his death."

A consular report on October 23 states that the Indian media had reported Parmar's ashes were given to family members and goes on to say, "The government of India has not confirmed this to the High Commission despite repeated requests for information."

A briefing note prepared the same day by P.M.R. Johnson to assist External Affairs Minister Barbara McDougall to respond to questions in the House of Commons claimed Canada was "vigorously" pursuing "an account of the circumstances surrounding the death of Mr. Parmar." But an unsigned Canadian consular report from early November 1992 indicates that the Indian government was stonewalling and had not delivered a promised report by the agreed-upon deadline.

The official Indian report finally arrived on November 16, 1992, but even it was suspicious, according to a Johnson memo from Ottawa to the High Commission in Delhi, which reads in part, "Thanks [for] copy of report provided by Indian authorities on Parmar's death. As you point out, report contains no letterhead or signature and is clearly inadequate." The memo urges the High Commission "to continue to press strongly for a formal accounting of events."

But the subsequent November 23 letter to the Indian government maintains the polite tone of the earlier notes, with none of the "vigorous" demands that were promised in Ottawa. "The High Commission appreciates the information respecting the death of Mr. Parmar received from the Ministry on Nov. 16. In addition to this preliminary information, any further Indian Government report provided to the High Commission on the circumstances surrounding his death would be most helpful," the letter reads.

A few days later, India provided Canada with more "details" about the incident, falsely claiming that the body had been turned over to the family, who had arranged cremation.

The Indian government seemed to be offended that Canada was demanding an official diplomatic explanation. A Canadian

High Commission report said Indian officials called Canada's request for more details about Parmar's death "preposterous." "The Indian authorities concluded that the three foreign citizens involved had entered India illegally, intending to carry out terrorist acts," it said.

By the middle of December, more than two months after Parmar's death, Canada had still not been able to obtain the inquest report, results of the postmortem examination, or the death certificate. A December 18 consular report said that an Indian official had corrected the earlier comment that the body had been turned over to relatives: "The Indian official explained that it was their policy to cremate the remains of terrorists and Mr. Parmar's ashes – not his body – were handed over to his mother. The official stated that Mr. Parmar had not been held prisoner prior to his death nor was he tortured in any way."

Another letter was sent from the High Commission to the Indian government on February 24, 1993, again requesting the death certificate, postmortem, and inquest reports. In May, the death certificate was finally provided, but the other two reports were not. No cause of death was listed on the certificate.

For the next four years, there appear to have been no further inquiry from Canada to India on what happened to Parmar. Only when the issue arose in a news report in June 1997 did the government look at it again. A panicked Canadian diplomat in New Delhi, Donald Waterfall, asked some colleagues to look into it.

"This is of some urgency and we had better search the consular files to see what we did/learned/etc. in 1987 at the time of the incident," Waterfall wrote to Margery Landeryou and Jacqueline Nigel in June 6, 1997. He was five years out in stating when Parmar died.

External Affairs official Keith Fountain seemed relieved when he wrote a memo to his New Delhi colleagues a few days later saying there had been nothing in the media for five days.

"Svend Robinson called for the matter to be examined by the Standing Committee of Foreign Affairs and International Trade, but it is uncertain how far that will go, especially since public interest in the issue (if there ever was any outside of the World Sikh Organization) seems to have dissipated," Fountain wrote.

As there was no public interest, there was no need to find out the truth.

Years later, the RCMP received what it considered reliable information that Parmar had been arrested by Punjabi police, held in custody for two weeks, tortured, interrogated, and killed. Canadian investigators were so worried about protecting the lives of the people who disclosed the information about Parmar's execution that it was not used when the Air-India case finally went to court. Before his death, Parmar was asked repeatedly about the Air-India bombing. Under torture, he eventually admitted that he had played a role in it. He also named Inderjit Reyat as being involved. He did not name Bagri, Malik, or anyone else.

The RCMP quietly went to Parmar's family and told them that what it had suspected a decade earlier was indeed what had happened. Police passed on the news to Sikh community leaders as well.

The Indian government's version of Parmar's death has never been changed to reflect the truth.

CHAPTER 5

Politics and Power

FOR MONTHS AFTER his death, friends and relatives of Talwinder Parmar lobbied anyone who would listen. Two of the campaigners were Prem Singh Vinning, who would go on to hold senior political positions in both the B.C. and federal Liberal parties, and Ranjit Dosanjh, the ISYF leader who was involved in drug trafficking and would be slain two years later in a gangland hit.

Both men spoke at one of the first demonstrations after Parmar's death. They were joined by Svend Robinson and Conservative Vancouver South MP John Fraser, speaker of the House of Commons. Each politician called on the federal government to scrutinize the official Indian account of Parmar's slaying. There was always a politician willing to take the stage with the Babbar Khalsa, it seemed.

Others whose names had surfaced in connection with the Air-India investigation also spoke from the same podium: Babbar Khalsa International leader Gurdev Gill claimed the Canadian government didn't want to investigate Parmar's death simply because he was a Sikh. Daljit Sandhu, the Air-India suspect who spoke on behalf of the World Sikh Organization, also appealed to the government to investigate: "Mr. Parmar was not afraid of death. He said he wanted to embrace martyrdom. He wanted to lay down his life and was one hundred per cent prepared for it."

But with Parmar dead and Reyat found guilty only of manslaughter in the Narita bombing, other suspects in the Air-India plot were able to carry on their lives without fear of repercussion. It was probably the darkest period for police investigators. They were stumped as to where else they could pursue witnesses and evidence, and they were frustrated that after seven years of investigation they had managed just one conviction, which was immediately appealed by Reyat.

Inderjit Reyat did not have to look far for help. Just nine days after he was sentenced, Ripudaman Malik deposited $10,000 in an account belonging to Reyat's wife, Satnam. It had been opened for her at Malik's Khalsa Credit Union. A second account in the name of Reyat's cousin, Piara Singh Panasar, was also opened with Mrs. Reyat as the only signing authority. The deposit was the first of regular monthly payments made to her under the table for helping out in the Khalsa daycare centre. They would continue undeclared for years while she and her children were on social assistance. Both accounts were opened with the help of Malik follower and Khalsa Credit Union manager Aniljit Uppal.

Malik also arranged for Mrs. Reyat and her children to move into the large two-storey house next door to the Khalsa School in Surrey, where the Khalsa daycare centre was located on the main floor. The name on the deed was Hardial Johal, the Air-India suspect who had talked on the phone with Parmar and Reyat so many times in the days immediately before the bombing. But Johal told me he had never once stepped inside the house and only agreed to put it in his name so that a mortgage could be obtained.

Really the house belonged to the Satnam Trust – the charitable trust that operated out of Khalsa School. Mrs. Reyat's electrical bill was paid by the other charity in the school, the Satnam Education Society, and her four children attended the Khalsa School for free.

Both the school and credit union were growing by leaps and bounds. As the B.C. government contributed 50 per cent of the public school funding for each student at Khalsa and other B.C. independent schools, the more students who registered, the more money came in. The daycare was growing as well. And Malik hired his old banker at the State Bank of India to run the fledging credit union. Harbans Singh Kandola, who signed the papers for Malik's $2-million loan at the Indian bank in March 1984 moved over to become the chief financial officer of Khalsa Credit Union when it opened in February 1986.

Malik was careful to give all the Sikh separatist groups representation on the nine-person credit union board. The Babbar Khalsa, the ISYF, and the World Sikh Organization were each assigned directors' seats for which they could put forward candidates. Relatives of Air-India suspects won board positions. Talwinder Parmar's brother Kulwarn held one seat. Daljit Sandhu's brother Avtar held another.

Despite being designated a terrorist group by India and several western nations, the Babbar Khalsa managed to get charitable status from Revenue Canada in the early 1990s, while both Ajaib Bagri and Kulwarn Parmar were directors. Other Kamloops members who made regular calls to Talwinder Parmar just before the bombings also held official positions with the Babbar Khalsa, according to its annual reports filed with B.C.'s Ministry of Finance and Revenue Canada.

Babbar Khalsa wasn't the only charity with terrorist links that was operating with the blessing of the Canadian and B.C.

governments. The Akhand Kirtani Jatha – the group headed in India by Malik's spiritual adviser, Bhai Jiwan Singh – drafted a constitution at its founding meeting at the Khalsa School in the fall of 1992 and was incorporated by the B.C. government a few months later. Bagri had told Keith Weston, of Scotland Yard, in the fall of 1985 that Babbar Khalsa International had evolved from the AKJ. Dr. Chohan, the founder of the modern Khalistani movement, told me the two groups were virtually the same. Yet the AKJ, despite its links to the Babbar Khalsa, also got both provincial non-profit and federal charitable status.

Its founding directors included Balwant Bhandher, the Air-India suspect who was also a Khalsa School trustee, and Gurdev Gill, the Babbar Khalsa leader, also a Khalsa school trustee, who had publicly demanded action by the Canadian government in the death of his ally, Talwinder Parmar.

As charities, these organizations could give receipts so that donors could get tax breaks for their contributions. More than $50,000 went from the charities toward Reyat's unsuccessful appeal of his conviction in the Narita bombing. The money was funnelled secretly through Mrs. Reyat's Khalsa Credit Union account while she collected welfare.

A complex web of common members, directors, donors, and ideology linked several of the groups. Malik headed the credit union and both the Satnam Education Society and the Satnam Trust. Gurdev Gill was a director of the AKJ and the Satnam Education Society. Aniljit Uppal worked at the credit union and was on the board of the AKJ and of the school. Hardial Johal was an Air-India suspect and treasurer of Satnam Trust.

Relatives of the close-knit and loyal group were also employed by both the school and the credit union. It was a tight cell to penetrate. No wonder investigators had such difficulty making headway as the power of the inner circle continued to grow.

Not only was the school used to house visiting delegates to conventions of the Babbar Khalsa, ISYF, and AKJ, it was visited regularly by city councillors, MLAs and MPs at every level of government, and candidates seeking nominations for every major party. Indian politicians also made the school a mandatory stop on their tours to Canada.

Malik's personal business empire was growing too. His clothing company, Papillon Eastern Imports, was doing record business by the mid-1990s. For the most part, his wife, Raminder, ran the business. His company Khalsa Developments began work on a hotel in the resort community of Harrison Hot Springs, 125 kilometres east of Vancouver. He began a condominium project on Vancouver Island, not far from where the test blast for the Air-India bombing was done by Parmar a few years earlier.

Surjan Gill, the former Parmar disciple who appeared to back out of the Air-India plot at the last minute, steered clear of the other suspects. He ran into financial trouble when he ran up a series of debts in the mid-1990s, which led creditors to file four civil suits against him. The petitioners won judgments that resulted in the forced sale of several of his properties, according to B.C. Supreme Court records.

Malik, an admitted financier of terrorists, including Parmar and Reyat, applied for and received several government grants for the Khalsa school and the daycare next door. He cultivated relationships with politicians from all parties and at all levels, donating to their campaigns and inviting them to his school for photo ops. He even travelled to India, getting a visa by paying a U.S.$1,000 bribe to a corrupt official in the Vancouver consul general's office. Many others with links to the separatist movement also paid bribes to get their visas. The corrupt official was eventually exposed and removed by the Indian government, sources in New Delhi later confirmed to me.

When the RCMP announced a million-dollar reward in the Air-India case on May 31, 1995, the suspects did not seem fazed at all. They took it as a sign of the desperation of investigators. I tried to reach all of them to get their reaction, but I only managed to talk to Gill and Bagri. Gill accused Parmar of ruining his dream to achieve Khalistan. And he cryptically said the police investigation would arrive at the right person – "One day the truth will be known," he said. Bagri said the police reward just showed they were trying to buy someone. And he said the police should quit blaming the bombing on Parmar – "He is not in this world any more. Why are they talking about him?"

There was trouble at Malik's Khalsa School. Parents protested in June 1996 after a staff member was forced to prove she had not shaved her body hair by allowing an inspection. Malik justified the inspection, saying the teachers had agreed not to cut their hair. "All we were doing is making sure they were keeping this commitment," he said.

Parents were also concerned about excessive discipline, if not the school's links to terrorism. One mother videotaped children being slapped on the back of the head for not sitting up straight during an extended prayer session in the school's temple. She complained in a letter sent to B.C. Education Minister Moe Sihota, the first elected Indo-Canadian, and someone who was close to Malik and other directors at the school. Sihota wrote back saying children being hit was an issue related to discipline and religion, which "do not come under the jurisdiction of my ministry."

Another ministry official said that all the government monitored was whether the school followed the B.C. curriculum, hired certified teachers, and met municipal guidelines for the

buildings. Links to terrorism or the teaching of terrorist ideology weren't on the checklist.

The victims' families became increasingly frustrated as the years
ticked by and little progress seemed to be made in the investigation. Most of the victims had been from Toronto, Ottawa, and
Montreal. Just a handful came from British Columbia. So the
majority of families was unaware of the suspects' growing political power and influence.

The families did not hear a word from the RCMP. They grew
more and more doubtful that anyone would ever be brought to
justice. The million-dollar reward was announced two days before
the families were set to meet Canada's Solicitor General, Herb
Gray. It looked like another federal plot to silence their criticism.

The years had been difficult for many of the family members.
They were not offered free grief counselling or therapy. They
didn't get much financial compensation in their out-of-court
settlements. Some of them had become politically active, but
others were just overwhelmed with pain.

Dr. Bal Gupta became the public face of the families. The electrical engineer from the Etobicoke suburb of Toronto was the
spokesman for the Air-India 182 Victims Families Association –
the lobby group that represented as many of the relatives as were
able to find each other. He tirelessly campaigned for a public
inquiry or a royal commission, but the politicians always found a
reason to say no – the criminal investigation continues or it would
affect national security or . . . the excuses went on and on.

Gupta lost his wife, Ramwati. It just so happened that he and
his two sons were booked on a later flight. He was the one relative that reporters called for comment any time there was a hint
of an Air-India story.

For the Paliwal family of Ottawa, who lost fifteen-year-old Mukul in the bombing, the tragedy was compounded when his father, Dr. Yogesh Paliwal, dropped dead of a heart attack on June 23, 1988, close to the hour that the plane had gone down. He had been painting protest signs for a demonstration later that day on Parliament Hill to demand a public inquiry. There had been no warning signs. He was a healthy forty-six-year-old at the time. His brother Jagat later told me he believed the stress of losing Mukul to terrorism had been too much for Yogesh. "He was keeping it inside too much," Jagat said. "Otherwise, he was a very, very healthy man. In our community he was known as a healthy person. In general, people say move on. But [for] the person whose son is gone, it is not easy."

Jagat, the rest of the family, and the other politically active victims kept the lobby alive. They had two people to fight for after 1988: Mukul and Yogesh. Just a month after Yogesh's death, they hosted a meeting of the Citizens Alliance for a Public Inquiry into Air-India.

Minutes of the two-and-a-half-hour meeting show the great dignity with which the families pursued their cause. There was no hateful rhetoric or destructive calls for revenge. "The idea of the Citizens Alliance came out of the growing frustration caused by the lack/absence of justice in the Air-India tragedy," the minutes state. "An analysis of the situation revealed a feasibility of a public inquiry in parallel with the ongoing criminal investigation."

Not only did they want a public inquiry, they also decided to ask the government to declare June 23 a Victims of Violence day "so the government cannot hope for the issue to die with time . . . It will create a spiritual memorial for the victims," the minutes say.

The minutes reflect the relatives' optimism that they would achieve some of their objectives. They could not possibly have

imagined just how long it would take to make progress, how deaf
successive governments would be to their cries for justice.

Perviz Madon, the North Vancouver woman widowed by the
bombing and who was raising her children, Eddie and Natasha,
alone, worked on the West Coast to bring attention to the victims'
issue. She allowed her grief to be profiled by reporters, year after
year, on the grim Air-India anniversary. She wanted the families'
despair to have a public face. She surrendered her privacy and
became that face. But it was hard. The media cared only about
the bombing victims whenever the anniversary approached. Then
Madon's phone would ring off the hook with requests for interviews from people like me, asking such asinine questions as,
"How are you feeling this year?" "Are you still upset?" "What
about the fact that no charges have been laid?"

A few years after the bombing, Perviz let me have it over the
phone one day. She was frustrated that the media was not embrac-
ing the families' cause with free full-page newspaper ads and
continuous coverage. "You call us once a year to do anniversary
stories and that is it," she said. I explained that we had to remain
neutral and that editors would tire of the issue until the anniversary rolled around. But I sounded pathetic. She was right. I felt
embarrassed about my profession and my own part. I also felt that
I should try to write more.

I was hurt after the call, so I sent her an ill-conceived letter about
how she didn't understand our role and I was just doing my job.
We didn't speak for a couple of years after that. I got a colleague
to call her on the following anniversary to ask the same old tired
questions. But Perviz Madon was an amazingly resilient woman
and I was a stubborn young reporter. We got over our differences
and spoke more and more often as the years passed. We grew more
aware and accepting of our roles in this historic event.

When the RCMP began meeting with the families in 1995 and 1996, Doug Henderson sat in the living room of the Madons' North Vancouver home and laid out the entire investigation for Perviz, Eddie, and Natasha. They were stunned at how much the police had actually done. For the first time since 1985, they felt they were not being ignored.

"We became very active, and I think the RCMP wanted us to be involved. They wanted to put a face to the crime and the victims. We were the first ones they contacted, and we were always ready to help out in any way we could," Eddie said. "Again, it was part of our healing."

Rattan Singh Kalsi lost his daughter Indira – a beautiful twenty-one-year-old pharmacy student with the face of a model. She was on her first trip to India alone. Her father was already in Punjab waiting for her, making sure everything was safe. Kalsi completely collapsed after Indira died. He had built a successful business in Georgetown, Ontario, where he taught others the trade of tool-and-die making. He couldn't continue. He lost his company.

He got a letter from Prime Minister Brian Mulroney after Indira was murdered. It said: "All Canadians share your immense grief and a sense of shock at this terrible tragedy. I wish to assure you that the Government will do everything possible to determine the cause of the Air-India disaster and bring any guilty parties to justice." Kalsi wanted to believe the prime minister, but the years kept passing and no one was being held accountable, no one was being brought to justice. Overcome by despair, he began to lose faith. A therapist suggested he might find solace in Ireland, on the rocky coast of west Cork near where the plane went down. Kalsi took the advice and together with other families built a beautiful garden there. It helped him and his wife, Harbhajan, find some peace.

Dr. Padmini Turlapati and her accountant husband, Narayana, of Markham, Ontario, also found comfort in west Cork, in the village of Ahakista, population 350. The locals welcomed them year after year, putting them up, feeding them and crying with them over the loss of their bright-faced boys, Deepak and Sanjay.

They worked with the Irish to construct a memorial near the site and also bought plants and flowers for the surrounding garden Kalsi had built. The azaleas are in bloom – pink and yellow – every year on June 23. Dr. Turlapati gave up all feelings of motherhood after she lost her boys. She just worked and coped, worked and coped. The doctor in her kicked in and she looked after her distraught husband. They broke off contact with all but three close friends. But every year, when she returned to Ireland, she allowed herself to be a mother again. She talked to her boys and told them about what had happened during the year. She felt peace and comfort.

Parkash Bedi of Detroit spent years looking for his daughter, Anu. The bodies of his son, Jatin, and wife, Saroj, were recovered, but because Anu wasn't found, because she was a good swimmer, he imagined she had someone survived, had been picked up by a Spanish fishing boat and taken to Spain. He went there to find her. He took out ads in the newspapers offering a $100,000 reward. He made posters with her picture on them. She must have amnesia, he thought. That was why she hadn't yet called him.

He also wrote to his president, Ronald Reagan, demanding help in the search for justice for this diabolical act of terrorism. He did not get a return letter. Instead, the FBI contacted him, concerned about the tone of the desperate man's missive to his country's leader. For a long time, Bedi stopped praying. He also cut off contact with all his friends. He did not want to be reminded about what he had lost. Eventually he tried to turn devastation to something positive. He founded a sports tournament in New Delhi in the name of his nine-year-old son, who had loved to play soccer. The tournament has grown to be the biggest of its kind in India. Many of the athletes use it as a starting point for a college scholarship. It made Bedi feel a bit better. But he still did not move or change his phone number – just in case Anu tried to contact him.

Amarjit Bhinder, who lost her pilot husband, Satwinder, was left without an income to look after her son and daughter. After months spent lying in bed unable to cope, she picked herself up and asked Air-India for a job. Every spare moment she was not working, she spent with her children. She took them to the pool, to games, to school. But she remained devastated by her loss. She couldn't bear to change the sign outside her pleasant house in the Punjabi capital, Chandigarh. "Captain S.S. Bhinder," it still reads.

Those relatives far away from Canada, such as Mrs. Bhinder, knew even less than the Canadian families about the Air-India investigation. Nor did they have other family members of victims close by to comfort them. Adding to her burden were silly media speculations that her loving husband, a Sikh, might have unknowingly carried a bomb-laden package on board the plane as a favour to a friend in Toronto.

The loss for all of them was overwhelming, unbearable, but if it could be worse, it was for those who lost everyone in their family, as Lata Pada of Toronto had. The classically trained Indian dancer went back to India after her husband, Vishnu, and daughters, Brinda and Arti, were killed. No longer a mother, no longer a wife, she felt stripped of her identity.

Then she turned to dance to recover – performing her own story, which she called *Revealed by Fire: A Woman's Journey of Transformation*. It began in the temple, where Pada, in widow's white, performed around a square the way the ancient Bharata

Natyam dancers would have. It told her story of marriage, immigration, motherhood, widowhood, and rebirth. It allowed her to
find a life to live again, a way to heal. And it was a powerful
message against terrorism.

Drawn together by fate and grief, the families, as united as they
could be, pressed for justice. They begged their government to
treat their loved ones like all Canadians should be treated. But they
did not have the political clout to get an inquiry. They did not
have the power to get answers. They watched the politicians on
the television news on Sikh holy days visiting the *gurdwaras* and
standing in front of Punjabi signs proclaiming Long Live
Khalistan. The families began to lose faith.

The RCMP officers on the Air-India Task Force had been working
for years to get approval for the reward that was finally announced
on May 31, 1995. It was a last-ditch attempt to stir things up in the
Sikh community and maybe, just maybe, get someone to come
forward with information to break the case wide open.

It is not that investigators didn't know who did it. They had
known who the suspects were since shortly after the two bombs
exploded on opposite sides of the globe in June 1985, resulting
in the biggest criminal probe in Canadian history in British
Columbia, halfway between the two blasts. What they didn't
have was evidence.

The reward announcement, made at a special news conference with pieces of the plane propped up behind the task-force
members, brought international attention to the case the likes
of which had not been seen since Reyat was convicted four
years earlier.

The task force had been winding down at this point. Some
investigators believed the file should just be closed so that the

families would not have any obstacle to their demands for a public inquiry.

The RCMP's major crime division in British Columbia had a new officer in charge. Insp. Gary Bass was a committed career Mountie who had arrived in British Columbia just a week after Parmar was killed in October 1992. He ordered a review of the entire Air-India file – a massive undertaking. He hoped that fresh eyes would see some new avenue of pursuit in the stalled investigation. Bass called one of his most respected homicide detectives, Doug Henderson. Henderson's cellphone rang as he sat in a car doing surveillance in the high-profile Rafay-Burns murder case, in which two parents were killed in Seattle by their son, Atif, and his Vancouver buddy, Sebastian Burns.

Henderson was swamped with work, but he wanted the Air-India job badly. He had been involved in the case as a corporal in Duncan back in 1985. He had known Reyat socially and interrogated him when Reyat was first arrested in November 1985.

Just as Henderson was beginning the review in the summer of 1995, he was struck by a personal tragedy that dramatically affected his approach to Air-India. His son Tom was killed by a hit-and-run driver as the sixteen-year-old chatted with friends at the bottom of the family driveway in the Vancouver suburb of Ladner. The driver was eventually caught and convicted. Henderson and his family lived with the pain of their immense loss during the police investigation and later court proceedings. It gave him a good perspective on what the Air-India victims' families were going through. He did see new investigative approaches after looking at the file. But one of the first things he decided to do was reach out to the grieving families, who had been waiting for ten years for an outstretched hand.

Henderson set up meetings in Ottawa, Toronto, Montreal, and later Vancouver. At first the relatives just let loose with their anger and frustrations. One by one, in the style of a support group, they told Henderson and the other RCMP officers about who they had lost. They described their last contact with their loved one – waving goodbye at the airport or just before they got into a car. They gave Henderson photographs. Henderson took all their stories back to his new team of investigators. They put up the pictures of the victims to motivate them. It was a new beginning.

Henderson was off to a good start with a much better relationship forming between the police and the families that would remain. Many of the relatives had feared not much had been done. They were surprised to learn police investigators had been all over the world, that they had uncovered a great deal of evidence about the conspirators, but not enough to make their case.

From an investigative point of view, Henderson hoped that a decade had brought enough change in the Sikh community that more people would be willing to talk. Bob Wright, a senior Crown prosecutor, was assigned to the case to help put together the report for charge approval. Having a dedicated prosecutor was a new idea back then and it helped move things forward.

Henderson also thought it would be worth going back to CSIS to see what else the agency had. He knew the relationship between the RCMP and CSIS had not been the best in the initial stages of this investigation, but he felt it had dramatically improved since. He was still surprised to learn, a decade after the bombing, some information from CSIS for the first time.

Bass came up with all the necessary resources. At times, the new task force had more than a hundred people working on it. They started almost from scratch, doing everything that had been done before and then more: undercover operations, wiretaps, developing sources and witnesses. No stone was left unturned. Not only did the new task force want to rely on the CSIS wiretaps, investigators re-interviewed everyone who had provided information either to the police or to CSIS at any point since the bombing. They wanted to turn informants into witnesses.

One of the main differences between the old task force and the new one was its approach to the massive terrorism investigation. The earlier team had handled it like a homicide investigation, albeit one of unprecedented scale. But by 1995 and 1996, investigators believed they should focus more on the conspiracy component of the crime.

They developed what became known as the one-two theory – that single actions led to both the Air-India bombing and the Narita explosion. One phone call booked both tickets used to load the bomb-laden suitcases. One person picked up both tickets. If a bomb had exploded at Narita, then one had exploded on Air-India Flight 182 too. Looking at it as a conspiracy, Bass thought the police could make great use of the CSIS wiretaps made before and after the bombing of phone calls between Parmar, the mastermind, and the other suspects, including Bagri, Malik, and Reyat. It was already public knowledge that hundreds of hours of those tapes had been erased by CSIS, leaving only logs with basic information about what had been said.

Bass wrote a scathing memo to CSIS in February 1996, criticizing the erasures, calling the lost wiretaps of "highly probative value," and saying that charges could have been laid years earlier if the tapes had been preserved. By late 1996 and early 1997, the RCMP was getting confident about making arrests, even before some key witnesses were on board.

Investigators were prepared to do a deal with someone involved in the plot. Henderson visited Reyat several times in jail to try to get his co-operation. As well, in November 1996, police picked up Surjan Gill, the former consul general of Khalistan who had split with Parmar in the days before the bombing. He was nabbed driving near the U.S. border with his girlfriend and interrogated for hours. Both Reyat and Gill indicated to police that they would consider co-operating. Gill told police he would definitely make a deal, but wanted to consult his lawyer, David Gibbons, first. As soon as Gibbons got involved, the deal was off. Gibbons had also represented Reyat, Bagri, Parmar, and Daljit Sandhu over the years.

At the time police were talking to Reyat, he was represented by Kuldip Singh Chaggar, who was a close friend of Malik. Chaggar claimed he wanted to make a deal to help Reyat. The RCMP was doubtful. It put a surveillance team on the controversial lawyer and followed him from Gary Bass's office at police headquarters right to Malik's house. The police decided that no deal could be worked out as long as Chaggar was involved. The British-born lawyer was later convicted in the United States of witness tampering in an unrelated drug case.

"It is unfortunate for the Canadian justice system that there was inappropriate conduct by Gibbons and Chaggar," Bass says. "It goes back many years. Certainly over the years I was involved."

The Air-India Task Force moved forward with dogged determination. They convinced an FBI informant to meet with them, even though the man had told his handlers that he would never give evidence about an alleged confession he said he heard from Bagri in 1985. The RCMP pursued him for months and finally made a deal.

Investigators went back repeatedly to Bagri's close female friend – Premika – who had once incriminated him to CSIS. She continued to refuse to co-operate, but bit by bit her story came out in several police statements.

And Henderson did something else police had been reluctant to do since June 1985: He predicted in the media on December 10, 1996, that charges would soon be laid. "One thing is for sure: We certainly know who did everything," Henderson told Canadian Press. "There is no doubt in my mind who was involved, who the main players and the principals were. As quite often is the case, the next step is: Can you prove that beyond a reasonable doubt in court? That's what we are dealing with right now."

Without a doubt, the RCMP was trying to turn up the heat on the Air-India suspects. There was the arrest of Surjan Gill, which soon got back to the other suspects. There was the media frenzy that ensued after Henderson's comments to the Canadian Press. And then in early 1997, a search warrant was executed for some of Gill's material. It named six bombing suspects: Parmar, Bagri, Malik, Johal, Reyat, and Gill.

Even before the Air-India reward was announced, Tara Singh Hayer, the *Indo-Canadian Times* publisher, was fretting. He had been sitting on some potentially deadly information about who had been involved in the Air-India bombings, some information that he believed led to the 1988 plot to assassinate him. But he also was worried about how talking to police would affect his life and his job as the leading Punjabi-language journalist in Canada.

He had seen a number of serious terrorism-related cases bungled – the ISYF conspiracy to kill the visiting cabinet minister, the Hamilton conspiracy case involving Bagri and Parmar, his own 1988 shooting, where the real motive had never come out in court.

He had even been frustrated with me when I wrote a story in April 1993 saying that Harkirat Bagga, the teenager who had shot him, was really sorry about what he had done and wanted to go back to India. Bagga had called me from jail to do a story on his plight. He had been granted parole, but had to be deported to his native India as a condition. But India didn't want him, so he could not be released. He claimed to me that he was now a mature twenty-two-year-old who realized that what he had done to Hayer was wrong. He sounded sincere, but when I called Hayer for comment for the story, he didn't buy it. Hayer said that, if Bagga were released, "I would be very much afraid." I did not know at the time that Bagga had been visited in jail by Ajaib Bagri.

Hayer got some devastating news in early January 1995. His old friend Tarsem Purewal had been gunned down outside his newspaper office in Southall, England. Hayer knew the motive behind the assassination better than anyone else. Purewal and Hayer both knew about a key conspirator in the Air-India bombing who had confessed in Purewal's office a decade before.

Purewal had kept the secret. But he had hinted in a December 1994 edition of his paper that he would be turning against his former Khalistani allies, whom he had decided were corrupt and had misappropriated donations. Three weeks later he was dead. Scotland Yard didn't have a clue who did it.

Hayer had also written about what he had heard, though not directly. He had alluded in two Punjabi-language news stories in 1987 and 1988 that, in front of others, Ajaib Bagri had confessed to a role in the Air-India bombing. But Hayer did not say in either article, which were missed by the police at the time, that he and Purewal had both heard Bagri first-hand. There was a disconnect between the Punjabi world of the Air-India suspects, and those around them, and the English world of RCMP investigators and reporters like me.

Hayer had once disclosed his secret about Bagri to a member of the Air-India Task Force. But Hayer had not wanted to be a witness at the time and the information was not passed on to subsequent investigators.

Now, with Purewal dead, Hayer felt he had to reassess his earlier position. He told the RCMP he was not prepared to testify, and he gave his first formal statement to the Air-India Task Force on October 15, 1995. He kept his decision to himself for years.

By the following August, Hayer was having second thoughts. The case against the Babbar Khalsa in Montreal over the conspiracy to bomb an Air-India jet in New York, which had been appealed to the Supreme Court of Canada, was thrown out one final time, meaning Santokh Khela and Kashmir Dhillon would not be forced to endure a third trial.

This time, though, a Quebec judge said the issue was not the identity of the confidential informant Billy-Joe, but rather that the prosecution had withheld evidence from the defence teams. Khela and Dhillon's lawyers had been told the informant claimed the pair paid $8,000 to have the Air-India jet blown up. But an earlier statement he made suggested the money was not to bomb a plane, but to assassinate Hayer.

The development unnerved the wheelchair-bound publisher. Not only could there have been another attempt on his life, but the culprits were once again free and clear.

"The people are very much insecure. If every time the judge is going to throw the charges out, then I guess this country would not be a safe haven for innocent people but a safe haven for crooks," Hayer said.

As Henderson had hoped, there had been a shift in the politics of the Sikh community in British Columbia. People who once may have feared the Air-India suspects had grown to see them for the opportunists they were. And others who had at one point been sympathetic to the movement, if not its tactics, had shifted away from demanding the separate state of Khalistan. Even Hayer now said the dream of a Sikh homeland was ruined – destroyed by the violence of groups like the Babbar Khalsa and the ISYF.

But the original suspects had been discreet. They had kept the secret within their inner circle for more than a decade.

Less than two weeks after Henderson publicly predicted Air-India charges would soon be laid, a gang from the ISYF gathered at Malik's Khalsa School on December 21, 1996, for a meeting. They vowed to race over to the Surrey Sikh temple they had controlled until a few months before and remove the tables and chairs that filled a communal dining hall on the lower level of the complex. The action was being pushed by the same people who had put the tables in place years earlier.

Now they were saying that real Sikhs – orthodox Sikhs – would never have the furniture in the hall and that they had to remove it to defend their faith. About a hundred people moved in, three of them brandishing swords, and smashed the furniture as stunned onlookers called police.

It was the beginning of a B.C.–based holy war between moderates and fundamentalists for control of lucrative temples. But it was also much more than that. Supporters of the Air-India suspects wanted to mobilize the faithful. In 1996, Khalistan did not raise the passions of many any more.

On January 5, 1997, a crowd gathered at Malik's school to plan their next move on the tables-and-chairs front. Six days later, they headed to Surrey's Guru Nanak Sikh temple a second time to take care of the new tables that had been brought in. Hundreds rioted with swords, baseball bats, metal pipes, and bars. Police were attacked with boiling liquids, pointed umbrellas, and ball bearings from powerful slingshots.

Four were injured in the bloody melee. Fourteen ISYF members ended up being charged after the two incidents, including Reyat's cousin Piara Panasar, who faced an attempted murder charge. He was the same cousin who had opened up the credit union account that allowed Mrs. Reyat to hide some of her money from welfare authorities.

Supporting the temple attackers for being defenders of the faith was Hardial Johal, the Air-India suspect. He contacted Ranjit

Singh, *jathedar*, or high priest, of the Akal Takht in Amritsar, to get an endorsement for the temple attackers' violent actions.

A new flashpoint had been successfully ignited.

One morning in September 1992, a newspaper ad caught the attention of Rani Kumar. It was advertising for staff for a new daycare for children aged three to five in a Sikh independent school in Surrey, just outside of Vancouver. (I have renamed her Rani because her real identity is shielded by court order.) As Rani later told me, she had been born a Sikh, but she was married to a Hindu man and no longer connected with her birth religion or culture. Even though she was already working, she decided to apply.

She met with a director of the Khalsa School and he offered her the job on the spot. The pay was less than what she was earning, but she was intrigued by the idea of starting a brand-new facility that would pay special attention to culture. The daycare was to operate on the ground floor of a house next door to the school. It was in a mess, but Rani began spending evenings and weekends there, cleaning the place, while she finished at her old job.

She soon met Ripudaman Malik. The two hit it off immediately. She found him full of ideas and inspiration; he was impressed by her commitment to the new job and kept giving her additional responsibilities. He told her she could depend on a woman named Satnam Reyat for help. Malik referred to Mrs. Reyat affectionately as a "sister." She lived in the upper three-bedroom apartment of the house in which the daycare was located.

Rani soon learned that Mrs. Reyat's husband was in prison for his role in a 1985 bombing. As awful as the crime sounded,

Rani did not pay much attention to it. Despite her Sikh heritage, she knew little of the Sikh separatists who had sometimes used violence in their campaign for a homeland. Even when the battle spilled over into Canada, Rani had not been aware of it. She had been living for years in a small, remote B.C. resource town that did not have much of a Sikh population. (Publication of the name of the town and other details of her life have been banned by court order.)

Rani and Mrs. Reyat quickly became good friends. Together they got the daycare centre ready for its opening a month or so after Rani started working there in the fall of 1992.

Rani saw members of the ISYF and Babbar Khalsa around the school and daycare. Some of their children were registered in both programs. The grandson of Talwinder Parmar attended the Khalsa daycare as a toddler. His famous grandfather was killed just weeks after Rani started.

The Khalsa School crowd was a closely knit group, and even though Rani did not agree with the Sikh separatist philosophy, she was admired for the skill with which she developed and expanded the daycare program. But she was seen as an outsider. She went beyond the call of duty, travelling to religious camps that the school held around British Columbia during winter and summer breaks.

Malik soon started to include her in non-school functions as well. He invited her to his luxurious Vancouver home for religious programs. She began to accompany him to political events involving municipal, provincial, and federal politicians. In turn, those politicians often visited the parochial school and were treated to Indian treats such as chai and samosas.

Rani, then an attractive, slim thirty-two-year-old, later said she and Malik started falling for each other. He was her boss, but she could tell him exactly what she thought and he respected that. She didn't understand why some people feared Malik. They shared a sarcastic sense of humour and a love of hard work. She says they each had something lacking in the marriages that had been arranged for them years earlier. They were drawn to each other like magnets.

Sometimes he would call her at the daycare from meetings he was in and they would chat on the cellphone. Malik became more and more reliant on her organizational skills and began to ask her to help him at the school and in some of his business dealings, on top of her regular daycare duties.

She had no clue that Malik was regarded by police as a suspect in the 1985 Air-India and Narita bombings, although she knew that Parmar and Reyat had both been associated with the terrorist attacks.

About a year after Rani began work at the school, Malik invited her to a religious program at his house. She started to see him more and more outside the daycare and school setting. Many who knew them both, including several directors at the school, saw the increasing amount of time Rani and Malik were spending together.

In the fall of 1994, Malik invited her to lunch at a vegetarian restaurant on Main Street in Vancouver. They shared dosa and other Indian delicacies, and he told her the part of India where each dish originated. He also gave her a white cotton blouse. Other times, he would take her to the White Spot for snacks. He loved junk food – fries, shakes, and so on.

Rani said later that Malik professed his love for her as they prepared for a gathering at the daycare one morning in January 1995. She wasn't surprised that he felt it, but she was surprised that he said it.

He had already given her a beautiful basket he had brought
back from California, stuffed with goodies. A month later, he
organized a birthday party for her. He gave her an emerald-green
dress. She said he also began to give her little gifts on Valentine's
Day – flower arrangements that contained birds of paradise, which
she told him she loved. And ginger flowers. He called her his
exotic princess, Rani later told me. She said they never consum-
mated the love they shared, but they had held hands and hugged.
Malik later denied through his lawyer that they had anything
other than an employer-employee relationship.

Rani said she was not prepared for the events of April 1996.
A young student at the Khalsa School had been accused by a religious teacher of cutting her hair against Sikh doctrine. In fact,
the girl had a medical condition that had made her hair fall out.

The distraught girl, Preethi Cudail, was so upset at the accu-
sation that she had violated her religion that she swallowed thirty
Tylenol pills and was rushed to hospital. Rani and many other
staff members were very concerned about the girl. Her parents
were angry about Malik's attitude. He didn't even bother to visit
the girl in the hospital.

Rani confronted Malik about his apparent indifference to the
girl's plight. She later told police that their heated conversation led
to his first admission that he had had something to do with the 1985
Air-India bombing. Devastated, she made notes of the discussion
in a journal she kept about daily events at the daycare centre.

But Malik soon conceded that he had not handled the girl's
suicide attempt well. He relented and wrote an apology letter to
the Cudail family. He tried to make amends, but the family went
ahead and filed a human-rights complaint against the school.

His gesture was enough to win Rani back over, she would later
tell both me and a B.C. Supreme Court judge. He could always

convince her she was better off with him. She had her work. She had her friends. She felt special and appreciated. But her feelings changed a few months later, in the spring of 1997, when she says Malik implicated himself in the Air-India bombing after she confronted him again. She wanted to stay at the job she loved, but it was becoming increasingly difficult.

Some of Malik's associates began to spread the rumour that she was a spy for the Canadian Security Intelligence Service. Ironically, several people connected to the Khalsa School had already provided information to CSIS by the time of these allegations against Rani. She was not one of them. But she was becoming increasingly desperate about her plight. She wondered what would happen if she left the school. Would she be in danger? She decided she had to stay in her job until she could prove she was not a spy.

She did not feel safe. Friends at the school warned her that she was getting too close to Malik, and that she didn't know him as well as she believed. In late summer 1997, she wrote a desperate note and tucked it in the back of the binder she used as her journal. The note was a macabre document. Addressed "To whom it may concern," it said that if she were found dead, she had not committed suicide.

CHAPTER 6

Guerrilla Journalism

I GOT THE CALL just before noon on November 5, 1997. It was a Wednesday. The speaker said she had been running the daycare associated with Surrey's Khalsa School. I knew the school, knew it was an elementary–junior high that had received millions of dollars in government funding even though it was linked to some of the most extreme Sikh militants in the world. I also knew that several close relatives of the suspects in the 1985 Air-India bombing worked there.

The caller identified herself as Rani Kumar and said someone had given her my name because of my years covering the Indo-Canadian community for the *Vancouver Sun*. I was also the *Sun*'s education reporter at the time and had an interest in how the controversial independent school was operating. Rani said she had been at the school since 1992, but had recently been fired and she believed it was very unfair.

"What went wrong?" I asked flippantly. "Were you not fundamentalist enough for them?"

She laughed.

I told her that I had been digging around for information on the school for a number of months but had been running into walls everywhere. It was so bad that when I made an inquiry to the Ministry of Education in the summer of 1996 about the school's funding and told the media officer that Sikhs linked to terrorism had been meeting there regularly, instead of looking into the terror connections, a ministry official contacted the school's president, Ripudaman Malik, and told him what I had said. Without my knowledge, the official gave Malik my name. He sent off a polite response denying my claims, as he would many times in the months ahead.

Rani and I agreed to meet a few days later. There was no talk of the 1985 Air-India bombing, though a few cryptic comments we both made indicated we knew the school was a symbol of something much greater than her problems with it.

On the appointed day, I drove out to the Vancouver suburb of Surrey, where I met Rani in a coffee bar. I found her to be a pleasant, attractive woman who was very westernized – not like most of the Punjabi immigrants associated with the Khalsa School. She told me she had never been to Punjab or India, but was born to Sikh parents in a country that I am not allowed to name because of the same court order designed to protect her. Her father had run a Khalsa School there, but a very secularized one that had been attended by Sikhs and non-Sikhs alike.

I told her I was interested in doing a series of stories on the Surrey school and the government money it was receiving. There were two charitable – and questionable – societies operating out of the school: the Satnam Education Society, which received $2 million a year in government funding for the school's 840 kids, and the Satnam Trust, which collected the fees for the school and donated the money back to the education society. Both were headed by Malik, who was also the chairman of the Khalsa Credit Union.

Rani told me about several improprieties she had seen since she began working for the education society as head of the school's daycare. But she also had a great deal of affection for the school and many of the people employed there. She appeared to be extremely conflicted, so I told her what I'd already found out about the school. With or without her help, I planned to do a series of stories, I said.

We agreed that she would come down to the new *Vancouver Sun* building at 200 Granville Street a few days later. When she arrived by SkyTrain, I gave her a brief tour of our newsroom with its spectacular views of the North Shore Mountains and Burrard Inlet. We then headed to a little café in the building for lunch. She ordered a vegetable sandwich on eight-grain bread – she is vegetarian – and a cup of tea. As we spoke, she seemed nervous, turning her head repeatedly to check out everyone entering the café.

We quickly learned we were the same age and both had two sons. We also knew many of the same people in the Indo-Canadian community, as well as on the provincial political scene. Rani had helped on several campaigns, including that of former New Democratic Party cabinet minister Penny Priddy.

When she applied for the Khalsa job, Rani had been running a secular daycare for a number of years. It wasn't that Rani had turned her back on Sikhism, she explained. She was a very proud Sikh. But it was not a culture she was immersed in. One reason why she had been interested in the job at the school's daycare was that it would allow her to reconnect with Sikhism and the Punjabi language and introduce it to her children.

She loved the job. She felt she was in at the beginning of something new to the Sikh community – the establishment of its own institution, where language, culture, and religion could all be taught. She had grown extremely fond of Malik, whom she found quick-witted and intellectually stimulating. At the time she did not know how twisted the relationship would become or that she would end up in the Witness Protection Program, identified by Crown prosecutors as "the lynchpin" in its case against Malik in Canada's worst mass murder.

Over lunch, we talked mostly about the school and daycare. She leaned in and spoke in a whisper when describing how she had become the person Malik depended on most, both for his school-related decisions as well as in business matters. She had even picked the tile colour for the lobby of the hotel he was building in the resort town of Harrison Hot Springs.

I suggested that she might want to move to a more private location, and took her to the reading area of the newspaper's library, a seldom-frequented room, where we could talk more openly about a school with frightening links to terrorists.

She told me that in the last few months, Malik and his supporters at the school had begun calling her a spy, a CSIS agent. She felt extremely isolated and fearful. She had been cornered by a school trustee in a threatening manner at the Surrey campus one day. Many of the friends she had made at the school – including Satnam Reyat – had begun to shun her. Satnam and the children were being well looked after by Malik while Reyat was serving his ten-year sentence for the Narita bombing. Satnam had been given work at the daycare, but continued to collect welfare while being paid under the table by Malik, she said. A few days before our first meeting, Rani had been fired.

I had a lot of questions for Rani, but also did not want to freak out someone who was potentially a gold mine of information about the people involved in the Air-India case – a case that had obsessed me since the day it had happened. I sensed that she needed to talk to someone about all the things that were happening to her and around her. She seemed very trusting of me – in part because

I had some knowledge and understanding about the Sikh community and the militants linked to the separatist movement and
the school.

She confided a lot about what she had been through, though,
as I later learned, not everything. She also told me about some of
the scandals waiting to be uncovered at the school. She explained
how government money was being misused and misdirected.
She said politicians of all persuasions would visit the school,
despite its terrorist links, and share Indian delicacies with Malik,
herself, and other staff members.

I was surprised when Rani told me a convicted hijacker from
India had been living in the school and working with the children
for two years. Malik had fondly dubbed the man – Tejinder Pal
Singh – "the hijacker." And I was shocked when she told me about
how some of the children were being abused, both physically and
sexually. She told me that members of the Babbar Khalsa and the
International Sikh Youth Federation had been meeting regularly
at the school, something I had heard from other sources in the Indo-
Canadian community. And she told me how the families of
identified suspects in the Air-India bombing – Talwinder Parmar
and Inderjit Reyat – were being looked after there. Parmar's son-
in-law, Sartaj Singh Chima, worked at Khalsa School; his son
Narinder had also been employed there; and his grandson
attended the daycare. Mrs. Reyat was receiving support in the
form of free accommodation and money, and her children were
getting free tuition.

I asked Rani about the allegation that she was an agent for
CSIS or anyone else. She admitted she had spoken to the spy
agency, but only after she had started to be ostracized at work.
She showed me a business card for Staff Sgt. John Schneider of
the Air-India Task Force and said that she had attended several
meetings with the RCMP at various locations around the Lower

Mainland. She said that investigators from both agencies had not trusted her at first. They thought she might be an agent for Malik, trying to see how the ramped-up police investigation was proceeding, but that investigators were now pressing her for more information. It was hard, she said, especially when Malik had been such a good friend. She felt very conflicted about talking to police.

At one point as we stood there looking out over the mountains and water, Rani said the most startling thing, that Malik had told her he had been involved in the bombing plot. My heart began to pound. Canada's libel laws make it dangerous to imply someone is involved in criminal activities if the police have not publicly named a suspect or laid any charges. I didn't know what I was supposed to do with the information. To publish it would be libellous. To possess it was perilous.

I asked Rani what she was expecting me to do. Did she want a story on her plight? She asked me to hold off writing anything as she was preparing a wrongful dismissal suit against Malik and the school with her lawyer, Ravi Hira.

After Rani left, I talked to my editors about preparing a series of stories on the school and the allegations against it. We knew that anything we wrote would likely affect the Air-India case. It was our Al Capone approach to journalism – we had not been able to get people to reveal details about Air-India, so we thought we would publish some of the other allegations involving the suspects. The notorious American gangster – suspected of ordering dozens of murders – had been convicted only for tax evasion, after all.

The more I investigated, the more links between the schools and the Air-India case I uncovered. There were the connections to the families of Parmar and Reyat I already knew about, but there were others. School trustees Balwant Bhandher and Satwant Sandhu were suspects. The RCMP had interviewed Sandhu shortly after the bombing about his relationship with Parmar. He had lied about knowing him. Hardial Johal, seen at the airport the day the bombs were checked in, was a director of the Satnam Trust. Other school trustees, including Kewal Nagra and Gurdev Gill, were prominent members of the Babbar Khalsa.

Rani and I spoke many times over the following days and weeks, meeting on a few other occasions. She had been receiving a lot of threatening calls and warnings from her former associates at the school. While I knew she was talking to police, I never asked her for details of those conversations. I assumed she had told them about Malik's admission to her, though she never said that she had.

By early December, I had come up with several stories that I had documented thoroughly enough to publish. The school had been charging families mandatory fees, then giving tax receipts for the full amount, calling the payments donations. Revenue Canada confirmed that the practice violated tax law. Volunteer school treasurer Narinder Singh Gill told me he had expressed concern about it to Malik.

I was able to confirm that the International Sikh Youth Federation, linked for years to terrorist activity, held monthly meetings at the Surrey school. And I found out that several parents had complained to the B.C. government about harsh punishment meted out by strict religious instructors. Ministry staff had faxed the complainant's letters directly to Malik.

And then there was the hijacker, Tejinder Pal Singh, who had been living in the school's basement and volunteering to work with the children for two years while he pursued a refugee claim to remain in Canada. I learned that Singh was one of the members of the Dal Khalsa terrorist group who had hijacked an Indian Airlines plane to Pakistan in 1981. He had been tried and convicted, and while in jail, he received a care package from Talwinder Parmar, delivered by his wife and sister-in-law. Another supporter was Ajaib Bagri, who had endorsed the hijacking in speeches and on the phone to Parmar. So not surprisingly, when Singh was released after a fourteen-year sentence, he travelled on a false Pakistani passport to Canada, where he received support from Malik at Khalsa School. When his refugee claim was examined, the federal government decided Singh was too dangerous to stay in the country. He was arrested at the school two days after I began making inquiries about him.

Singh was not the only person with terrorist links who had stayed at the school. The widow of the Babbar Khalsa leader in Punjab, Sukhdev Babbar, and her children had been brought to Canada on false passports and stayed in the school for several months using fake names. When Narinder Gill complained, the family of the man whom India once considered its number-one enemy bolted to Calgary and made a successful refugee claim.

I called Malik to get his response to what I was writing in my series on December 12 – the day before the first article was published. He was charming and chatty and confirmed most of what I had uncovered. But he defended the practice of issuing charitable tax receipts, saying he believed government policy was being followed. Then he pleaded with me not to write anything. "Kim, as a good Christian, I beg you to look into your heart at this special time of year – Christmas – and don't do anything to hurt our little school," Malik said. "I am not saying we are 100 per cent right in everything. All we are trying to do is educate these children." He also admitted that the ISYF had been meeting at the school, saying that anyone, from any Sikh group, was welcome to use the facility after school hours.

After the first story appeared on December 13, my phone rang off the hook. People were surprised that I was exposing Malik and the school. A flood of new tips came in.

One of the other stories I stumbled upon confirmed what Rani had told me. I found it more disturbing than the school's

links to terrorism. Two confidential sources told me that some
girls at the Khalsa School had complained to staff and their parents
that a priest, Beant Singh Sekhon, had sexually assaulted them
repeatedly during a class to teach them how to play the tabla (a
round drum) and the harmonium – both used in *kirtan*, or hymn
singing. I spoke to two of the mothers, who said they didn't think
the allegations had been presented to police. They were ready to
call the police themselves, but held back because they were hesitant to involve their children in an investigation.

I called the local RCMP, which confirmed that it had heard
nothing. I called the school administrators and the B.C. Ministry
of Education. Within hours, the Khalsa School administration
phoned the police – twelve days after the allegations had first been
reported to staff.

The series had an explosive effect in the community. The
RCMP announced it was investigating the school's financial
irregularities and the sex-abuse allegations. The B.C. government
launched a probe of the alleged misuse of government funds. And
the Immigration department began a deportation hearing for the
hijacker – all within a week of my first story.

In retrospect, I realize Malik must have known that one of my
sources was Rani. A few days after the first story, I was preparing
a feature on the Sikh leader, who was keeping a low profile in
the broader community despite his powerful position among
Indo-Canadians. When I called him about the story, Malik said,
"People are using you to do things. The only goal I have in the
Sikh religion is to educate these children." He claimed his only
political affiliation was Sikhism, but admitted knowing all the militant leaders, including Parmar. "I am very close to them," he said.
"I am saying to you there is not a leader here in the Sikh community that I did not know from 1972 to 1997 and that includes
everybody, including Mr. Parmar."

I needed people to comment in my articles. But few in the Sikh community would publicly criticize Malik, despite privately providing me with information about the controversies. When no one else was prepared to be quoted, I turned to Tara Hayer. The outspoken and controversial publisher never shied away from speaking his mind. When we first talked, he told me that Malik had too much control over the Sikh community through the school and credit union. He gave me a letter he had received from the credit union a few months earlier, cancelling all the ads in his newspaper because he had refused a request to support in his newspaper the fundamentalist slate in a temple election. "He has been controlling the community for a long time, either because people need money to buy a house or because they want to make sure their kids know a little about Sikh culture and religion. Both are available through him," Hayer said.

As Beant Sekhon made last-ditch attempts to avert deportation, several people linked to my stories began getting threats. Rani received more calls designed to intimidate her. Narinder Gill, the school treasurer I had quoted, had rocks thrown through his living-room window at 3:30 a.m. by a former Khalsa School student named Mindy Bhandher. Mindy, who would later admit in court that he was a gangster and drug trafficker, considered Malik a father figure. He had lived with Malik as a thirteen-year-old when he wasn't getting along with his own father, Balwant Bhandher, a school trustee and Air-India suspect.

My contacts at the RCMP had already warned me that I might receive threats because of the stories. They were right.

The first threatening letter arrived in the newsroom late on a snowy afternoon two days before Christmas 1997. It was mailed in a business-sized envelope with no return address. The author had written on white foolscap in neat handwriting: "You are bad man Kim Bolan. You stop lies about good Mr. Malik. You are bad. You stop or you will die." Then, farther down the page were the words: "You die Hayer man. You die like Gandhi woman."

I called Hayer immediately and faxed him the letter, but he wasn't worried. He was used to threats. He was still paralyzed from the 1988 assassination attempt. I joked that at least the letter-writer wrongly thought I was a man. Then, instead of leaving work early to finish my Christmas shopping and attend a neigh-bourhood caroling party, I called the police. I didn't even know who to call. It seemed silly to dial 911, so I phoned the media officers for the RCMP and Vancouver police to ask for advice. RCMP Sgt. Russ Grabb advised me to call the emergency oper-ator. But he also said he would notify the Air-India Task Force about the letter.

Even though my series had been about Khalsa School and its links to terrorism, the backdrop to everything I was writing was the 1985 Air-India bombing plot. The RCMP understood. Many in the Sikh community understood.

As I awaited the arrival of the Vancouver police on December 23, 1997, I got an unexpected call from a leading RCMP officer, Gary Bass, who oversaw the Air-India Task Force. He said he appreciated the stories I had done and suggested that I take some security measures. The Vancouver beat cops who eventually came knew nothing about Air-India, let alone the controversial school in Surrey I had written about.

They got me to type out a statement. When I included a line about Malik being an Air-India suspect, the beat cops told me to remove it. They didn't explain why, but I think they were nervous about my making the link to the ongoing terrorism investigation in an unrelated complaint to a different police force. They bagged the letter and envelope and said they would send it to the RCMP – specifically the Air-India investigators – for forensic testing. I was never told whether police found anything.

In the following months, I continued to cover everything related to the militants running the school who were supporting the Air-India suspects. The hijacker was deported and the priest was charged with twenty counts of sexual assault and interference on students. He later pleaded guilty to two counts.

Rani's wrongful dismissal suit against Malik's society was filed in January 1988. A few days later, the RCMP raided the school in connection with its fraud investigation. The B.C. Minstry of Education released its report, which backed my stories and showed the school was not in compliance with the law. Almost $1 million in payments to the school would be withheld until improvements were made.

There were so many allegations coming out against the school that I found it hard to imagine how government officials could have handed over millions every year without noticing the problems. Only after my stories appeared did they demand an explanation of years-long practices and links to terrorism.

For each and every story I wrote, I called Malik. Sometimes he gave me a comment and chatted a little, sometimes he refused to say a word and slammed down the phone. I had not intended to turn my series on Malik's school into a full-time reporting beat. Nor did I know that the RCMP's Air-India investigation was nearing completion with a recommendation for charges against several people, including Malik. But I am stubborn. I felt I had to continue reporting so that it didn't look like I was caving in to threats. Letters of support were pouring in. Tara Hayer sent one to my editors, urging me to keep my "eagle eye" on Malik and the school.

I began investigating the Khalsa Credit Union, and I uncovered several allegations of conflict-of-interest and inappropriate financial transactions. Government regulators put the institution under supervision after my series.

The threats continued along with the articles. Malik called a special meeting at the school to allay the concerns of parents over all the investigations. I went to the meeting and was verbally abused by a few Malik supporters. Outside the school, I ran into some people who had gathered to see what was going on. Rani Kumar was one of them. I spoke to her about the escalating hostility. A young woman whom Rani recognized wrote my licence plate down in front of both of us and then said, "[Rani Kumar] and Kim Bolan. Mr. Malik is going to kick your ass."

In February a young Sikh man wearing a bandanna approached Rani as she stood on the platform at a Surrey SkyTrain station. He drew a finger across his throat and said both she and I were going to get it. She was on her way to meet me at the time. Later in February, on a call-in program on a Punjabi radio station, school trustee Satwant Sandhu declared that I was going to "fall into a grave" if I didn't watch out. Sandhu made the comment in English although he was using an old Punjabi adage. He said that if both I and a Punjabi journalist named Sukhminder Singh Cheema didn't stop digging up dirt on people, like gravediggers, we would soon fall into the graves we'd dug. I would later learn that Cheema, a former member of the ISYF who had split from the group, was also on the Air-India witness list. Cheema's son was a student at Khalsa School. When Cheema attended a parents' meeting that month, a Malik supporter shouted that he would be "cut into bits and spread around" for the dogs. Several journalists taped the comments.

All these threats were reported to the RCMP and the Vancouver police after they were made. But no one was charged in any of the cases, even when police were provided with tapes of the threatening comments. In my case, the Vancouver police suggested the *Sun* publish an article about the threats as a warning to those responsible. My editors agreed and a colleague wrote it in March 1998.

Mike Porteous, a detective constable from the Vancouver Police Department, was quoted in the story saying police are "treating the threats very seriously . . . From a police perspective, we're investigating any criminal aspects to it. We're taking steps to ensure her safety." While Air-India wasn't mentioned, Porteous hinted that the people associated with the Khalsa School had used violence to settle scores in the past. "I believe that they are trying to intimidate her into not writing the stories," he said.

I think Rani's daily calls to me during this time were a sign of the desperate situation she was in. I had become her sounding board. Other journalists had been pressing her for interviews ever since her civil suit was filed. They knew she was talking to me. But she politely refused their interview requests. She was concerned about the growing level of intimidation. She felt thrust into the camp of the police, but was also worried about trusting investigators. She did not want to be a witness, especially if charges were laid for the Air-India bombing. She thought it would be a death sentence. But she also felt a moral obligation to do something about what she had seen at the school.

I understood her fear. But I told her that if I knew something about the bombing plot, I would probably tell the police. More than three hundred people had died. Those families deserved answers. I never asked her what she had provided to the investigators about Malik and Air-India. She had mentioned to me the names of several people Malik had said were involved. I already knew about the obvious ones: Parmar, Bagri, Surjan Gill, Johal, and Reyat. But she mentioned some I had never heard before: Daljit Sandhu of the World Sikh Organization, Bhandher from the school, Satwant Sandhu, another school director. I never asked for details, but I think she wanted to get it off her chest. In February or March 1998, she asked me to consult the *Sun*'s lawyer about whether someone could be forced to be a witness.

I told her I would ask others around the newsroom with more expertise than myself. Without relaying too many details, I talked to our deputy managing editor, Patricia Graham, who had been a lawyer. She commented that prosecutors don't really like to have uncooperative witnesses because it can backfire on a case. I also talked to my assignment editor, Graham Rockingham, again without giving too much information. He said someone could always call Crimestoppers if they didn't want to be a witness.

I passed all this over to Rani and then piped in with my own thoughts: How could you be a witness to Air-India when you didn't meet Malik until 1992? Wouldn't anything he told you be hearsay? I told her I was sure it would not be admissible. I was just thinking out loud, completely ignorant of the laws concerning evidence.

I knew she had her own lawyer, so it didn't dawn on me that I was giving her legal advice that she would heed. I was having a chat with a source. But I would learn eighteen months later that she had told the RCMP about the main confession she alleges Malik gave her only after I provided my inaccurate and naive opinion about the admissibility of evidence. In part because of me, she had been forced to become a witness in the biggest case in Canadian history.

From the time I met Rani until she fled into the Witness Protection Program, she had hoped that Satnam Reyat, a woman she had grown to respect and admire, would back her up and co-operate with the police. She told me Mrs. Reyat was frustrated at being forced to live in poverty with four children when the other Air-India suspects lived in large homes and had fancy cars. At one of her husband's parole hearings, I approached Mrs. Reyat and said I had been talking to Rani. Did she want to meet me? I asked. She said she would think about it and call me later.

Reyat's counsel was still Kuldip Chaggar, the controversial lawyer who was married to Malik's goddaughter and had remained loyal to Malik while representing Reyat. Chaggar complained at Reyat's parole hearing that Mrs. Reyat had had to put a fence up around her house after Air-India investigators had broken in to remove a listening device. I wrote a story based on what some insiders at the school told me – that government money from the Satnam Education Society had paid for the fence. The police investigations into the school and the Air-India bombing were becoming increasingly entwined. It would become impossible to untangle them.

Malik and the other suspects were getting worried about finally being arrested in the bombing case. Hardial Johal – a director of Malik's Satnam Trust – told me so when he invited me to his house to hear his criticisms of Malik's lending practices at the credit union. RCMP Insp. Gary Bass wrote to the warden at Reyat's prison, saying it would be dangerous to release him on parole because charges were imminent in Air-India and other suspects might see Reyat as a liability.

Narinder Gill, the school treasurer who had tried to expose the financial wrongdoing, was working at a construction site for a new credit union head office when Parmar's brother Kulwarn stopped by for a chat. The subject soon turned to Air-India, and Kulwarn said he didn't understand why everyone was always blaming his dead brother for the bombing. "Hardial Johal kept the bombs overnight in the school where he worked," Kulwarn blurted.

Gill told me he was startled by the admission. He took it as a sign the suspects were getting agitated. Gill also confirmed for me that Malik had been using charitable money to make the under-the-table payments to the Reyats while they were on welfare.

Shortly after I published a story about the illegal payments, a search warrant was executed on Mrs. Reyat's accounts at the

Khalsa Credit Union. I was upset to see that the warrants named my story, as well as Rani, as sources of the information as the police had heard about the allegations months earlier from other sources. It struck me as dangerous for both of us to be named in warrants that would lead to criminal charges against Mrs. Reyat for welfare fraud.

Almost every day, I wrote stories for the newspaper about the school, the credit union, Air-India, or the various investigations into each. In March, my city editor commented that he thought senior editors were suffering from a little "Khalsa fatigue" and that I should change gears for a while. I told him that Khalsa meant truth and that newspaper editors should not be tired of the truth, and I continued with my coverage.

But in April the story took a complicated and potentially deadly turn.

Jathedar Ranjit Singh – the high priest in Amritsar – was contacted again by Hardial Johal and other Air-India suspects. They asked him to put into writing his position on the issues of tables and chairs. They asked for an edict, or *hukamnama*, banning the furniture outright. Singh was a wild card in Sikhism. He was an uneducated man who had been in the same group as Malik, the Akhand Kirtani Jatha. And he had killed a rival religious leader who was linked to the 1978 murders in Punjab that spurred Parmar to form the Babbar Khalsa.

Singh was made one of five *jathedars* while still in jail for the murder. He was eventually pardoned, but continued to admit openly to the bloody slaying and said he would do it again in the name of his faith.

So what could tables and chairs possibly have to do with the investigation into the 1985 Air-India bombings? I believe they were deliberately made an issue by the Air-India suspects, who were concerned by the increased activity of police, and were becoming desperate to hang on to their power base in the Sikh community. That meant portraying themselves as the only true defenders of their faith. A surge in moderate Sikhism in the mid-1990s had seen separatist leaders lose their hold on the Sikh temples that had been so important to them for more than a decade. They also lost access to millions of dollars a year in temple donations.

When the separatists ran the temples, they had tables and chairs in the dining halls where communal meals are shared after prayer as a symbol of the equality of all Sikhs. They objected to the use of the furniture in late 1996 and early 1997 only after losing temple elections. The two bloody melees in the Surrey temple that happened the year before Ranjit Singh's edict resulted in charges being laid against fourteen men, all connected to the International Sikh Youth Federation. But then the issue had died down for several months – that is, until April 1998, when the Air-India suspects feared they were on the verge of facing charges.

Ranjit Singh did not follow religious doctrine and consult the other four *jathedars* of Sikhism before faxing off his edict ordering the removal of all tables and chairs by May 29, 1998. The edict was sent to Hardial Johal to deliver to temple leaders. That, in itself, was suspect. Why would a person of interest in the Air-India bombing be receiving the orders of a high priest in Punjab? Johal admitted to me later that he had talked to Singh by phone before the edict was issued. So had Malik.

Armed with Singh's edict, the fundamentalist Sikhs, including some linked to the bombing, began forcing the issue at temples around Vancouver. They persuaded several Sikh priests from the temples to strike. The strikers held a big meeting at the home of Balwant Bhandher, across the street from the Khalsa School.

The moderates were also motivated by politics unrelated to the actual issue of furniture. They refused to compromise because they felt the edict was a last-ditch effort by the separatists and

Air-India suspects to intimidate them into submission, as they had been doing for years.

As is so often the case in the Sikh community, this apparent religious issue was really a political one, and the potential for violence was so great that Ujjal Dosanjh, who was now B.C.'s Attorney General, made a public plea for calm. He also said police would be on standby on May 29, just in case.

I tried to explain in the *Sun* the underlying story, but it was difficult for non-Sikh readers to comprehend. Hayer was writing the truth as he saw it in his newspaper, criticizing Singh for breaching the religion's protocol in issuing the edict.

Around this time, Hayer invited me for lunch at his favourite restaurant on Scott Road in Surrey. He told me he wanted to talk about all the stories I had written in recent months and their effect on the community. While we spoke often by phone, we had not met in person much since the threats began in December.

I met him at his office and we drove to a nearby restaurant in his large black Cadillac with special hand controls. He ordered lunch for both of us and a rye for himself. Then he told me I could not back down now, that there were principles at stake. He pulled out a two-page document and asked me to read it. It was his first formal statement to the RCMP's Air-India Task Force.

It described how in the fall of 1985 – three years before he had been paralyzed in the assassination attempt – he had been at the newspaper office of his old friend Tarsem Purewal in Southall, London. Purewal had looked out the window and remarked to Hayer, "One of your countrymen is coming." It was Ajaib Bagri. Because Hayer was not on good terms with Bagri, he sat with some other employees behind a partition while Bagri talked to Purewal. According to the statement, Purewal asked for details of the bombings, and Bagri laid it all out.

I was stunned. I knew Hayer had always known a lot about Air-India, but I had not known until that moment that he claimed to have overheard a confession.

Hayer had published this allegation against Bagri in the *Indo-Canadian Times* in August 1988, a week before he was shot and paralyzed. He told me he had agreed to be a witness in the Air-India case after Purewal was assassinated in January 1995. Purewal had finally become disillusioned with the ISYF and the Babbars and had begun to publish stories against them just before he was gunned down outside his newspaper office.

I had heard similar stories over the years about Bagri's alleged involvement, but never in the detail Hayer provided me that day. I couldn't do anything with the knowledge except store it away and use at some point in the future – either after charges were finally laid in the bombing or if Hayer were ever killed.

The situation at the temples went from bad to worse. The moderate leaders issued statements linking the edict to the separatist movement and vowing not to back down. Riot police were stationed at temples in Vancouver, Surrey, and Abbotsford. They wore bulletproof vests and had dogs ready to intervene if necessary.

Both sides tried to get large crowds out to the temples to muscle the other side with superior numbers and strength. People such as Manmohan Singh, the old ISYF spokesman who rarely attended temple, showed up to voice support for the edict. Police began to complain about tens of thousands of dollars it was costing to have officers stationed at the temples for days at a time.

Hayer spoke out about an ad in a local separatist newspaper asking for donations to buy Ranjit Singh a new car. Hayer said the fundraising proved the edict was given in exchange for some payback to the priest.

Bagri made the trip down to Vancouver from Kamloops, where he made an impassioned speech at a fundamentalist temple in Surrey for the immediate removal of the furniture. His statement was carried live on a radio station owned by Malik. That same weekend, the houses of six moderate temple leaders, and also Rani's house, were attacked by vandals in the middle of the night. She called me, telling me her family was terrified by the eggs smashing into the windows.

"My little boy wakes up screaming," Rani would later recall in court. "Our whole house was in a panic. We didn't know what was coming next."

Bagri came to Vancouver a second time in June, when Malik and others organized a rally of five thousand pro-edict supporters at a Vancouver high school. In late June, Ranjit Singh had issued another edict ordering Hayer and five other moderate Sikh leaders to appear before him in Punjab in July. They never received the order, but it was broadcast on the Punjabi radio stations that had been threatening Hayer, Cheema, and me for months. It said: "The above listed people have been punished for not obeying the *hukamnama*."

All six men were excommunicated from their faith within weeks by a killer priest egged on by B.C. militants linked to the Air-India bombing. It was insane. Police were now publicly expressing concern about violent retaliation from fundamentalist Sikhs. The RCMP cancelled a huge religious parade in Surrey in early July because they feared Hayer or moderate leader Balwant Gill would be attacked. Air-India suspect Daljit Sandhu had met with the RCMP and warned them about possible violence in the parade.

I was told by a few people, including Rani, that a hit list had been discussed at a meeting of fundamentalist leaders. Her name was on it. So was mine. Hayer, Balwant Gill, and other moderate Sikh leaders were also named. For the first time, I felt really nervous.

Reporters are always reluctant to call police about information we have heard from our sources. The gulf between collecting information and providing it to police can get very narrow at times, and I had come close to telling police what I'd learned several times that year. But now I was worried that someone was going to get killed. I asked editor-in-chief John Cruickshank if it would be appropriate to call the RCMP to give them information about a hit list. He said to go ahead. That night, I contacted RCMP Staff Sgt. John Schneider of the Air-India Task Force and told him about all that I had heard, without identifying sources. I said I was concerned. He promised to get some investigators to check it out.

A few days later, I was lying in bed at about 1:00 a.m. when a blast in front of my house shattered the quiet. I knew it was a gunshot, as did my neighbours, who called police. I heard a car race away, but did not look out for fear that they would see me. Within minutes, several squad cars arrived with lights flashing and began checking the wet pavement for shell casings. They didn't find any.

The police who arrived did not make the connection between the shooting and my expanding police file regarding the threats. I didn't want to go outside in my pyjamas and suggest I might have been the intended target. Maybe it was just a coincidence, I rationalized. I waited almost an hour before I called 911 and talked to a rather abrasive operator who didn't seem to know my house was on high-alert status. She made me feel stupid for phoning.

The next day I called Det. Const. Mike Porteous of the Vancouver police, who was alarmed to hear about the shooting and the response of the operator. He insisted that police panic buttons be installed in the house immediately. I was due to meet Rani for lunch that day in a place east of Vancouver where she was working as a daycare supervisor. I arrived two hours late because of the trauma of the night before. She couldn't believe it.

When two messages were telephoned to the *Sun* newsroom a few days later, John Schneider became convinced that the shooting on my street was meant as a warning to me. The first message was left on John Cruickshank's voicemail about 3:00 a.m. The anonymous male caller sarcastically expressed concern about the shooting at my house, even though the incident had not been publicized. He went on to say, "I hope she never gets shot or burnt or anything along those lines because that would be such a tragedy to lose a woman of her nature."

The second call was full of derogatory language and was somewhat rambling, as if the caller had been drinking. It was definitely the same voice, but the caller was not as overtly threatening as he had been the first time.

Schneider told me to give him the tapes of the calls. As we chatted in his office at RCMP headquarters, he told me the police wanted Rani to go into the Witness Protection Program with her family but that she was resisting. He wanted me to talk to her, but I refused. I asked why police couldn't just protect someone right there, at their home. Why should they have to leave everything, everyone they know and start again? She didn't do anything wrong, I said. "There is only so much we can do for someone," he told me.

I would soon learn how true that was. Tensions were so high now that when a suspicious box was seen outside Hayer's office in July, the bomb squad was called and a city block was evacuated. It turned out to be garbage.

Rani went to meet Hayer one day at his office. He had heard about her, and she certainly knew his work. She told him what she had been through at the school. He told her it was not worth the risk to stay in British Columbia

"Run away, daughter. Run away from here. It is not safe for you any more," Hayer told her.

Rani decided to heed Hayer's warning after the most frightening threat came that summer. She was out shopping with her youngest child at a Surrey mall when she met an acquaintance she had known at the Khalsa School. The man threatened to kill her and her children with an AK-47.

" 'Nobody will be able to recognize you when we finish with you and your family,' " she later quoted the man as saying. "I was shaking. . . . It was scary because [my son] was standing there and listening."

Rani and her youngest son were whisked away into the Witness Protection Program. Her husband and eldest child, who was going into university, refused to go. She left me a voicemail message saying she would contact me when and if she could. I felt very alone and nervous.

Throughout the summer, there were arrests and stabbings at the temples. The border police were on the lookout for fundamentalists arriving to bolster the numbers of those who wanted to forcibly remove the furniture. Vancouver police got so worried about the potential for violence that it closed the city's Ross Street temple, which was run by the oldest and largest Sikh society in North America. The battle ended up in the courts. Malik wrote a letter of support for the fundamentalists' court challenge and warned me not to write anything when I called him to ask about it.

In September 1998, several Crown lawyers joined lead prosecutor Bob Wright on the Air-India file. The Khalsa Credit

Union was raided by the RCMP, who took documents relating to Malik's account, Hardial Johal's accounts, and the accounts of both the Satnam Education Society and the Satnam Trust. The suspects had to know that Air-India charges would be coming some time soon.

Tensions at the temples calmed down in advance of hotly contested fall elections between the moderates and fundamentalists. Police obtained injunctions so they could arrest anyone loitering around those temples that continued to have tables and chairs. Courts ordered special procedures to be put in place for the election to curb controversy and tensions.

I relished the break in the storm and was enjoying some overdue extra time with my family. On Thanksgiving Monday, relatives and friends had gathered at my house for dinner. The smell of turkey wafted through the rooms. Then the phone rang. It was a desperate call from Rani, whom I had not spoken to in weeks. She said she was sick in bed without proper food or sufficient blankets for herself and her child. She said she had had to send her young son out by himself to buy milk because she was so ill.

"Why aren't the police helping you?" I said.

Nobody had checked on her in a while and, being a proud woman, she did not like to ask for help. But she sounded horrible. I told her she should call the B.C. RCMP officers and tell them I would write a story about how she was being treated. There was nothing else I could do as she was in witness protection, and I had no idea where she was. I felt guilty sitting down to a comforting meal with family and friends when she had lost everything.

In the midst of the calm, Hayer's daughter, Rupinder, called me about a petition that she had been circulating, demanding a tough new approach to criminals and terrorists who immigrate to

Canada. She had founded a group called the Canadian Grassroots Community Association and collected eleven thousand signatures. She told me she was motivated by the shooting of her father in 1988 and by the Air-India bombings. I did a story on her petition, which she presented to several MPs on October 15, 1998.

Coincidentally, two other related events also happened on the day the Hayer family petition was presented. The RCMP announced it had turned over its findings in the Air-India investigation to Crown prosecutors to decide if charges would be laid, and the refugee board granted the founder of the International Sikh Youth Federation, Harpal Nagra, landed immigrant status in Canada over the objections of the Immigration department. Nagra's name had surfaced in the Air-India investigation. He had also been watched by the RCMP as he met with Harkirat Bagga, the youth who shot Hayer in 1988, months before the attack.

I quoted Hayer ripping into the Nagra decision in an article I wrote. Nagra was so mad that he called me to complain about Hayer the next day.

A week later, another Air-India suspect was dead. Kamloops Babbar Khalsa leader Avtar Narwal, a close associate of Bagri, had driven his brand-new car into a lake and drowned. There was no mechanical failure nor medical emergency. Witnesses said he made no effort to get out of the vehicle as he sank to his death.

On November 16, federal Immigration Minister Lucienne Robillard followed Hayer's lead and criticized the refugee board ruling that had allowed Nagra, the founder of a terrorist group, to remain in Canada. She said an appeal would be launched.

A year to the week that I first met Rani Kumar, I got another life-altering telephone call. It came on November 18, 1998, just before 7:00 p.m. while I was sitting in a movie theatre, loaded down with buckets of popcorn and drinks, with my two young sons, then aged two and eight. We were waiting for a preview of the Rugrats movie to begin. I had left work early for a change after months of late nights at the office, but I had forgotten to turn my cellphone off. I was annoyed when I saw the newsroom number on the call display, but answered anyway, ready to give them an earful for bugging me after hours again. It was Dan Cassidy, an assistant city editor at the *Sun*.

"Tara Singh Hayer has been shot," he said. "He is dead."

"Are you sure? I just called him today," I said, as if somehow that meant he could not have been murdered. I started babbling and repeating myself, not really believing what Dan was saying. After he hung up, I got another call, this one from a source who had the same information. I was terrified. Was someone making the rounds that night to take out everyone on the hit list? I didn't know what to do. But I did know I had to grab my kids and get out of there.

We got into the elevator to the movie theatre parkade. There was a young Sikh man with his turban tied in the fashion of a Babbar Khalsa member. I freaked out. I held the kids close as we spent mere seconds in the elevator with the man. I did not take my eyes off him. We all got off on the same level and, like us, he turned to find his car. He was just a movie-goer. I felt horrible.

In the car, I tried to reassure my children that everything was okay. "A man I know has been shot by some bad guys. But the police are looking for them and they will catch them, I am sure," I said.

I don't know how much trauma I inflicted on my kids that night. I had always been careful not to talk about work in front of them, let alone the threats that had become commonplace in recent months. But I was in shock and desperate to find out what was going on. So I worked the phones in front of them as we raced to the home of a friend who had agreed to babysit them while I rushed back to work.

I called political contacts in the Sikh community and friends of Hayer. I assumed people had already heard the terrible news and I was breathless as I spoke. Because of my mental state, I was not particularly sensitive in my approach. I didn't realize until later that I was giving several people the news and they reacted with as much shock as I was experiencing. Many had trouble believing it.

I called the campaign office of the moderate Sikhs running for the temple election and spoke to Jagdeep Sanghera, who had passionately fought the table-and-chairs issue. A decade earlier he had been the national spokesman for the International Sikh Youth Federation, but had turned away from the group after becoming disillusioned by the violence he saw. "Hayer's dead. They killed him," I blurted.

He was stunned. I could hear him turn and tell the people gathered there, "Mr. Hayer has been shot." In the background I could hear men burst into sobs. I told him I would come by and that we should go out to Surrey to Hayer's house.

I paged John Schneider at the RCMP. I had contacted him about the hit list just three months earlier. He wouldn't say much when he found out I was on a cellphone except, "Be careful, Kim. Watch yourself."

Hayer's death was the first-ever assassination of a Canadian journalist. It had happened about 5:45 p.m. when he arrived home in his black Cadillac. He drove into the garage as he always did. As he was getting out of the car and lifting himself into the wheelchair, he was shot. The person or persons must have slipped under the garage door as it was coming down. A bullet to the head killed him, but Hayer was also stabbed in his midsection. That made the killing personal.

I had known Hayer for fifteen years, ever since I started at the newspaper, and I had come to know him much better in the months before his death, as we were both being threatened. I had grown to rely on his assessment of those threats. Given all that had gone on in the previous year, I should not have been surprised by his murder, but I was stunned. I had believed the threats were designed to scare and were not some forewarning of a plot to kill people.

A number of his friends and supporters congregated at Hayer's home, where media trucks were arriving outside. His wife of more than four decades was devastated. She had heard the shot fired and ran downstairs to find him dead.

Hayer's only son and eldest child, Dave, somehow remained poised in the chaos. He told me that he was going back to the newspaper office to produce a special insert for the paper so readers would know of the assassination. If the killers thought they would silence the Hayer family, they were wrong. "He fought for the freedom of human beings here. He always said if they were going to kill him for what he published, so be it," Dave said.

There was immediate anger and frustration from Hayer's friends and political allies who had known of the escalating threats and tensions in the community. "It's tragic that he's been killed. The police should have acted on the threats against Mr. Hayer and others before an assassination," said former Ross Street Temple president Bikar Dhillon, himself a victim of a 1991 assassination attempt. "There have been rumours of hit men in town for weeks and police have done nothing."

Many of Hayer's friends said the killers knew that they could get away with murder in Canada. I didn't want to believe their cynicism.

Rani also called me on my cellphone – something she had never done since she entered witness protection. But she had heard of Hayer's murder from the Air-India Task Force, as they didn't want her to learn of it on the news. She understood more than anyone exactly what the assassination meant. "If I had stayed there, Kim, I would be dead right now," she said.

I had to agree.

CHAPTER 7

Paralysis, then Death

I WAS UP for most of the night of the shooting. I couldn't stop seeing the image of the wine-coloured sheet covering Hayer's lifeless body as he was removed from his house for the last time. I paid my condolences to his stunned family. They were stoic and found the strength to comfort Sikh leaders and friends who poured into their home through the night and early morning.

When I finally got home, the BBC called from London wanting to do an interview. The national media was on the phone from 3:00 a.m. onwards. And the police called me before the sun was up. A Vancouver detective named George Kristensen, who had taken over my threat file, asked me to come to the police station on my way to work. I liked Kristensen. He was an old-fashioned detective who did not mince words. He had followed up on the shooting the previous July by having investigators go door to door in my neighbourhood to get a description of the car that was seen racing away from my house.

At Vancouver police headquarters that morning, I was too exhausted to be nervous. But Kristensen said that John Schneider

The Golden Temple at Amritsar, India. (Bill Keay, *Vancouver Sun*)

A demonstration for the separate Sikh country of Khalistan outside the Indian consulate in Vancouver, March 25, 1984. The circled figures are, left to right: one of Talwinder Singh Parmar's children, Ajaib Singh Bagri, Ripudaman Singh Malik, and Jaswinder Singh Parmar. (Peter Battistoni, *Vancouver Sun*)

Surjan Singh Gill (left) at a June 11, 1984, demonstration outside the Indian consulate after the Indian Army's assault on the Golden Temple in Amritsar. Nine-year-old Devinder Singh is spearing an effigy of Indira Gandhi that was later burned. (Dan Scott, *Vancouver Sun*)

The June 18, 1984, demonstration in Vancouver over the raid on the Golden Temple. Note the "Death to Indira" signs. (Peter Battistoni, *Vancouver Sun*)

Dancing on the plaza in front of the Ross Street temple after Indira Gandhi was assassinated on October 31, 1984. This is the plaza that the judge at the Air-India trial said did not exist.
(Brian Kent, *Vancouver Sun*)

Ripudaman Singh Malik entering the front door of Talwinder Singh Parmar's Surrey home on June 18, 1985, three days before the bombing.
(CSIS photo)

Rescue workers from Irish Navy ship *Aisling* pull a victim from the Atlantic Ocean near the west coast of Ireland on June 23, 1985. (Thomas Smyth)

Bodies of the victims are laid out in the makeshift morgue at Cork Regional Hospital on June 24, 1985. (Denis Minihane, *Irish Examiner*)

On the night of the bombing, the author visited the Canadian family of Shinghara Cheema, who died on Flight 182 on his way back to India. His mother, Reshaw Cheema (left), is being comforted by Dilraj Cheema.
(Greg Kinch, *Vancouver Sun*)

Left to right: Ajaib Bagri, Talwinder Parmar, and translator Chattar Singh Saini at a July 1987 press conference about 174 Sikh boat people who were dropped by a freighter off the coast of Nova Scotia.
(Mark Van Manen, *Vancouver Sun*)

The author in Amritsar in 1988 with an AK-47 given to her by police to fire.
(Bill Keay, *Vancouver Sun*)

Narinder Singh Parmar holds up a photograph of his father, Talwinder
Parmar, holding a machine gun and surrounded by rifles, shells, and a rocket
launcher. (The barrel of the rocket launcher can be seen in the foreground.)
(Ian Smith, *Vancouver Sun*)

Indo-Canadian Times publisher Tara Singh Hayer was left paralyzed and in a wheelchair after an assassination attempt in 1988. Hayer had turned against the two organizations that promoted a separate Khalistan, the Babbar Khalsa and the International Sikh Youth Federation, accusing them of corruption. (Steve Bosch, *Vancouver Sun*)

Hardial Singh Johal, the school custodian suspected of involvement in the Air-India bombing, was never charged. He died in 2002. (Ian Lindsay, *Vancouver Sun*)

Des Pardes publisher Tarsem Singh Purewal (left) and his old friend Tara Singh Hayer were both assassinated. Purewal was shot in the heart at the front door of his newspaper office in Southall, London, in January 1995. Less than three years later, Hayer was gunned down in the garage of his home in Surrey, B.C., on November 18, 1998. No charges have ever been laid in either shooting. (*Vancouver Sun* archives)

The Sikh community in the Lower Mainland, B.C., was wrenched apart by the edict that tables and chairs be removed from all Sikh temples. On January 11, 1997, Sikh purists, some waving sabres, charged into the dining area of the Guru Nanak Sikh temple in Surrey. Four people were injured. (Rob Kruyt, *Vancouver Sun*)

The death threat sent to the author on December 23, 1997. (The loop around Hayer's name was drawn by the author when she first skimmed the note.)

Inderjit Singh Reyat, seen here in March 1998, was convicted in the Narita airport bombing, which killed baggage handlers Hideharu Koda and Hideo Asano, and pleaded guilty to manslaughter in the bombing of Flight 182. (Photo courtesy CBC)

Ripudaman Malik in 1998 at a rally in support of his Khalsa School. (Peter Battistoni, *Vancouver Sun*)

Four of the trustees of the Khalsa School were considered suspects in the Air-India bombings. Circled, left to right, Kewal Singh Nagra, Ripudaman Singh Malik, Satwant Singh Sandu, and Balwant Singh Bhandher. (*Vancouver Sun*)

Sukhminder Singh Cheema, a journalist with the Punjabi-language media in Vancouver, was formerly a member of the International Sikh Youth Federation and received death threats for agreeing to testify for the Crown at the trial.
(Glenn Baglo, *Vancouver Sun*)

Balwant Bhandher and Ajaib Bagri, both suspects in the bombings, at the Vaisaiki Day celebrations in 2000. (Craig Hodge, *Vancouver Sun*)

Dave Hayer and his wife, Isabelle, in October 2000 at an RCMP news conference announcing the arrest of Malik and Bagri for the Air-India bombings. (Bill Keay, *Vancouver Sun*)

"Roman" Narwal leaving the courtroom at the bail hearing for Malik and Bagri in December 2000. Narwal is a suspect in the murder of Tara Hayer.

"Mindy" Bhandher, an admitted gangster and son of Balwant Bhandher, testified for the defence at the Air-India trial. (Ian Lindsay, *Vancouver Sun*)

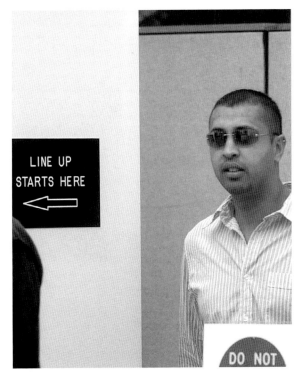

Cab driver Kulwarn Singh Parmar, seen here in 2002, was present at several meetings with his brother Talwinder Parmar and Ripudaman Malik in the mid-1980s. (Peter Battistoni, *Vancouver Sun*)

Daniel Brown, the merchant seaman who helped recover the bodies of victims, came to Vancouver with his wife, Louise, to hear the verdict in the Air-India trial. (Glenn Baglo, *Vancouver Sun*)

At a press conference held by the victims' families after the acquittal of Malik and Bagri on the grounds of reasonable doubt, Rattan Singh Kalsi held up a portrait of his daughter, Indira, who died in the bombing.
(Ian Smith, *Vancouver Sun*)

Every year the families of the 329 passengers and crew who died aboard Flight 182 gather in Ahakista, Ireland. For the twentieth anniversary of the bombing, in June 2005, they were joined for the first time by Canadian politicians. The sundial (centre) is part of the memorial built on the Irish coast closest to where the plane went down. (Denis Minihane, *Irish Examiner*)

Lata Pada, who lost her husband and daughters aboard Flight 182, at the twentieth anniversary gathering in Ireland. (Denis Minihane, *Irish Examiner*)

At the end of the anniversary ceremony in 2005, lanterns for the victims were set on the water of Dunmanus Bay and floated out to sea. (Denis Minihane, *Irish Examiner*)

had called and warned that there might actually be something to the hit-list rumours circulating in July. "Well that is really smart, now that somebody on it is dead," I responded flippantly.

I called Schneider after I got back to the newsroom. He had told me two months earlier that investigators could not nail anything down about the hit list. Now he was saying they were re-examining the intelligence about the list in the wake of Hayer's murder. I told my editors what both police forces were saying. We decided to publish the information, which angered some RCMP officers. They had assumed I would keep it quiet because they had told me for security reasons. The page-one headline on November 20, 1998, blared: "POLICE EXAMINING SIKH HIT LIST IN THE WAKE OF HAYER ASSASSINATION."

One RCMP sergeant called me and started yelling about the article. I was so upset, I slammed the phone down. Another RCMP officer denied to other reporters what I had written about the hit list, which infuriated me because the police had given the information to me and my editors the day after the murder.

It was true that there was no piece of paper with the names carefully spelled out. There was just talk about certain people whom extremists linked to the Air-India case were said to want eliminated. Until Hayer's murder, it was easy to believe it was only talk.

My editors paid for my children and their father to leave the country for a week, but I continued working, and watching my back everywhere I went.

On the advice of the police, we adopted new ways of living. Window coverings had to be closed at all times. I spent a night madly sewing new curtains for two windows that we had never covered. The children were no longer allowed to answer the phone or the door. Calls were carefully screened. There were no more late-night walks with the dog. We learned to vary our routes to work, school, and other destinations.

We asked for our names and phone number to be removed from class lists at my son's school. We kept it off the parent list for the upcoming little league season. It made me think of how much information we give out about ourselves all the time. In some stores, you can't even buy groceries without giving a phone number or a card to indicate your "membership." Your personal data flashes up on the checker's computer as she thanks you by name. But, as Hayer had always told me, you can't do much to stop someone bent on attacking you. Just a week before he died, he told me there was no point in being afraid. For the most part, threats were just supposed to scare you, to stop you from writing. He would never stop, he said.

I was shocked by Hayer's murder, even though I knew about the threats. The one eleven months earlier had been made against both of us. He had told me about the February 1998 radio broadcast saying he deserved the same fate as a Hindu editor assassinated in India. And then there was the rumoured hit list.

Hayer had told police at least three times the previous year about the threats to him. I had called them myself twice, in December and in July. He had also contacted the Canadian Radio-television and Telecommunications Commission about the threatening Punjabi radio programs. Two days before Hayer was gunned down, a caller to the station owed by Ripudaman Malik cryptically said the "lame" man was going to get what was coming to him.

If Hayer's murder was designed to frighten people into silence, the plot seriously backfired. Condemnations came from around the world. Moderate Sikhs were furious and pledged to expose the terrorists once and for all. They vowed to win upcoming Sikh temple elections in Hayer's memory and to maintain the tables and chairs in the temple dining halls that had become a lightning rod of the battle between moderates and fundamentalists, led by the Air-India suspects.

I felt guilty about Hayer's death. I wondered whether I had contributed to it by repeatedly quoting his criticism of the militant separatists. I had found it hard to get people to speak out about the problems at the Khalsa School and Khalsa Credit Union, let alone the Air–India bombing, but Hayer had always been willing to take a public stand when others feared to do so.

On November 28, the day of Hayer's funeral, the skies were grey and threatening. More than twenty-five hundred mourners jammed into the Valleyview Funeral Home in Surrey, a short distance from Hayer's home. Dozens of police officers and private security guards monitored the event. At the service, Premier Glen Clark said he was proud to call Hayer a friend. Liberal leader Gordon Campbell called the assassination a violent act that hit right at the heart of our Canadian values. Many of the politicians who lined up to praise Hayer had also enjoyed close relationships with his foes in the Sikh extremist movement. The irony would not have been lost on Hayer.

Two leaders from England, Ajit Singh Khera and Iqbal Singh, came to the service wearing the tall saffron turbans that in British Columbia are associated with militants. They were separatists affiliated with Dr. Chohan, the founder of the movement, but they had always condemned violence. They were the men I had met in London nine years earlier. They were shocked at the hostile stares they received as if they were enemy infiltrators. I explained to them afterward what their turban style had come to symbolize in British Columbia.

I broke down when I walked past Hayer's open coffin and saw him there, quiet for the first time in the fifteen years I had known him.

I felt an obligation to the controversial editor to find out what had happened and whether his murder was linked to the information he had about the Air-India bombing – the information he had eventually passed on to police and that he had given me just a few months earlier. I re-examined the failure of police to investigate adequately the August 1988 conspiracy to kill him. That shooting had so obviously been part of a political conspiracy. The RCMP knew it at the time. The accused youth, Harkirat Bagga, had initially confirmed it, and only later pleaded guilty and claimed that he acted alone out of personal revenge. Crown prosecutor Sean Madigan had said Bagga was just the triggerman in an international scheme to kill Hayer.

"It is clear from the evidence of the police, which the accused now brands as lies, that this was a conspiracy, in which he was a willing part, to murder a man," Madigan said at Bagga's sentencing hearing in December 1988. "It is destructive of civilization to permit assassins, and that is all he is, free rein in any country, least of all in a democratic country such as this."

Hayer had told me many times that the 1988 plot to kill him had been hatched in Pakistan and involved members of the Babbar Khalsa and the ISYF. He was frustrated that police did not pursue other suspects after Bagga pleaded guilty and was sentenced to fourteen years in prison. He also said he believed Bagga was much older than seventeen, but was advised to claim to be a teen so he could be prosecuted as a youth offender. The judge overseeing Bagga's sentencing hearing also thought the young man, who represented himself, was older. "Judging by your maturity and intelligence you've displayed in court I would have thought you to be several years older," Judge Patrick Hyde said.

After Hayer's murder, Surrey RCMP confirmed that the file on the 1988 shooting had been closed when Bagga was convicted. Neither the RCMP nor the Crown would explain why, especially when the relationship between Bagga and the suspects in Air-India could be documented. I had found the young man's associations with the two terrorist groups that had branded Hayer their enemy easy enough to uncover.

Bagga's family left India after Operation Blue Star. His father, Santokh Singh Bagga, ended up in Princeton, Ontario, where he made a successful refugee claim. But the boy was living in Singapore in April 1987 when he met a British Babbar Khalsa leader named Gurdeep Singh Sivia. Though he was just sixteen, according to the age he later gave Canadian police, he provided Sivia with a contact in Bangkok to aid the Babbar Khalsa in opening a cell in Thailand. A month later, Air-India suspect Ripudaman Malik was searched by police. On him, they found a letter written by the teen to his father in Ontario.

Later in 1987, Bagga made his way to England, where he claimed asylum under Sivia's sponsorship. After Bagga was nabbed by police in 1992, Sivia described assisting him to Indian interrogators. He told them Bagga had enjoyed his hospitality for three months.

Bagga was also supported by Dr. Chohan, the colourful founder of the separatist movement. Chohan told me that Bagga also stayed with him in London in 1987 and was desperate to become a fighter for Khalistan. Chohan had persuaded the youth to return to India to finish his studies instead. "I said, 'Listen, you are not going to become a leader if you don't study.'" Chohan told me. "'What will you do? Supposing Khalistan becomes a reality – what will be your role in that Khalistan?' He said, 'Yes, that is right.' I said, 'Listen, I can get you a ticket, go back to Punjab, go back to your school.'" Chohan gave Bagga about $1,000 for the ticket. He planned to return to India via Pakistan.

In September that year, Hayer hinted for the first time in a magazine called *New Horizons* about Bagri's alleged confession to

Tarsem Purewal. He didn't name Bagri, but said one of the bombers admitted "in the presence of at least four other men that we are responsible for this tragedy and this is how we did it."

Within two months, Bagri was in Pakistan, where he met with Bagga. The two were photographed together, not knowing the pictures would one day land in the hands of the RCMP's Air-India Task Force. Chohan told me that the Babbars, who had gathered in Pakistan from Canada and elsewhere, frightened Bagga into doing what they wanted. "They said, 'We are going to kill you tonight. The only way you can be saved is to come along with us.' They brought him back [to England]. They brought him back here because they wanted to use him. They could use him to kill anybody. Luckily, I was saved."

Bagga stayed with several Babbar Khalsa leaders in London in late 1987 and early 1988. Sikh separatists in the United Kingdom got a rude awakening when Inderjit Reyat, then living in Coventry, was arrested in early February 1988 and charged with manslaughter in the Narita bombing.

On both sides of the Atlantic, Sikhs speculated that there would be more arrests, not just for the Narita bombing, but for the Air-India bombing as well. As he always had, Hayer spoke out publicly, linking the two bombings in my page-one story and saying that more arrests were expected.

It must have been a trying time for nervous Air-India suspects. They must have thought they would soon face prosecution – especially when a man who claimed to possess a confession was speculating about charges being laid in front-page articles. Malik told the CBC's Carol Off in a radio interview that arrests in the Air-India bombings were imminent. He said he would raise money to defend all the suspects.

During this period of speculation and high tension, Bagga arrived in Toronto on a false passport. It was March 2, 1988.

Within a month, the teen was in Vancouver, where police sur-
veillance photographed him visiting the offices of the *Chardi
Kala*, the ISYF newspaper, then run by federation founder Harpal
Nagra. Bagga stayed at the home of another ISYF member.

He returned to Ontario, but left again on August 16 by bus
and crossed into the United States. He stopped at Dayton, Ohio,
then Toledo, then made his way, still on a Greyhound, to Detroit,
Michigan. He caught an American Airlines flight under the name
Singh to Seattle on August 21, 1988, and then crossed back into
Canada a day later. One has to wonder about how a teenager from
a Third World country could have made such complicated travel
plans without help.

On August 22, 1988, Bagga checked into a Surrey motel
under the name H. Singh. The next night he stayed at a hotel in
Vancouver, moving to another Vancouver hotel under the name
Upinder Singh for August 24.

The next morning he called the *Indo-Canadian Times* office
and spoke to Surjit Singh Madhopuri about advertising rates.
Bagga booked an appointment with Madhopuri for 11:00 a.m.
August 26.

The teen was half an hour late. He chatted with Madhopuri
for about forty minutes until Hayer arrived. Bagga asked
Madhopuri who the editor of the newspaper was and the loyal
ad salesman pointed to Hayer, whose desk was a couple of metres
away. Bagga walked toward the front door as if to leave, then he
pulled out a handgun from his jacket, gripped it with two hands,
and fired several times directly at Hayer from two metres away.

The boy assassin was arrested after fleeing the building. He told
police that the ISYF and the Babbar Khalsa had aided him, and
that Bagri had provided him with the .357-calibre revolver he had
used to shoot Hayer. The police found some evidence of what
he had claimed. There was the surveillance of his meetings in

April with ISYF leaders. And investigators searched his luggage, which he had stowed in a locker at the Vancouver bus depot. In it, they found a piece of paper with the names and numbers of two Kamloops residents – one of whom was Bagri's brother-in-law. The Crown's handwriting expert concluded that Bagri could have written the note.

In September, the teenager's father, Santokh Bagga, travelled from Ontario to British Columbia to meet his son. He made an inflammatory speech at Surrey's Guru Nanak temple, in which he praised his son's violent actions. "It was the right thing to do, the shooting. He deserved to be shot because he wrote about everyone. He wrote about my good brother Talwinder Singh Parmar and my good brother Ajaib Singh Bagri and my good brother Jagtar Singh Sandhu."

Shocked temple worshippers called me to write a story about the speech. I called Santokh Bagga and some of the temple leaders, who all confirmed what he had said.

The unfair targets of Hayer's journalism, according to the father of Hayer's would-be assassin, were two Air-India suspects and the Canadian president of the ISYF. There was no mention of a problem Bagga may have had with the *Indo-Canadian Times* publisher over an article about his father. The elder Bagga also raised money for his son.

Shortly after Santokh Bagga's B.C. visit, the RCMP interviewed Bagri about the boy's claim that the Kamloops Babbar Khalsa leader had provided him with the gun. Bagri claimed he did not know the youth, despite having met him a year earlier in Pakistan. But police would only learn about that critical meeting much later.

At the end of November, Bagga decided to plead guilty to attempted murder for paralyzing Hayer. As part of that plea, he denied all the earlier information he had given police about the aid of Bagri's group and the ISYF.

"This is the first time that I shot a man," Bagga told the court. "Your Honour, I would like to indicate here that I don't really feel sorry for the man I was shooting. This is going against me, but I am saying the truth."

His family, however, maintained close connections with leaders of both groups, I would learn as I probed deeper after Hayer's murder. When his mother, Gurjinder Kaur, came to visit Bagga in jail, she stayed at Parmar's Burnaby home. She later stayed several times at Malik's Vancouver mansion even after her son was paroled and deported to India.

Bagri, who told police that the teen was a stranger to him, called and visited the boy while he was in jail. He brought a television for Bagga's cell.

While he was in British Columbia, Bagga's father, Santokh, would stay at the Surrey home of ISYF leader Satinderpal Gill. Gill was the avid separatist I had met in Pakistan – the one Indian intelligence officers accused of being a major terrorist leader there. He was based at Dera Sahib Gurdwara – the same temple where Bagga, Parmar, and Bagri had stayed together in the months before Hayer was crippled.

Former ISYF members, disillusioned with the violence of the group, confirmed to me after Hayer's slaying that the 1988 shooting had been jointly financed by the federation and the Babbar Khalsa. The connections seemed obvious, yet startling. I wondered why they were not aggressively pursued by the police when Hayer himself had called for action so many times.

In 1995, when I obtained a copy of the secret interrogation report of Sivia, the British Babbar Khalsa leader who aided Bagga, Hayer told me he was frustrated the truth had never come out about the plot. "I believe the conspiracy to kill me was hatched in Pakistan. Bagga was only the one to pull the trigger. I would have been much more happy if the real person behind this conspiracy could have been caught," Hayer said.

Ajit Khera, the British Sikh leader who attended Hayer's funeral in his orange turban, said it was obvious Bagga was a troubled young man when he fell into the clutches of violent militants. "It is certainly not something he did on his own. There were forces working on his mind to carry out this assassination attempt. I think the Canadian authorities are to be blamed to a very large extent. They have let matters go so far. Something has got to be done. The community is crying out for it."

At least in Canada, Hayer's 1988 shooting and 1998 assassination received widespread condemnation and plenty of media coverage. At least journalists here tried to expose what had really gone on and the link to violent elements within the Sikh separatist movement.

In England, Scotland Yard had also done little to solve the January 1995 assassination of Hayer's long-time friend Tarsem Purewal. There were uncanny similarities between the two slayings. It was a cold evening when Purewal, then sixty-one, locked up the office of his weekly Punjabi newspaper for the last time. He had stayed late, as he often did, to finish an article. Just before 8:00 p.m., as he stood in the office doorway of *Des Pardes*, Purewal was shot in the heart. It was a professional assassination. No eyewitnesses came forward in either shooting. Hayer lived in a busy Surrey neighbourhood. Purewal's office was in one of the busiest spots in Southall.

Hayer had told me during our spring 1998 lunch that he believed Purewal was killed because he had inside information about the Babbar Khalsa. In fact, Purewal knew what Hayer knew, if Bagri's alleged 1985 admission of guilt in Purewal's newspaper office is to be believed. Hayer told me he decided to give police a statement because of his friend's violent demise. Hayer did not say much more than that, but within days of Hayer's assassination, my Sikh contacts who knew both men began to believe the murders were linked.

Ajit Khera, Dr. Chohan, and others in England told me that Purewal had made a visit to Pakistan in late 1994 that changed his view about the Khalistani leaders there. On his return, Purewal confided to friends that he was disillusioned, that he had seen money misappropriated and other corruption within the movement. He wrote an article that was extremely critical of the ISYF and promised more exposés on the Babbar Khalsa. And he told some associates that he was going to print information about who was responsible for the 1985 Air-India bombing. Purewal claimed that he learned the details of the bombing plot from Hayer, his old friend of the *Indo-Canadian Times*. In fact, Hayer and Purewal had learned the information from the same source.

"I think there is a connection there. The information about the other will come out when one is solved," said Gurbax Singh Virk, who took over as editor of Purewal's paper after the assassination. "The culprit is not in the forefront."

Purewal and Hayer were friends for more than thirty years before both of their lives were cut short by an assassin's bullet. Like many Sikhs around the world, they had embraced the separatist movement for Khalistan after the Indian Army attacked the Golden Temple in Amritsar in June 1984. Despite Hayer's printed attacks on the ISYF and the Babbar Khalsa, he remained a separatist until a few years before his murder. Purewal remained close to both groups until a month before he was killed.

"He was trusted by the Babbar Khalsa," Gurbax Virk said. "Tara Hayer and Mr. Purewal were personal friends. . . . Sometimes Purewal gave news to Tara and sometimes Tara gave news to

Purewal. They helped each other. They visited each other so many times."

Hayer had talked confidentially to the RCMP about Bagri's alleged admission a few months after his visit to England. But he did not want to be a witness or give a formal statement at the time. Instead, he agreed with a member of the police task force, Bob Solvason, that he would call Purewal and talk with him about Bagri's 1985 conversation while the RCMP was listening. Solvason taped the call, but Purewal did not say much. Though the British editor talked to Hayer several times about Bagri's comments, Purewal said he did not want to get involved in a police investigation.

Even though Hayer spoke regularly to police, he did not always tell them the things he was writing in his paper. And the Air-India Task Force did not have someone monitoring Punjabi-language articles that were published about the case. So police missed Hayer's cryptic September 1987 *New Horizons* article describing the Air-India suspect, who was not named, disclosing his crime to four others. Hayer's article appealed to Sikhs to provide police with information about Air-India. The suspects may well have concluded that he had already done the same.

Hayer's most pointed reference to Bagri was published in the *Indo-Canadian Times* on August 19, 1988, just a week before the first attempt on his life. He wrote, "In 1985, in England, Ajaib Singh Bagri was talking noisily about his involvement in the blowing up of the Air-India air plane and in another section of the room, four men were listening to him and expressing their remorse by saying: Could a man in the Sikh appearance murder countless innocent people?" Bagri must have known from this that Hayer himself had overheard his comments.

It wasn't until early 1997 that the RCMP's Air-India Task Force asked Hayer for copies of articles that he had written about

Bagri and Parmar that might have caused the duo to be angry with the *Indo-Canadian Times* publisher. Hayer handed over two packages of articles, including the August 1988 report alleging Bagri had confessed to the Air-India bombing. The RCMP sent the articles out for translation. You'd think police would have had a Punjabi-speaking investigator. But they did not.

After some of the articles were translated, the RCMP sent a report to Crown prosecutors, recommending that an attempted murder charge be laid against Bagri for Hayer's 1988 shooting. In June 1997, the Crown decided there was not enough evidence to charge Bagri in the 1988 plot.

A key article – the one in which Hayer boldly proclaimed to know that Bagri had admitted his part in the biggest crime in Canadian history – was mysteriously left out of the pile that was sent for translation. Neither the RCMP nor the Crown realized the mistake until 2002, four years after Hayer's murder. The police missed the critical story, even though Hayer had told investigators during a 1997 interview that he had written about what Bagri had said in his newspaper in the summer of 1988. "So he knew that I knew this. Bagri knew, I think," Hayer told the RCMP on May 1, 1997.

There certainly would have been a greater likelihood of Bagri being arrested and charged in June 1997 had the critical article been part of the evidence translated and included for the prosecution. Instead, the two men who allegedly heard Bagri's ominous confession in the fall of 1985 were permanently silenced. Ironically, the omission was the kind of blunder that would have enraged Hayer journalistically.

The RCMP had tried to get Purewal to co-operate with its investigation when he visited British Columbia for a tournament featuring the popular Punjabi sport of *kabaddi* in August 1991. He was invited to a meeting with the police at a Surrey hotel, where he was asked specifically whether Bagri had ever spoken to him about his involvement in the Air-India bombings.

"Purewal stated Bagri had never discussed the topic with him," the RCMP report of the meeting said. "However, he quickly added that no one will ever talk to us about Air-India as they are all afraid. Purewal added that the ISYF/BK have long arms. Purewal cited the example of Indian Foreign Minister Ribeiro and his attempted assassination in Romania. Purewal went on to say that Ribeiro was at one time a Punjab police chief and thus the reason he was targeted.

"Purewal appears, at least on the surface, to be a strong supporter of the Khalistan cause and yet recounted several threats Dr. Jagjit Chohan, he and his family had received from Sikh extremists in England. Although these threats had no basis in Canada, Purewal was critical of the lack of assistance provided by British authorities."

Like Hayer, Purewal had been threatened by the most extremist elements of a movement he generally supported. Like Hayer, he felt police had not done enough to respond to the threats. Like Hayer, he was eventually proven right. But Purewal also played games with the RCMP. When he talked to them, he indicated that Bagri was still a friend of his and that he had visited both Bagri and members of the ISYF on his 1991 trip to British Columbia. Pressed by police, he also admitted that Bagri had indeed visited him on the 1985 trip through England to Germany. "Purewal at this stage was notably uncomfortable and eluded further questioning in this regard," the RCMP report reads.

Hayer later tried to explain to the RCMP why Purewal was reluctant to co-operate with police. "Mr. Purewal told me that these are very dangerous people . . . you should not criticize them in the newspaper about what they are doing wrong. You should not tell the public."

The RCMP appeared careful not to cite Hayer as the source of the tip about Bagri's 1985 visit to the *Des Pardes* office. It was not until ten months after Purewal's murder, on October 15, 1995, that Hayer provided his first formal statement to police about Bagri. It was a critical break in the Air-India investigation. Just months into the rejuvenated task force, a key insider who had known the suspects for years was willing to testify that he had over-heard a confession by one of them.

Hayer signed the two-page statement that had been typed out by Sgt. Bob Solvason.

In late 1985, I was in England to attend an International Sikh conference and had occasion to visit my friend Tarsem Singh Purewal at his offices of the Des Pardes newspaper...
I am not certain of the dates at this time, but I think it was the latter part of October or the early part of November. Present at this time with Tarsem Singh Purewal and myself were employees of Des Pardes: Avtar Singh Jandialvi and Pritam Singh Sidhu. A part-time employee of the paper Manmohan Singh Bajaj was also there but only for a short time.

All of us were sitting talking when Bagri showed up by himself later that evening about 7 p.m. Bagri was on his way to Germany where there are a lot of Babbar Khalsa follow-ers. Purewal said that he would talk to Bagri alone because Bagri did not like non-baptized Sikhs. Then Purewal went to speak to Bagri at one end of the room and the rest of us remained at the other end, divided by office dividers.

We could clearly hear the conversation between Bagri and Purewal. Bagri stayed talking to Purewal for about one hour during which time the subject of the Air-India disaster came up. Purewal asked Bagri how he managed to do that. Bagri replied that they (Babbar Khalsa) wanted the government of India to come on their knees and give them Khalistan. Bagri then said that if everything would have gone as planned, the plane would have blown up at Heathrow Airport with no passengers on it. But because it was a half an hour or three quarters of an hour late, it blew up over the ocean.

Purewal then asked how he managed to have the bomb inside the plane. Bagri said that when the device was ready, Surjan Singh Gill was supposed to take it to the airport but when it was ready and shown to him, he got scared and resigned from the Babbar Khalsa. Bagri then suggested to Talwinder Singh Parmar that they should kill Surjan Singh Gill, but Parmar said no because that would bring suspicion on them and so they just warned Gill not to say anything. Bagri then said that he got someone else to take the bomb inside a suitcase to Vancouver airport and put it on the plane. Then the talk shifted to other topics regarding Sikh politics in general.

All of us, except perhaps Manmohan Singh Bajaj, heard Bagri admit to this. I asked Purewal about this afterwards. I asked him why is he a friend of these people who blow up 329 people and he said they (Babbar Khalsa) are very dangerous people and he has to be careful. He also said they pay him well and so he prints everything that they want.

The RCMP was thrilled at getting the statement from Hayer. The dates of his trip to England could be corroborated by his passport stamps. And investigators knew Bagri had landed in London during the same period because he had been interviewed by Keith Weston of Scotland Yard's anti-terrorism section. And the story also matched elements of statements Bagri's old girl-friend, Premika, had provided to CSIS.

Hayer's next statement to police was given on June 6, 1996, in a Vancouver-area hotel room. In it, he repeated all the key infor-mation he claimed Bagri said to Purewal about the Air-India bombings. There were a few inconsistencies – he could not remem-ber the date of the trip, but said he could confirm it by checking his passport and the newspaper reports he had done about the con-ference. He also said Bagri had arrived with two British Babbar Khalsa members whom he did not know, but identified by their outfits. And he said that Gurbax Singh Virk, who would take over Purewal's newspaper, was present for the meeting.

At the end of the interview, RCMP Cpl. Bart Blachford asked Hayer for any other information that might help the Air-India investigation. The veteran journalist said the culprits had been involved in many acts of violence, but "the laws are such that the police could not lay charges." Hayer said people with informa-tion were too afraid to come forward but might do so if charges were laid. "I can only pray that somebody should come [forward]. You know some people know about this."

His final statement was given at Surrey RCMP headquarters on May 1, 1997. Hayer told police that he was still afraid. The statement was almost identical to the one he had given a year earlier, repeating the detail about Bagri being with two others and Virk being present in the room.

Virk later told the RCMP that he was not there, as he had not arrived in England until January 1986. He said Hayer must have been mistaken, since they had met on many subsequent trips, and that Bagga had visited the offices of *Des Pardes* before heading to

Canada to shoot Hayer. The new editor also thought the young man was a suspect in the 1995 Purewal murder, but he could not explain to the police why he believed that. The RCMP also asked Virk about another man whom Hayer claimed had overheard the conversation – Pritam Singh Sidhu – but Virk said Sidhu had gone to India and could not be reached.

Investigators did talk to another of the men supposedly there at the time, Avtar Jandialvi. He said he had been at the office on a number of occasions, but claimed he had never heard anyone take responsibility for the bombing.

Hayer did not keep it a secret that he would be a witness in an eventual Air-India prosecution. He told me in the spring of 1998, having alluded to much of the information about Bagri, Parmar, and Surjan Singh Gill years earlier. He told his son, Dave. He also told many of his closest associates.

The more details I published about the links between the Air-India suspects and the assassin who shot Hayer in 1988, the angrier the fundamentalists got. I received an interesting e-mail from Malik's son Hardeep just four days after Hayer was gunned down. Hardeep objected vigorously to any suggestion that the militant Sikhs were linked to Hayer's murder. He said the fundamentalists would win the temple elections and remove the tables and chairs. And he made a strange comment referring to Hayer and two other moderate leaders, who had also been threatened: "For Balwant Gill, Jarnail Bhandal and Mr. Hayer to have thought they were going to challenge Sikhism, they were sadly wrong," Malik's second son wrote. There was no condemnation of Hayer's assassination.

In the two weeks following Hayer's murder and under heavy police guard, tens of thousands of Sikhs voted in temple elections in Vancouver and Abbotsford. In both places, despite the edict from Ranjit Singh to remove the tables and chairs, moderate slates swept all the seats of power.

But the separatists and the Air-India suspects and their supporters continued to enjoy political connections at the highest level. Malik and other suspects attended a fundraising dinner on December 8, 1998, for Prime Minister Jean Chrétien. It was held in a ballroom at the Hyatt Hotel as riot police surrounded anti-Chrétien protesters outside. Many of Hayer's friends were at the dinner and were frustrated by the coziness of militant separatists and top federal Liberals.

At the time, Hayer was still being attacked regularly on the unlicensed Punjabi radio stations, including the one owned by Malik. Fundamentalist critics said Hayer's family should not be allowed to hold the funeral service in a Sikh temple because he had been excommunicated by Ranjit Singh. They said his family and newspaper should continue to be shunned and spread the rumour that his son had killed Hayer for insurance money.

Just as Bagga once shifted his motive from the political to the personal, Hayer's foes attempted to shift the emphasis from Hayer's political attacks to the personal ones he had made against opponents in the Sikh community over the years in the pages of his newspaper. They pointed to the gossipy nature of his journalism, which sometimes included insults and sordid details of the personal lives of his subjects, such as drunkenness, wife-beatings, and extramarital affairs.

Hayer's venture beyond the realm of what would have been acceptable in the mainstream media was typical of the Punjabi newspapers and radio stations. They all indulged in rustic insult-hurtling and innuendo. The verbal battles were sometimes taken to the B.C. Supreme Court, when competing news outlets with different agendas would sue each other over the tit-for-tat stories. Hayer had been a claimant and a defendant in such suits. He had won and he had lost.

But none of the other Punjabi journalists had been targeted for physical attack as Hayer had been. It was his political journalism and his insiders' knowledge of the Khalistan movement and its most violent adherents that set Hayer apart from other Punjabi journalists. It was the knowledge he had developed as a one-time sympathizer to the movement.

Like Sikhs around the world, Hayer had initially endorsed armed struggle after the Golden Temple attack. In his newspaper, he ripped into moderates like Ujjal Dosanjh and Gurcharan Rampuri. But Hayer's support ebbed away from the Babbar Khalsa and the ISYF when he saw them misusing funds that had been donated to the separatist cause. He pulled away more rapidly after he began to suspect their role in the Air-India and Narita bombings.

He remained sympathetic to the idea of a separate Sikh country even after Bagga shot him. But he thought it should be achieved by a Quebec-style referendum, not by violence. By the mid-1990s, after Purewal was assassinated, Hayer abandoned his support for Khalistan altogether. His political evolution was complete.

The assassination of Tara Hayer shifted the destiny of his family. Not only was their adored patriarch dead at sixty-two, but his murder was inevitably linked to the fact he had agreed to be a witness in a future Air-India prosecution. Hayer should have been given more protection – an escort to and from his newspaper office at the very least.

After the slaying, RCMP spokesman Grant Learned said that it was hard for police to do something about ongoing threats against any individual. "It is like trying to arm wrestle with a shadow. It is there, but you can't get at it." It was also like trying to fight against powerful people with connections at the highest political level in Canada.

The family's healthy distrust of the police hit me when Dave Hayer called me to come out to his father's house on January 2, 1999. He asked me to bring a photographer from the *Sun*. When we got there, he said he wanted us to take pictures of the RCMP security cameras that had been installed to protect his dad. The Air-India Task Force was coming to remove them and Dave wanted their existence documented, just in case someone later tried to deny they were there.

He wanted a witness.

We took the pictures – one of a camera hidden in a flowerbox at the front of the house and a second facing out into the back-yard. There was nothing in the garage, even though it was the only place Hayer was able to get in and out of his house. He never used the front door or the back as there were stairs in both locations.

Hayer's blood still stained the garage floor.

CHAPTER 8

My Year of Living Dangerously

A FTER HAYER WAS MURDERED, I was desperate to see Air-India charges laid. I hoped it would end the violence. But police told me they were at least a year away from charging people. I knew it would be a dangerous year if I continued to write about the case. But I felt compelled to carry on because Hayer had already died for the cause. I knew the people who had started speaking out against the suspects would not let me abandon them. I had to do my *sewa*, my service, just as they did.

Still, despite shootings, a murder, a hit list, and several threats, I was not prepared for what would happen.

In early 1999, the rhetoric against me reached an unprecedented level. The controversial high priest Ranjit Singh had managed to get a visa to the United States for his first-ever foreign visit, despite his admission to having killed in the name of Sikhism and his threat to do so again. His supporters planned a rally on the B.C.–Washington State border, which had moderates fearing more violence. Malik's radio station was promoting the visit. A local Punjabi newspaper ad listed both the Babbar Khalsa and the ISYF as sponsors of Singh's trip.

I called the U.S. State Department for my story and asked how a man with Singh's record could get permission to visit the States. Balwant Gill and Jarnail Bhandal, who were on the hit list with me, Hayer, Rani, and others also contacted State Department's Asia desk to explain their concerns. They sent them a copy of a CTV interview with Singh, in which he justified the use of violence and the excommunication of the six Canadians. The Americans said they would carefully monitor Singh's visit, but a day later, his visa was revoked.

Reporters love "gotcha" journalism, when a story leads to some action, whether it is an investigation being launched, a political resignation, or the revocation of a visa for a notorious religious leader. I may have made a mistake, however, when I quoted the State Department official saying, "After you called Monday, we called the embassy in New Delhi. The decision has been made to revoke the visa."

The response was immediate. Singh supporters blamed me for the Americans' change of heart. A woman at the U.S. embassy in Delhi told me they received calls from people who held me responsible. The suggestion that I had the power to control U.S. foreign policy would have been laughable if it weren't so dangerous.

I travelled to Phoenix in early January 1999 for a conference of Sikh scholars that was attended by another of the five *jathedars* of Sikhism, Prof. Manjit Singh. He was a moderate, educated Sikh scholar who told me that Ranjit Singh had made a mistake both in the way the original edict banning tables and chairs had been implemented, as well as the second one expelling the Canadians – including Hayer – from their faith. The professor greeted two of the excommunicated Sikhs who had travelled from British

Columbia for the meeting, which was in direct defiance of what
Ranjit Singh, his fellow high priest, had ordered. Manjit Singh's
position got big play in my newspaper. It also increased the schism
among Sikhs in Canada and in Punjab.

As Ranjit Singh's supporters continued to try to get him
special dispensation to make his trip, a court case over the bloodiest of the table-and-chairs battles got underway in January 1999
in B.C. Supreme Court. Four men associated with the ISYF,
including the cousin of Inderjit Reyat, were on trial for various
assault charges related to the attack on moderates at a Surrey Sikh
temple two years earlier.

The fundamentalists must have felt attacked on several fronts.
They had faced criticism over Hayer's murder, their leader was
not allowed to touch down in North America, and some of their
peers were on trial for serious and violent crimes.

Against this backdrop, the former ISYF spokesman Manmohan
Singh, who had called me for advice the night of his 1985 arrest,
went on Malik's radio station on January 16 and urged separatists
to protest against me the following week. But he let down his
guard and exposed the real issue. It had nothing to do with tables
and chairs:

"If Kim Bolan is not stopped at this moment – it's fine to
postpone or cancel or whatever, but I am warning the Sikh
community – the visa of Ranjit Singh has been cancelled and
Ranjit Singh has decided to sit at home or whatever – but the
case for Air-India is about to be opened and it is the full intent
of Kim Bolan to put on trial the front-line leading four, five or
six Sikh leaders.

"They will be made sacrificial goats and put in the position
of having to prove they are innocent instead of being proven
guilty. She has already named them and the first name that came

up is of Malik Sahib. She has named him that he paid money. Even after this we are thinking about cancelling the demonstration?"

Some of my contacts taped the program and translated it for me. I was stunned. I had never identified Malik in print as an Air-India suspect, although I had written about his financial support of Parmar and Reyat. So now I was accused not only of controlling U.S. foreign policy, but also the Air-India prosecutors! It was ridiculous.

I told John Schneider about Manmohan's comments. I thought it should be part of the threat file, and I wanted police to know there was a demonstration in the works. Instead, Schneider told me the Crown wanted to meet with me about being an Air-India witness. I refused. "I am a reporter," I said. "I can't be a witness. I want to cover the trial."

Ranjit Singh lost an appeal of the ruling to revoke his visa. Canadian diplomatic staff visited the high priest in Amritsar in late January to discuss the volatile situation in Canada. But Ranjit Singh was not backing down. He summoned Prof. Manjit Singh to appear before him and explain his contact with the "heretics" he had met in Phoenix. It was as if he was reading my stories and reacting on the other side of the world. The more Ranjit Singh tried to control things, the bigger the storm clouds got.

The protest against me changed dates several times in January and early February, but appeared to be going ahead on February 19. Manmohan Singh continued to call me "sweetheart" when we spoke on the phone, telling me privately that his call to have me "stopped" was all politics and that he didn't mean any of it. Still, he placed ads for the demonstration in Indo-Canadian newspapers and continued the rhetoric on radio. He didn't give an official affiliation, but called himself "servant of the Sikhs." Many Sikhs – even from the fundamentalist side – told me that they had tried to stop the organizers but that they were hell-bent on going ahead.

The protest took place outside the *Sun*'s downtown Vancouver offices on the scheduled date under the watchful eye of police. Among the demonstrators were four or five Air-India suspects. My colleague Doug Todd was sent to cover the story. I was not allowed to have any input. Manmohan claimed the crowd topped 4,000. Police said it was between 200 and 300 people. As the group gathered, a coalition of thirty-three Sikh societies issued a statement saying they supported the *Sun*, me, and our continued coverage.

My Sikh community sources told me that most people in the crowd were employed at the Khalsa School or the credit union and had been told to go. Many could not speak English and probably had never read one of my articles. They carried signs, which I found out were all made at the Khalsa School. The slogans were creative at least, referring to me only as Kim – like Cher or Bono. "KIM IS ANTI-SIKH." "IF KIM IS GOLIATH, SIKHS ARE DAVID." "KIM TO GO."

The newsroom found the demonstration fascinating, but I was frustrated. I couldn't stand being the subject of a story, instead of the reporter covering it. I couldn't even go near the window. Security was high. The Air-India Task Force was videotaping. Co-workers joked that all the Kim references would make people think it was a protest against the North Korean dictator.

Throughout this period, I had contacts within the school who would call me and let me know what was happening there. They told me they liked their jobs, but they did not necessarily agree with Malik and the other directors.

The demonstration was reported across Canada. But none of the reports mentioned Manmohan's suggestion on radio that I was going to somehow put Malik and others on trial for Air-India.

Manmohan arranged a meeting with *Sun* editor-in-chief John Cruickshank the following Monday to complain about me. He brought along lawyer David Unterman, who represented the Khalsa School, the credit union, and Malik personally. I was not invited to the meeting. I could scarcely believe that Manmohan – once the spokesman of a terrorist group linked to violent acts in Canada – was given the chance to air his grievances with the head of a major Canadian newspaper. How Canadian, I thought.

Cruickshank assured me he didn't sell me out in the meeting. That didn't stop Manmohan from claiming to have won on Malik's radio station that night. He said, incorrectly, that I would not be assigned to cover the upcoming three-hundredth anniversary of the Khalsa – a sacred religious event. And he said that any statement he wanted to make would be published in the *Sun*. The propaganda war was heating up.

A second e-mail came from Malik's son Hardeep five days after the protest. It was to Graham Rockingham, the *Sun*'s assignment editor, ordering him to send another reporter out to do a story on the temple turmoil, one who would write it from young Malik's angle. He claimed the moderates were non-Sikhs. "East Indians," he called them, adding, "In no way are traditionalist Sikhs going to let non-worshippers change their religion, or tell the worshippers how they should worship. That would be ludicrous, but in the *Vancouver Sun*'s and Kim Bolan's narrow-minded way of thinking, you expect that."

He said if an article were produced to his liking, then "maybe the in-the-plans Saturday, March 13, protest outside the *Sun* building won't happen," adding, "this time, there won't be 300 people. It's going to be a Saturday and 1000 to 2000 is an easy estimation."

It was blackmail. Rockingham ignored the e-mail.

The next day, I was invited to speak to a journalism class at the University of British Columbia. A bright group of graduate students peppered me with challenging questions about the effect of my reporting on the Sikh community and whether I was getting too involved in the story. They really made me think. When I got home that evening, I was surprised to get a call from Schneider, who rarely called me at home. He said the RCMP had received some information they wanted to discuss with me. It was about new security concerns. He was frustratingly vague. He said Malik's people were not happy with me.

"Obviously. There were 250 protesters outside my office last week," I retorted.

He said he wanted to meet me the following day – that he would come to my house to pick me up. I wanted more information. I didn't like to meet the RCMP for any reason other than a story. And I told him he could not come to my house.

I checked with Rockingham in the morning and he advised me to go. So I met Schneider at E Division headquarters. He drove me to Surrey to meet with Gary Bass, the head of the major crime division, including the Air-India Task Force. During the twenty-five-minute drive, Schneider gave me a toffee and made small talk, asking me what my hobbies were. I wanted to say catching Sikh terrorists and sewing, but I made up something else. I was extremely uncomfortable. I still didn't know what this meeting was about.

We chatted for about an hour in Bass's office about my articles and the fact I had stirred up so many issues in the community. Bass indicated that the RCMP had some information about possible threats against me, but did not provide anything specific.

"If someone is plotting against me, why can't you charge them?" I asked naively. He said the threat was less direct than that. Because I lived in Vancouver proper and out of the RCMP's jurisdiction, he said he would call Vancouver police to let them know what security he and Schneider thought I needed.

I felt as confused driving back into Vancouver with Schneider as I had driving out to Surrey. The picture became a little clearer a few days later when my Vancouver police contact, George Kristensen, came to my house on a Saturday morning.

"They have a coded informant who says there is talk of doing to you what was done to Hayer," Kristensen said. "This is very serious."

He suggested a host of severe security measures, including bodyguards and relocation. I felt sick. I didn't really believe I would be attacked, but I was embarrassed at the attention and worried how it would affect my kids and my ability to do my job.

Kristensen said that as an interim measure he would get an old squad car and have it parked outside my house as a ruse. And he did. I thought it was a bit silly, especially as the detailing on the car didn't match the current paint job the Vancouver police were using. And because it was out of commission, it didn't run well, so someone would come by every few days and start it up, much to my chagrin.

Kristensen was great. He told me everything he knew and he provided me with a real assessment of the situation. He wasn't in a conflict, like the RCMP, which had to guard its Air-India investigation at all costs. But I told the veteran detective that he would have to let my bosses know about the recommended security measures. I worked for the *Vancouver Sun* after all, and I was being targeted because of my reporting.

Kristensen came to the newsroom a few days later and met with John Cruickshank, managing editor Patricia Graham, someone from head office, and me. He had a single piece of paper outlining the concerns of police.

He said, "These guys have already killed 331 people. We have to take it seriously."

I piped in, "332. You should include Hayer."

I had learned over the past year that many people mistakenly think the police can protect you if your life is in danger. That is what I had suggested to Schneider the summer before when he told me the RCMP wanted Rani to enter the Witness Protection Program. That's what I thought should have been arranged for Hayer. That's what I had thought should be done for me now that I had received threats. But the police don't have the resources to provide someone with protection. They give you alarms and cameras and panic buttons, but they tell you to hire a security company if you need more protection.

So that's what my newspaper did. It hired a private security firm of ex-RCMP officers to escort me around and find somewhere for me to stay. As professional as the men were, they did not understand what my job entailed. We were constantly at loggerheads. I couldn't be driven around by bodyguards to meet potential sources. It just wouldn't work.

They found me an executive condo to move into with my two boys. Everything about the place was unsuitable for children – light carpeting, glass-top tables, large vases standing in the corners. I was miserable, but for the sake of the kids I pretended that everything was all right.

Kristensen wanted the paper to print a story about the fact I was getting protection. My editors agreed and a colleague wrote it. But just as it was going to press, the RCMP complained about the tactic. I had the story pulled. I constantly felt pulled, as well, between the sometimes conflicting advice of the two agencies.

Within days of the police telling me I had renewed reasons to worry, two strange things happened that alarmed me. First, a suspected Sikh terrorist named Ajit Singh, affiliated with the ISYF, landed at Vancouver International Airport at the end of February 1999. He claimed to be a U.S. resident who was visiting a friend here and said he had no criminal convictions. In fact he had been deported from the United States for shooting two people at a California temple in 1994. Singh was nabbed at the airport by

CSIS and immigration officials. He tried to make a refugee claim, but was deported to Bangkok on March 5 without revealing the real purpose of his B.C. visit.

The next day, Davinder Singh, another suspected terrorist from the Babbar Khalsa, tried to cross into British Columbia at the Washington state border. Immigration officials had received a tip about his trip and arrested him. Singh said he was coming to British Columbia to visit a cousin, but Immigration officials believed he was here to meet other members of the Babbar Khalsa. He openly admitted his associations during an interrogation with CSIS agents, naming a director of Malik's Khalsa School, Gurdev Gill, as his Babbar Khalsa contact in Canada. Singh was deported to the United States and told he was ineligible for further travel to Canada.

I called the RCMP to see if they thought either man could have had a more sinister purpose in coming to British Columbia, such as working on the remaining names on the hit list. Police had no information to link the men to anything specific, other than their connections to known terrorist organizations.

The *Sun* decided to print an article on the new threats against me. It ran on March 9, 1999, one day after Inderjit Reyat was denied parole yet again. This time the parole board had received a letter from the Air-India Task Force pointing out that Reyat had been found with an illegal gun acquired from the same California man who once owned the gun used to shoot Hayer in 1988. The board said it was satisfied Reyat was likely to "commit an offence by causing serious harm or death to another person prior to your warrant expiry date."

The same week I moved out of my house, four of the Sikh high priests in Amritsar sacked their fellow *jathedar* Ranjit Singh, in part because of the way he had handled the religious crisis in Canada. I felt pretty good about Singh losing his position, but I felt pretty uncomfortable over the publicity about my own plight. Other media were beginning to do stories on the threats I had received. Friends, sources and old family friends were calling constantly, and I didn't really want to talk about the peril I was in.

Canadian Press reporter Dene Moore quoted a UBC professor, Ken Bryant, saying that the divisive religious struggle in Vancouver had led to a showdown in Punjab "that is potentially very, very dangerous." He said Ranjit Singh had been turfed "in considerable part . . . for his failure to extend his powers here." Bryant was quoted as saying, "[Bolan] can claim some credit or blame, depending on which side of the table you're sitting at."

I didn't want either credit or blame. I just wanted to expose the people behind the Air-India bombing. I just wanted to write the truth about Hayer's murder.

Just before the April celebrations to mark the birth of the Khalsa, Reyat's wife, Satnam, was charged with welfare fraud of $109,054. The evidence had come from the search warrant that was executed after my story about her scheme was published in March 1998. Mrs. Reyat was supposed to be notified of the charge by registered letter, but learned about it when I called her to do a story. The charge involved one of the highest amounts of welfare fraud ever prosecuted in the province – more than ten times the average of $7,300.

The payments she had received while on welfare had come from Malik's company and the two charitable groups he headed – the Satnam Education Society and the Satnam Trust. Some of the monthly cheques were made out to her children; some had no name in the payee spot but were deposited in the Khalsa Credit Union by Aniljit Uppal, a branch manager and school director;

some were made out to Uppal but deposited in Mrs. Reyat's credit union account.

Later in April, as the celebrations of the Khalsa tricentennial continued, the Air-India prosecution team confirmed it was being more than doubled in size. I was able to state publicly for the first time that Hayer had been a potential Air-India witness, though for legal reasons, I could not mention the contents of the statement Hayer had shown me.

Then the RCMP's Air-India Task Force raided the Khalsa Credit Union in connection with its probe. Malik, Bagri, and the other suspects had to be feeling nervous. When I called Malik about the raid, he said he knew nothing about it. "I don't find these things out. How can I confirm these things?" he said, sounding agitated.

Things seemed to calm down in the late spring. There were no new threats and I begged police to allow me to return home. I couldn't stand living out of a suitcase and it was confusing and difficult for my boys to be displaced.

In June, Rani called me as she had done periodically since entering witness protection. She had just had her first meeting with Joe Bellows, the Crown prosecutor who would eventually lead the Malik portion of the case. She didn't really get along with Bellows, who peppered her with more questions than she felt comfortable answering. He told her he needed to know why she had waited so long – more than five months after she first started talking to the Air-India Task Force – before she revealed the main bombing confession she says Malik made to her.

"Because I had a dumb lawyer," she said to Bellows, repeating the comment to me.

I knew her lawyer had been Ravi Hira, a QC with an excellent reputation. "I thought Ravi was good," I said.

"Not Ravi. You!"

I was stunned. She reminded me what I had said to her in late February or early March 1998 after she had asked me to find out if someone could pass on information to the police without having to be a witness. I had told her Malik's incriminating comments to her were probably hearsay. But I had not realized at the time that I was giving legal advice that someone was heeding. I was just thinking aloud as I chatted to someone who had become a good source.

Now I was hearing her tell me how she disclosed the most important information in the whole Air-India case (months after she began to talk to the RCMP) because I had provided inaccurate information to her. I felt terrible. "Oh my God. Now I see," I said. "It is like a jailhouse informant."

I wanted her to know that I had not deliberately misled her. She had always told me she did not want to be a witness and she was reluctant to tell the police about her Air-India knowledge for that very reason. Now she was the key witness for the Air-India prosecutors because I had made her feel safe about disclosing what she knew. The thought that she was forced into witness protection over this deadly information, which she had told police because of me, made me feel sick. I wanted to reassure her that I was dumb, not manipulative. She was cheerful enough and said she didn't hold anything against me.

But I selfishly had another fear: Would I be compelled to testify if she had told both the RCMP and the Crown about my advice to her? She didn't know, but she said there was a written record of my involvement.

As soon as I got off the phone, I ran into the office of my editor-in-chief, John Cruickshank. I told him that I had unintentionally given out legal advice, bad advice, and that it might come up in the Air-India case once charges were laid. I was panicked, but he told me there was no point in worrying. If a subpoena arrived at the newspaper, we would deal with it then, he said.

Even after this, I did not ask Rani for any details about what Malik had told her. The only thing I knew was what she told me back in November 1997, which was that Malik had told her he was involved in the Air-India plot. And I knew she had been told about a few others from the Khalsa School who had been involved.

On July 13, I got word that the Federal Court of Canada had granted the Immigration department leave to appeal the refugee status given to Harpal Nagra, the ISYF founder, which had so enraged Hayer when it happened a few weeks before his death. When I called him for comment, Nagra said he wasn't worried about the development.

Later the same day, the RCMP in Surrey issued a strange media advisory. It told journalists about a news conference to be held the following day in both Surrey and Edmonton to announce a development in the investigation of the Hayer murder. I phoned a few sources and found out that investigators were looking at an Edmonton man as a possible suspect. I knew the ISYF was the big separatist group in that city so I called B.C. federation members to get a few contact numbers.

The first man I phoned knew exactly who police were targeting. His friend, a truck driver and cabbie named Inderjit Singh Kundan, had been interviewed in June. The ISYF leader gave me Kundan's cell number, and said that he used the nickname "Jassy." Kundan confirmed to me that he was the man police thought had something to do with Hayer's murder. He denied his involvement, of course, and I quoted him at length in a page-one story that scooped the RCMP news conference. Police were a little choked, as they had not planned to confirm Kundan's identity to reporters.

At the news conference, they claimed that the investigation showed the Hayer murder was not political, but motivated by personal revenge over a single editorial Hayer wrote. But Kundan told me he did not know Hayer personally. He was a leader in the ISYF and the vice-president of the federation's Edmonton temple.

I flew to Edmonton the next day to spend more time talking to Kundan, who was flooded by media requests for an interview after my initial story broke. He agreed to pick me up at a downtown location in his taxi and to take me to a location of his choice. He said that he feared the police were following him.

After he picked me up, we went to a food court in a mall and he ordered something to eat. As we sat down, he said the police were hassling him and that he had nothing to do with Hayer's murder. He claimed he was working for the City of Edmonton the night Hayer was gunned down and had a letter that proved it. What struck me as odd was that he had requested the letter in January, months before police started asking about him.

As I wrote notes on what Kundan was saying, a young Indo-Canadian man approached both of us. He said, "Hi, Jassy. Hi, Kim," causing me a split second of panic, as I had no idea who he was. Then he pulled out an RCMP badge and gave each of us a copy of his business card. His name was Const. Sean Gill, of the Surrey RCMP. Kundan had been followed.

Gill talked to Kundan about his being a murder suspect and told him that he could clear his name by taking a lie-detector test. Kundan agreed. I asked Gill how he knew my name. I was angry that police were making it look as if I were involved in the game they were playing with their suspect.

Kundan later told me that he believed I was working with the police – something I adamantly denied. If this man were involved in Hayer's brutal slaying, the police had done me no favours by making it look like I was in cahoots with them. I got my editor to write a scathing letter to the RCMP for endangering me. They wrote back claiming that I was at fault by interfering somehow in their investigation.

Kundan had admitted to me that he knew some of the most controversial ISYF leaders in British Columbia and that he had stayed at the Surrey home of Satinderpal Gill, the leader who was based in Pakistan for so many years and with whom Bagga's father had stayed.

I decided to check out the Sikh temple where Kundan was vice-president. As I arrived, I noticed a bus in the parking lot from Malik's Khalsa School. It had brought Malik's staff from British Columbia to teach in the summer camp, like the kind that Rani used to attend with Malik. Many of the Khalsa School teachers attending the Edmonton camp knew Kundan.

While I was in Edmonton, I got a call from the International Women's Media Foundation in Washington, D.C., telling me I was the recipient of a Courage in Journalism Award to be presented in October. I didn't know what to say. On the one hand, it seemed weird to be getting an award because people wanted to kill me. On the other hand, the foundation was inviting me to travel across the United States for two weeks, meeting the media, including the editorial board of the *New York Times* and the *L.A. Times*. It was a-once-in-a-lifetime opportunity.

Toward the end of August I received a strange call from a Surrey family I did not know. They explained that they had satellite television so they could watch the news from India, and told me about a news report of a Canadian woman, Gurbax Kaur, described as a Babbar Khalsa terrorist, who had been found shot to death in Uttar Pradesh, India. They had taped the broadcast for me so that I could see the local police exhuming her decaying body, together with a stash of explosives, some automatic weapons, and a day-planner from the Khalsa Credit Union. Indian intelligence was alleging Gurbax Kaur, also known as Baksho Kaur Dhillon, was the Canadian financier of Sikh separatists. I had heard from sources that she was from the Vancouver area.

I published a story the next day, prompting a call from the woman's teenaged daughter, who invited me to talk. When we met, she said her mother was no terrorist and had run an orphanage in India. But there were many things the young woman was not saying, such as why a mother would leave behind her three children to go back to India to live. The daughter confirmed that Dhillon had come back to Canada twice a year to fundraise at the Khalsa School camps. Some of the money from Malik's two charities had gone to the woman, who India claimed was a terrorist.

This was yet another instance of the Surrey school being connected to someone alleged by a foreign government to be a terrorist.

The troubles at B.C. temples continued throughout the summer of 1999 as moderates tried to hold referendums to reduce the number of board members. It was a tactic to ensure their long-term control, and Sikh separatists were not going to let it happen without a fight. The vote at the historic Ross Street temple was halted by police more than once.

The moderate members of the temple's board got an injunction prohibiting several fundamentalist leaders from protesting within a set distance of the temple. Among those named were Air-India suspect Hardial Johal and Manmohan Singh, the man who had organized the protest against me.

Meanwhile, I was taking a break from reporting on temple politics to cover a disturbing court case. Five young Nazi skinheads had kicked to death an elderly Sikh caretaker at Surrey's Guru Nanak temple. The five had admitted their guilt, but still all the terrible details of the crime were being recounted at their sentencing hearing. The case was due to wrap up just before I was to go to the United States to collect the Courage in Journalism Award. The trip would give me a bit of a break from the politics of the Sikh community, though I would be back in time for a temple election in Surrey in the third week in October.

On a lunch break one day in the skinhead hearing, I checked my voicemail. The first message was from a detective with the Vancouver Police Department, saying the RCMP had called regarding renewed threats. The second message was from John Schneider, from the Air-India Task Force. I returned both calls. The news was bad. The police had intelligence indicating that I would be targeted if the moderates won the upcoming election. Schneider suggested reimposing the extreme security measures – bodyguards and possibly relocation. I told him I was leaving town for two weeks in a couple of days and didn't see the need to do anything drastic. Then I called my office with the news and was told to return immediately for a security meeting.

I found this second warning by police worse than the first one the previous February. Back then I had known that emotions were running high over Ranjit Singh's cancelled visa, Hayer's assassination, and my stories about each. But there didn't seem to be any particular event or issue triggering the new threat. I began to realize that to a small element within the Sikh community I had become a symbol of opposition and that what I actually wrote in the newspaper didn't matter.

I wasn't the only one targeted this time. Balwant Gill, the moderate presidential candidate in the Surrey temple election with whom I shared a spot on the infamous hit list, was also threatened. I called him to see if the police had warned him. He said he still had the bulletproof vest they had given him the previous year.

I looked forward to getting away on the U.S. tour. There were to be two large awards luncheons – one at the Waldorf Astoria in New York and the other in Beverley Hills – attended by some of the most prominent media personalities in the United States, including Judy Woodruff of CNN, Maria Shriver, who would later become California's first lady, Helen Gurley Brown, and Howell Raines, who was then the editorial page editor of the *New York Times*. And there were speaking engagements in Boston and Washington, D.C., as well.

Two other journalists, from Afghanistan and Kosovo, were also being honoured for their work under arduous conditions in their wartorn countries. I felt silly being compared to these amazing women who had overcome so much adversity. But surprisingly, the Americans were fascinated by the story of a Canadian journalist being threatened for writing about a small terrorist group linked to an airline bombing.

I was glad for the chance to explain to editors from the *New York Times* and the *L.A. Times* about the Air-India bombing, which at that point was still the largest act of aviation terrorism in history, yet was barely mentioned by the U.S. media. And I was able to inform these powerful people that one Canadian journalist had already been murdered, likely by the same religious extremists who blew up the plane and killed 331 people.

A few days into the trip, my editor, John Cruickshank, called to explain that he had spoken with the head office of Conrad Black's Hollinger International, which then owned the *Vancouver Sun*. Apparently they disagreed with the newspaper about letting me travel without security. They flew in two bodyguards to meet me in New York, including Black's own head of security. He hand-delivered a letter from the company laying out what it intended to do. The letter seemed to have been written by a lawyer. For the first time, it occurred to me that my newspaper was worried about its liability in the event I was killed.

"The RCMP has heard via two independent sources that you may again be targeted for violence if the moderate Sikh faction is successful in elections on the 24th of this month," the letter read. "We understand that you found the previous security arrangements restrictive and frustrating. We will work hard with you to minimize them this time around."

The underlying tone of the letter was that I had not been co-operating and that I had better start. I was already aware of the risk I was facing, yet my editor-in-chief felt the need to have someone fly to New York to hand me a letter telling me of the risk. I thought it was an overreaction, but I had no choice but to accept their security arrangements. My editors also decided to fly me home for the weekend for a security meeting. I was pleased about that, as it meant I would be able to see my kids and also cover the Surrey temple election.

The moderates ended up winning again. Several of their leaders were wearing bulletproof vests on voting day. I had two body-guards. We stood together at their campaign office, which was next door to Hayer's newspaper office, and we talked about how out-rageous it was that, almost a year after Hayer's murder, no one had been charged and we were living with death threat after death threat. But we laughed too. Balwant Gill said he didn't really want to wear the protective vest because he had lost weight and didn't want to look chubby. I joked that the vests weren't all that helpful if someone decided to shoot you in the head. Someone piped in that we should patent special bulletproof turbans made from the same material as the vests. "There would be a big demand here in B.C.," Gill said, and we laughed, morbid as it was.

It had come to the point that being threatened was a mark of prestige in the Sikh community. It meant you were doing your *sewa*, your service, so well that extremists had targeted you. That led to some inane debates about whether certain people had done enough to land on the hit list – as if somehow they weren't deserving of this odious honour.

On the first anniversary of Hayer's death, a federal court dismissed the government's appeal to reverse the refugee status given to Harpal Nagra, the ISYF founder who had spent time in the spring of 1988 with Bagga. I missed having Hayer around to provide me with comments for my story this time.

Then, in December, a special prosecutor decided there would be no fraud charges laid in connection with the allegations against Malik's Khalsa School. He said, without a doubt, there had been problems, but there was no likelihood of conviction. He said that a civil suit by the government was in the works instead.

Since I had exposed the various wrongdoings in my initial series on the school, the hijacker had been deported, Satnam Reyat faced welfare fraud charges, a Sikh priest had pleaded guilty to sexually assaulting students, and another teacher had admitted to hitting students in the face. But the core allegation of misappropriation of funds never made it to a criminal court.

I began to think that there would never be Air-India charges laid and that everyone who had risked their lives to give information to the police had done so for nothing. The key players were so well connected politically to every level of government. People with information about the bombing often saw them hobnobbing with power-brokers from all three major parties.

Here we were heading into a new millennium, a full fifteen years since the bombings, and still nobody had been charged.

Malik began the new year by launching his re-election campaign for a board position in the Khalsa Credit Union. He sent a letter to supporters urging them to unite under his leadership. "It pained my heart to see the community divided over the tables and chairs issue," the letter said, prompting his opponents to publicly blame Malik for the divisions. When I called him for comment, Malik said, "I don't start controversies."

While he campaigned for re-election, Malik was freed of the burden of having to testify at Satnam Reyat's welfare fraud trial. On January 31, 2000, she pleaded guilty to having collected more than $109,000 in benefits over a seven-year period while being paid under the table by Malik.

Malik was at the courthouse waiting to testify at her preliminary hearing when he got news of her guilty plea, as was Inderjit Reyat's cousin, Piara Panasar, the man who had been acquitted of stabbing a moderate leader in the bloodiest temple battle in January 1997.

Mrs. Reyat's lawyer, Kuldip Chaggar, told the court that about $58,000 of the illegal payments was used to finance Inderjit Reyat's appeal of his 1991 terrorism conviction. He was trying to explain that she did not get the benefit of all the money. So money from charities – including one that was government funded – went to finance a terrorist's court case. I called Revenue Canada to check on the propriety of charities funding a convicted bombmaker's appeal. I was told it would launch an investigation. I also called the two lawyers who fought the unsuccessful appeal for Reyat – Richard Peck and Michael Tammen. Neither agreed to comment. And both would soon represent another Air-India suspect.

When Mrs. Reyat was sentenced to a year of house arrest, Chaggar blamed Malik and his key ally, Aniljit Uppal, the Khalsa School trustee and a manager at the credit union. Chaggar, who was an ally of Malik, nevertheless called Malik a "pious and pretentious" community leader who insisted that Mrs. Reyat be compensated illegally for the work she was doing at the Khalsa daycare. "That was the condition. That was the way they insisted it happen and that is the way it happened," Chaggar said in court, adding that he couldn't believe "how stupid they were or how stupid they are until this day."

The payments to Mrs. Reyat would become an integral part of the prosecution case against Malik in the Air-India bombing just a few months later.

Throughout the early months of 2000, a team of eleven Crown prosecutors pored through documents and evidence that totalled in the millions of pages. They made a decision to charge Malik and Bagri.

But Malik would face other challenges before being arrested in the biggest criminal case in Canadian history. The CRTC threatened to fine him if he did not get a licence for the radio station that had been the subject of numerous complaints for its violent rhetoric. And provincial regulators placed the Khalsa Credit Union under their administration after a scathing report accused Malik of misusing his position in the credit union to get high-risk loans and to borrow from members after checking the balances in their accounts. He also borrowed money from employees.

The report came on the heels of the exposure of the credit union's link to Satnam Reyat's welfare fraud, as well as two successive raids on the credit union by the Air-India Task Force. And there was my story about Gurbax Kaur, the B.C. woman who allegedly had been using the credit union to fund terrorists in India when she was killed.

But Malik had always been a fighter. He launched an appeal of the regulators' ruling and used the credit union's money to hire a lawyer to take on the government body. There was a month-long hearing in the summer of 2000 where witness after witness came forward and testified about problems at the credit union. Among them was Guru Raj Kaur Khalsa, a white Sikh and director of the credit union, who had always been a Malik ally.

However, she had become increasingly concerned about the problems at the credit union and thought they needed the regulators' help. Because of her views, she said she felt threatened by a motion put forward at an annual general meeting, which noted that Sikhs have always fought to the death to maintain control of their institutions.

"This [motion] hurt because I feel that this can put my family in danger," Khalsa testified at the hearing. "There are people who see this kind of thing and feel, Oh, they're betraying the religion. I had better do something about it."

She testified that Malik had said he would withdraw the motion if Khalsa agreed not to testify against him at the hearing.

The same belligerent sentiments were heard on Malik's radio station during the appeal hearing on who would run the credit union. A controversial radio host urged Sikhs to get the "white" regulators out. "Sikhs built this bank. They should get control back in their hands."

The most startling thing in the hearing was repeated reference to Malik as a suspect in the Air-India bombing. As far as I knew, that had never been stated in a quasi-judicial public setting, though many with inside knowledge knew Malik's suspect status very well.

In September and October 2000, there were a number of attacks on the homes of moderate Sikh leaders, as well as at the office of the *Indo-Canadian Times*. Most involved rocks being thrown through windows in the middle of the night. But one elderly man was the victim of a drive-by shooting. Dave Hayer said bluntly that the smashing of his newspaper's windows was likely an attempt to silence potential Air-India witnesses, just as his father had been silenced.

Hayer was now involved in provincial politics and was running for the Liberal nomination in a Surrey riding. His father's old enemies in the ISYF and the Babbar Khalsa, including Ajaib Bagri, aligned themselves with Hayer's opponent for the nomination, Surrey mayor Doug McCallum. Dave Hayer won by a large margin, in the first step toward his 2001 election to the B.C. legislature. He would become one of the most vocal critics of the tight relationship between some terrorists and politicians from every major party and at every level of government.

Just five days before the charges were laid for the Air-India bombing, Malik won back control of the Khalsa Credit Union. A panel of three commissioners ruled that the fact he was a suspect in a mass murder should not be held against him forever. In effect, they ruled that just because another director of the credit union testified that Malik had threatened her didn't mean he should be precluded from running his own financial institution, and just because his involvement in a welfare fraud had been well documented did not make him unsuitable to head a credit union with assets of $110 million. "We cannot think it is fair to hold a person hostage to a suspicion which could go on indefinitely," the panel said in its ruling.

Like I had always done, I called Malik for comment on his victory. He said, "Yes, I am pleased. The board is fine, that is what I heard. . . . All the allegations are removed."

Well, not exactly. The commissioners agreed there had been serious problems with the way Malik had been running the credit union. But they said they were "correctable" with the right amount of support.

Because of the panel's specific references to the Air-India bombing, I was able to ask Malik for the first time if he had thought of himself as a suspect. He said he had not noticed the

Air-India references in the ruling. But he added, "Because of the stories you were writing, I was thinking that I was one."

He later admitted that he had known since the day of the bombing that he was a suspect. And he later admitted he had hired a lawyer in 1997 because he feared charges against him were imminent.

Even though Malik expressed joy at regaining control of his credit union when he spoke to me on October 22, 2000, he already had other plans in the works. He had purchased an airline ticket to Pakistan and was planning a secret trip within days.

CHAPTER 9

Justice at Last?

E ARLY IN OCTOBER 2000, I began to hear rumours that, after
fifteen long years, charges in the Air-India case were imminent. The RCMP and Crown prosecutors called family members
of victims to meetings across Canada to tell them charges were
coming soon. They were not given a date.

I heard from Rani during the third week of October. She had
been told the investigation was intensifying. She had not been
told when the suspects would be rounded up, but she was optimistic it would happen soon. I also heard from some of my
sources in the legal profession that charges were coming soon. I
tried to prepare some advance stories for the big day, but I found
it hard to believe charges really would be laid. Rumours of imminent arrests had come and gone before.

But late on October 25, I received several phone calls that convinced me arrests would be made within days, if not hours. I drove
past the Vancouver homes of Malik and Johal to see if there was
any activity. There was none.

At 6:00 a.m. on Friday, October 27, CBC in Toronto phoned me at home to ask me to comment on air about the pending Air-India charges. CBC Radio news was already reporting that something was going to happen, and other radio stations also began reporting that there had been a break in the Air-India case. My cellphone was ringing like crazy.

I learned later that police were furious that the media was reporting this breakthrough before the two men were in custody. They worried that the suspects would flee before they were picked up. Malik had already purchased a ticket to Pakistan, which was found by the RCMP on the desk of his downtown Vancouver office after he was arrested.

Not only were reporters going to air with stories about the arrests before they happened, several of us were camped outside Malik's house and office, as well as the Khalsa School in Surrey, waiting for the RCMP to arrive. By late morning, police had moved in on several locations.

Malik's Shaughnessy mansion was searched, as was the Yaletown office of his company, Papillon Eastern Imports. Police also arrived at the Khalsa School in Surrey, much to the surprise of staff and students. Cpl. Doug Best asked staff where Malik was. Loyal supporter Aniljit Uppal at first said that Malik was not there, but then he succumbed to RCMP demands for information and led Best to a small room behind the school's temple, where Malik was. He was taken into custody shortly after noon.

Within an hour, Bagri was picked up at his luxurious home on Tranquille Road in Kamloops. He was flown to Vancouver for a weekend in custody before his first court appearance.

As it was on the day of the bombing more than fifteen years earlier, arrest day was absolutely frantic for those of us in the media as we scrambled to figure out what was going on, how many people had been arrested, and whether the police would be making any formal statement. The RCMP finally scheduled a news conference for mid-afternoon at its regional headquarters in Vancouver. Reporters packed into the room, as did several senior investigators on the file.

The official announcement of the charges was read by Const. Catherine Galliford, who had recently taken over as media liaison for Air-India investigators. There were eight counts for each man, among them conspiracy to commit murder and first-degree murder for both the Air-India and Narita bombings, and the attempted murder of all the passengers on the connecting flights, as well as those on Air-India Flight 301 – the intended target of the Narita bomb. There were also counts of endangering an aircraft by placing bombs on board.

"The RCMP allege that both bombs originated or were placed on respective flights originating from Vancouver, British Columbia, as a result of an alleged conspiracy taking place in part in the province of British Columbia," said Beverly Busson, assistant commander of the RCMP's E division. "These criminal acts marked the beginning of one of the largest and most complex investigations ever undertaken by the Royal Canadian Mounted Police. . . . This has been a worldwide investigation with extremely challenging logistical problems."

There were a few surprises in the charges, the first being that only Malik and Bagri were arrested. Not Reyat, not Johal, not Surjan Gill, whom we knew the police suspected were also involved. We had been expecting more. The other big surprise was that Bagri faced one charge that Malik did not, for the attempted murder of Tara Singh Hayer in 1988. Hayer's son, Dave, and daughter-in-law, Isabelle, were in the room for the announcement, surrounded by reporters. Tears streamed down

Isabelle's face. For the first time, police were publicly admitting a link between the first time Hayer was shot and the Air-India case. I felt a little choked up as well.

"We are very pleased with the arrest of the suspects, along with the rest of Canadian society," Dave Hayer said. "We are relieved. It is a very difficult, very sad, and very painful day today."

He was right. There was no joy at hearing that charges had been laid at last. The relatives of Air-India victims also had subdued reactions. They had waited so long, and they had suffered so much. It was difficult for them to find solace in the charges. I called Bal Gupta, the Etobicoke man who lost his wife, Ramwati, in the bombing and who had spoken out so eloquently for victims' families for fifteen years. "It is like somebody putting a needle in a wound that has formed a crust. It was probably bleeding on the inside, but you couldn't see it. Now it is bleeding on the outside," he said.

I called many other relatives. None were thrilled or elated by the charges. But they now had a faint hope that maybe, finally, there would be some justice.

Charges being laid in the deadliest act of aviation terrorism in history was big news. The American networks, Indian newspapers, and the British media all carried stories. My newspaper ran thirteen full pages of news, including a ten-page supplement in which I laid out details of the plot that I had never reported before. I wrote for the first time that Hayer had shown me one of the statements he gave the police about overhearing Bagri's alleged confession. I wrote that Hayer decided to tell police what he knew only after his old friend Tarsem Purewal was assassinated.

But the faint optimism that justice would be done, which the charges brought, came with increased tension as well. Some former separatist leaders declared that the charges were trumped up and that they would continue to support Malik and Bagri. Others quietly put the word out that it would not be safe to co-operate with police.

The RCMP stepped up security for the witnesses as well as for Sikh leaders who praised police for finally laying charges. The names of the witnesses had not been publicly disclosed, but those of us who covered the case had a sense of who some of them were. As did members of the Sikh community. I got extra patrols outside my house and some additional security. *Province* journalist Salim Jiwa got extra patrols. He had written extensively about the case during the 1980s and was close to Sukhminder Cheema, one of the people on the witness list.

Malik and Bagri each spent the weekend being questioned by a team of RCMP interrogation specialists, including Insp. Don Adam and Sgt. Jim Hunter, who tried to get each of them to talk. It came out later in court documents that the interrogators made some outrageous claims to the two suspects. Only partial transcripts of the recorded and videotaped interviews with the accused terrorists were eventually released to reporters. But the portions we got would prove to be nationwide bombshells.

At one point, Adam suggested to Malik that CSIS might have destroyed the tapes in a deliberate coverup. "Perhaps if your agent was right in the middle of it, and then it happened and now you were all going to look horrible, you might, you might, have a reason to cover that up, wouldn't you?" Adam said.

If the idea was to get Malik to admit guilt by making him enraged that he had been set up by CSIS, it didn't work. Nor was the tactic any more successful when Hunter used it on Bagri to suggest that CSIS had pulled its agent, Surjan Gill, out when all the others were set to go with the bombings.

"Why was he trying to back out? Well, because his CSIS agents have told him to back out," Hunter said. "They told him to get out of there. Things are happening and you can't be seen as part of that."

Both the RCMP and CSIS were later forced to publicly deny that Gill was a mole for the Canadian spy agency, but he remained a mysterious figure who disappeared from Canada on the eve of the Air-India arrests, despite having been a suspect since 1985.

Police tried other ways to get Malik and Bagri to talk. They showed them videos of the bodies being recovered from the ocean in the hopes of eliciting an emotional response – finding some remorse. Investigators even brought in children's toys that had been aboard the flight.

Nothing.

Malik munched away on a plate of cookies that had been put out for him. He asked at one point if he could take a shower. Neither he nor Bagri made any confession.

In British Columbia, there was a great deal of reaction to the historic arrests. Politicians quickly distanced themselves from the two men who had been prominent during so many fundraising dinners and campaigns. Fundamentalist temples attacked the RCMP and stood behind Malik and Bagri in Sunday speeches to the congregation and the Punjabi media did interviews. Victims' families made emotional statements to the press about their relief. Other suspects met at a temple in the Vancouver suburb of New Westminster – concerned about the possibility of more arrests.

Friends of the two men immediately started organizing on their behalf. At the Khalsa School, Malik supporters gathered over his first weekend in jail to sign letters of support. Bagri's comrades in the Kamloops Babbar Khalsa made the five-hour trip down to Vancouver to attend his first court appearance Monday morning, October 30.

On Sunday, Malik's lawyer, Terry LaLiberte, spoke to the media, suggesting the case against his client was pathetically

weak – nothing more than a few people with grudges against him.
When LaLiberte was brought in for the defence, Malik's eldest
son, Jaspreet, was articling for him. I had a brief phone interview
with the colourful lawyer, during which he assailed my reporting on Malik's school over the previous three years and said that,
if I called him again, he would file a criminal harassment complaint against me with the police. I told him it was my duty to
call him each time I wrote about his client, but that he was
welcome to refuse comment if he wished. He later joked to a television reporter about the threat he made to me.

I learned late Sunday that Hardial Johal, the school custodian
who had been seen at the airport the day the bombs were loaded,
had also been arrested. I called his house and got his wife,
Gurcharan, on the phone. I had met her on a couple of occasions
when Johal had invited me to his home. Gurcharan was distraught at his detention. Just as the police had promised, it looked
like others would also be charged.

Johal, too, was interrogated for hours by the RCMP, during
which he seemed most concerned about not having the financial
resources to fight the charges adequately, according to a partial
transcript. He was released without being charged on the Monday,
as the other two men waited for their first court appearance. The
drug-addicted and downtrodden in their usual place on the steps
outside the Vancouver Provincial Courthouse were stunned by
the media frenzy on their turf. Dozens of reporters added to the
bottleneck at the front door as sheriffs scrambled to get everyone
searched and through the metal detectors as quickly as possible.

Supporters of the two accused terrorists vied with reporters
for seats in Courtroom 101, where defendants usually appear for
less than a minute to fix another court date for charges like
trafficking, robbery, or soliciting. This was the first and likely last
international terrorism case to land in this dingy courtroom.

Malik and Bagri were supposed to be in and out of court shortly after 9:30 a.m., but ended up being two hours late because of a controversy over their attire. The two orthodox Sikhs had been forced to remove their turbans while being transported between the jail and court. They appeared in court in white plastic jumpsuits that looked like the kind painters wore and without the headdress that signifies so much in their religion.

"It's an outrage to Mr. Malik and his religion to hold him this way," LaLiberte bellowed to the media. "It's demeaning and embarrassing and it shows the way he has been dealt with by the RCMP so far."

LaLiberte's attack on the RCMP was sly, for it was misplaced. The experienced lawyer must have known that police had nothing to do with the transport of prisoners, something squarely in the jurisdiction of the Corrections Service, which later apologized for its actions.

Outside court, Sukhminder Cheema, the ISYF member turned journalist who was on the witness list, was yelled at by one of Malik's sons as Cheema snapped a photo: "Don't publish that picture or we'll fix you." Those of us who heard the comment thought it was threatening. Cheema reported it to police, but nothing happened.

The B.C. Sikh community was publicly divided over the charges. Supporters of the men claimed police were caving to political pressure and slammed witnesses and overjoyed moderate Sikhs. Punjabi radio stations, including Malik's, were full of rhetoric and threats. Police and community leaders appealed for calm. But it was hard for anyone to stay calm. People knew what was at stake. For fifteen years, intimidation had been a successful tactic to silence potential witnesses.

Cheema, who we later learned was not only on the witness list but also on the RCMP's payroll, had a late-night visit to his radio station by a group of men whom he said threatened him over his Air-India coverage. He received death threats in anonymous telephone calls. Rocks were thrown at his office window.

The chief minister of Punjab, Parkash Singh Badal, cancelled a trip to Canada for security reasons. He was to have been a guest of Ujjal Dosanjh, who was now the premier of British Columbia. Because Badal was in the same party – the Akali Dal – as Malkiat Sidhu, the minister shot by B.C. militants in 1986, he was advised it would not be wise to travel there in the inflamed environment.

Malik and Bagri had more immediate concerns – how to assemble a legal team and raise enough money to get bail. They printed up form letters asking supporters to put up their property and possessions as sureties. Fundraising drives began on Web sites. Some temples collected funds.

Bagri turned to the widow of Avtar Narwal, the Babbar Khalsa associate and Air-India suspect who had drowned himself two years earlier. Sources in the Sikh community told me his wife, Gurmej Kaur, had received a sizeable insurance settlement for her husband's untimely death. She did not hesitate to give her Kamloops neighbour and close friend tens of thousands so he could hire lawyers.

A Mississauga man named Balkar Singh Heir formed a group called the United Defence Council to raise money for the pair. Heir confirmed to me that he was the "Balkar Singh" who had been in an Amritsar jail in 1988, accused of being a financier to Sikh militants, and later released. I had been in Punjab in August of that year and had managed to pass him some questions through a mutual contact when police refused to permit me into the prison.

In response to those questions, Heir had claimed to be innocent of all the terrorism charges he was facing and said he had been tortured: "My legs were pulled apart more and more. I got electric shocks in my nose and my mouth. I was made to lie down and a heavy constable was jumping on me. The torture continued for 13 or 14 hours until I was almost unconscious," he wrote.

And here he was, twelve years later, raising funds for other accused terrorists. He told me that a fundraising dinner he organized in the fall of 2000 raised $70,000 for the Air-India defendants. Malik's radio station reported the dinner actually raised $300,000.

Both accused men lined up top lawyers – Bill Smart, who had been both a prosecutor and defence lawyer, would lead the Malik team, facing off against his old UBC classmate Joe Bellows, the lead Malik prosecutor. Bagri retained Richard Peck, another member of the same UBC law class, to head his defence team.

Malik looked to the school he founded for support. A letter was circulated requesting staff to put up their property or provide character references for Malik. After I published a story about the letter, the Ministry of Education intervened and advised school staff that they were not obligated to commit any resources to Malik's defence. But there must have been pressure. The staff knew who ran the school. Even with Malik in jail, the other trustees were loyal to him. Some of those trustees joined other Malik supporters going door to door to solicit funds for the defence teams.

Other Air-India suspects were doing their bit for the greater cause. Daljit Sandhu and Hardial Johal made speeches at a new temple in south Vancouver run by the Akhand Kirtani Jatha organization. They urged people to donate money to fight a court challenge against the moderates Ross Street temple election. Regaining control of lucrative temples continued to be high on their agenda.

Balwant Bhandher and Satwant Sandhu, also both on the RCMP's list of suspects and both trustees of Malik's school, worked with Aniljit Uppal to photocopy and circulate witness statements in the Sikh community. Family members and friends of the witnesses were approached about the statements. Some were given copies of confidential disclosure material to keep. Many of the people who reported this to me also said that they felt the move was designed to intimidate witnesses into pulling out. I actually got copies of three witness statements myself from a third party who had been given them. But, according to police, it wasn't illegal to expose the future testimony of witnesses in the country's biggest terrorism case. The RCMP said defence lawyers had the right to these statements in order to investigate witnesses.

While Air-India watchers like me had an idea of who some of the witnesses were going to be, we still expected a few surprises when the bail hearing got underway just before Christmas. But what surprised me the most was the lack of surprise. The Crown outlined its case against each accused, focusing on a few witnesses – Rani, Narinder Gill, and "the farmer" against Malik, and the FBI informant codenamed John, Sukhminder Cheema, and Premika against Bagri.

The Crown's most compelling evidence, which was a surprise to most observers, was a videotape that the RCMP had obtained of Bagri's infamous New York speech in July 1984, in which he called for the murder of fifty thousand Hindus. The whole tape was played at the bail hearing, with English subtitles, before Associate Chief Justice Patrick Dohm. Some of Bagri's young supporters in the gallery raised their fists in the air in solidarity at a couple of points of high rhetoric.

I had expected to hear all kinds of fresh evidence the RCMP and Crown had uncovered, but they revealed nothing that I didn't already know. I was a little shocked at the simplicity of the case as the prosecution laid it out at the bail hearing. Each man had confessed to a few people close to them, the Crown said. The defence immediately attacked the credibility of the witnesses.

Malik's counsel called as a witness to the hearing a forensic accountant who estimated Malik's wealth at $10 million. They were making a push for him to be held under house arrest at his mansion, with an electronic monitor on his ankle and security guards on his payroll watching him.

The bail hearing lasted several days throughout December 2000 and early into 2001. Dohm finally ruled that the two men would be held in custody. Calling the Air-India bombing "almost beyond human comprehension," Dohm said detention was necessary to maintain the public's confidence in the administration of justice in Canada.

"It is difficult to think of a more planned and deliberate act. The gravity of the nature of the offence of murder in this case is beyond question. The circumstances surrounding the murders are unspeakable," Dohm said. "Any reasonable fair-minded person, aware of all of these circumstances, including the curves and bumps in the evidence, and cognizant of the presumption of innocence, would not have confidence in the justice system if the accused were released from custody."

After the hearing, the B.C. government forced Malik to take a leave of absence from his position at the publicly funded Khalsa School, but he remained on the board of the credit union until September 2001, eleven months after his arrest. And even when he was obliged to step down from that position too, he made sure he kept his influence at both institutions through sympathetic directors who confirmed to me and to government regulators that they visited him regularly in jail.

I made a special arrangement to tour the jail in which both men were held as I wanted to get a sense of the dramatic shift in their lives in the months since their arrest. I saw that the officials from the B.C. Corrections Service had made every effort to accommodate their religious and cultural needs. They had weekly prayer services with a priest – Giani Swarn Singh – who had prayed with Inderjit Reyat when he had been in the same jail awaiting trial in

1990. Corrections staff told me Malik had also led prayer services for Reyat a decade earlier. They were allowed to bring in *langar* once a week.

The men had Sikh holy books in their cells and spent an hour a day in the gym with other inmates. I saw Bagri there pumping a little iron and walking a few laps. They wore the same green prison pants and red T-shirts as other inmates. Malik had received permission to hold an engagement ceremony in jail for his eldest son, Jaspreet, who was to marry a few months later at the Khalsa School.

Bagri was so enraged at my report of his jail life that he phoned up Malik's radio station and complained on air that everything I wrote was a lie: "It is all totally false . . . Kim Bolan has said that we are receiving good treatment, good food and good behaviour in jail. . . . There is no good treatment, no good food."

Bagri said that another inmate had left human feces on his turban when he left his cell to shower, something jail officials later confirmed. He also complained about substandard medical care and claimed that the RCMP had put me up to doing the story. In fact, I never even talked to police before going into the jail.

But bigger than their concerns about conditions in jail were their concerns about preparing for the expanding criminal case they faced.

In February 2001, the prosecution announced its intention to also charge Inderjit Reyat in the Air-India bombing. Permission first had to be obtained from the British government, as Reyat had been extradited from England in 1989 for just the Narita bombing. That meant the British home secretary, Jack Straw, had to consent to additional charges.

Mrs. Reyat did not seem pleased with the development when I called her. She had been waiting more than ten years for her husband to get out of jail.

"You know more than I do. You know everything. I have no comment. I don't want to talk to you," she said before hanging up.

For years, terrorist attacks in India and Canada had been attributed to militant Sikh separatist groups like the Babbar Khalsa and the ISYF. Still, western governments were slow to ban them or even publicly criticize the groups. Perhaps it was because no politician wanted to lose valuable Sikh votes come election time. Security agencies in other countries had taken a harder line against extremist groups like the Irish Republican Army and the Palestinian Liberation Organization, which had been proscribed. There was widespread condemnation of the Libyan connection to the 1988 bombing of Pan Am Flight 103 over Lockerbie, Scotland.

In early 2001, with two men linked to the Babbar Khalsa now charged with 331 murders, Canada was still hesitant to take action. But the British government, as it pondered whether to give Canada permission to charge Inderjit Reyat in the Air-India bombing, was changing its tune. In late February, over the protests of some members of the Labour Party, it placed the Babbars and the ISYF on a list of proscribed organizations.

Following the British announcement, Canada's Solicitor General, Lawrence MacAulay, said that his ministry was going to introduce legislation to ban charities that raised funds for known terrorist organizations. But his ministry spokesman, Dan Brien, told me he didn't think that terrorist groups could be banned here, as they could be in the United Kingdom, because of the Charter of Rights and Freedoms. "Our conditions here are different in terms of the legislative framework and the Charter of Rights and all that," Brien explained.

As there was a lull in court proceedings involving Malik and Bagri, I decided to fly to England to see what was happening there with the same groups that were operating in Canada. I had heard there was a lot of support for Reyat in his other adopted country and that a powerful Sikh lobby was trying to stop the British Home Secretary from granting Canada permission to charge the former Jaguar plant worker a second time. As well, Surjan Gill had not returned to Canada from his brother's home outside London. My sources told me he feared arrest. I wanted to track him down and ask him about the 1985 bombing.

Gill was an enigma. Clearly he had been one of Parmar's closest associates and an original Khalistani activist. CSIS wiretaps and surveillance showed him to be in the thick of the Air-India plot. But he had backed out at the last minute. If his conscience had got the better of him, the guilt was not so great that he ran to authorities to save 331 lives. He had been on the verge of co-operating with police more than once, but always backed down. Some RCMP officers told me they believed he was someone's agent. They just couldn't figure out whose. Some speculated he was an agent for CSIS, as RCMP interrogators Don Adam and Jim Hunter had suggested to Malik and Bagri. Others believed he was loyal to the government of India.

Many Sikh separatist leaders in Britain had close ties to Malik and Bagri. Dr. Chohan, the grandfather of the movement, had provided the ideological zeal to the Air-India suspects, and members of the Babbar Khalsa and the ISYF had maintained overseas relationships for years. I also wanted to investigate the 1995 murder of Purewal and its possible link to Tara Hayer's killing.

I arrived in London just in time to attend an elegant Vaisakhi celebration at the Palace of Westminster attended by many former members of the now-banned groups and MPs and ministers with a large Punjabi population in their constituencies. As they sipped drinks and munched on Indian finger food, the politicians listened intently as the Sikh leaders made their case for de-proscription. It was as if I were back in British Columbia, watching members of the same groups shaking hands and making donations at fundraising dinners for provincial and federal cabinet ministers.

In the wood-panelled Jubilee Room, Chohan sat on a velvet chair with his white beard loose and flowing. I watched politicians coming up to him, wineglasses in hand, almost bowing in reverence and grasping his left hand in greeting, so as not to touch his artificial right hand. Several promised him they would work to reverse the legislation banning the terrorist groups.

The MPs were not receptive to my questions about ISYF members being convicted in Britain of a plot to kill Rajiv Gandhi, including a man whose brother was running one of the B.C. radio stations that had been the subject of complaints.

Many of the British Khalistani leaders had close connections to their compatriots in Canada. Babbar Khalsa leader Joga Singh of Birmingham told me he had heard Bagri preach and had visited Malik's Surrey school on one of his trips to British Columbia. Former British Babbar Khalsa leader Gurmej Gill had also been to the school and was close to Malik. He refused to see me during my visit to England, cancelling two meetings even after he had agreed to them.

Chohan was more receptive. I had met him years earlier, in 1989, when I was in London for Reyat's extradition hearing. I had kept in touch with him through occasional phone calls whenever issues arose affecting the Sikh community. The soft-spoken doctor invited me to his small sixteenth-floor apartment near Buckingham Palace. There, he told me how he had worked with Air-India suspects Surjan Gill and Talwinder Parmar in the early 1980s. He said that he had even arranged for Parmar's escape from India in 1982 when the Canadian man was wanted on two murder charges. When Parmar was arrested in Germany in 1983, Chohan had pushed for his release, and he had hosted Parmar on his fundraising tour to England in 1992.

But in 2001, Chohan was expressing some concern about his once close relationship with the Babbar Khalsa, especially the Canadian branches. He was disturbed that no one had been charged in the murders of his two old friends Hayer and Purewal.

Purewal's newspaper was fighting a lawsuit in 2001 from an unusual source – Surjan Gill. The newspaper had called Gill an Air-India suspect who was close to Parmar. It was completely accurate, but the truth didn't stop Gill from filing a defamation suit against *Des Pardes* in the Royal Court of Justice, although it never went to trial. I don't know how he thought he could have disputed in court that he was not connected to Parmar, the Babbar Khalsa, or Air-India, considering what was about to come out about him in a Canadian court. It made me wonder whether Gill had made some kind of deal with authorities after his 1996 arrest that would have kept his role in the bombing secret.

He was confident enough to deny his role in his civil suit against *Des Pardes* and its new editor, Gurbax Virk. I had spoken to Gill a couple of times by phone since landing in England, but although he kept promising to call me back and arrange a meeting, he never followed through. The good news about Gill's lawsuit was that his brother's address in Hayes, Middlesex, was printed on the court papers. I could go to see him unannounced.

The predominantly Indian community where Gill lived was about a forty-five-minute train ride from London. I easily found the simple semi-detached brick home and knocked on the front door. Surjan Gill's sister-in-law invited me in and gave me a cup of tea and some biscuits. A pleasant woman offering typically warm Punjabi hospitality, she seemed not at all concerned about a visit from a Canadian journalist in connection with the Air-India case. Gill himself was not there, but she promised me that he would arrive home soon. About forty-five minutes later, I saw him walking down the street – his long white beard recognizable from a distance. He seemed stunned that I had found him. He immediately claimed he had another meeting to go to and hustled me out the front door.

"I'll walk you to the train station," he said, not offering me a choice.

I pulled out my camera and tape recorder, but he put his hand up to gesture no. So I scribbled down notes as I asked him the core questions.

"What about the arrests of your friends in the Air-India case?" I asked.

"I have been instructed by my attorney in Vancouver not to talk," he replied, mentioning that David Gibbons – Reyat's lawyer – was also representing him. "But I am definitely not hiding out."

He claimed that all the news reports suggesting he was a suspect were false and said that he would return to British Columbia soon. I asked him about the Air-India arrests and any role he might have played in plotting the bombing.

"Why should I be afraid?" he said. "So much garbage and lies are going on in the paper. . . . Please look into my heart. I never hide anything. I face any challenge."

He falsely claimed not to have had any contact with the Babbar Khalsa since 1983. But he had been captured on CSIS wiretaps and surveillance meeting and talking to other Babbar Khalsa members both before and after the bombings. "I know people here. I am a well-known person around the world. They honour me as a good person. Sikhs in U.S. and Britain have honoured me for my contributions to the community."

After my visit, Gill went underground. He stayed in England but lowered his profile. He never did make it back to his B.C. home. But he has remained on the radar of the RCMP.

A powerful lobby of British Sikh groups, many of them separatist, prepared petitions and sent off letters in support of Inderjit Reyat and against the Canadian government's request to have the dual citizen charged again. But the British government was not swayed by their arguments. As he completed his last week in jail for his role in the Narita bombing, Reyat received the news that the Home Secretary would allow Canada to charge him in the downing of Air-India Flight 182. He was picked up at his prison about an hour east of Vancouver on June 6, 2001, and driven to B.C. Supreme Court to answer seven new charges in the deaths of 329 people on Air-India Flight 182. He appeared wearing leg shackles before the newly appointed trial judge, Mr. Justice Ian Bruce Josephson.

Reyat had no trouble securing a government deal for legal aid. He had been in jail for more than ten years and even though his wife had defrauded the provincial government of $109,000 in welfare payments between 1991 and 1998, the family did not have sufficient resources to fund the kind of legal dream team that had been assembled by each of the other two defendants.

Reyat's lawyer, Kuldip Chaggar, persuaded constitutional expert David Martin to come on board as head of Reyat's defence. By July, Reyat was telling Martin he wanted to use some of the legal-aid funding to support his family, something that another member of the defence team would later call in a Law Society hearing a "shake-down."

Reyat argued that his wife and four children needed $15,000 a month to survive, which was a little steep given that the family welfare rate had been about $1,200 a month for years. Martin agreed to hire two of Reyat's children at $25 an hour even though they had no experience in the field. That would give the family about $10,000 a month. The commitment would come back to haunt Martin a few months later when the Law Society claimed he had submitted fraudulent bills on behalf of Reyat's children. A subsequent hearing revealed the details of Martin's arrangement with Reyat, which troubled eight lawyers enough to quit the team.

Reyat also asked Martin to hire a friend of his son as an investigator and asked if his old cellmate from the medium-security prison – Larry – could be paid to work on his defence as well. Neither were hired.

Reyat legitimately needed government help to pay for his lawyers. But it was questionable whether Bagri or Malik did. Bagri paid off the mortgage on his house in April 2001, several months after landing in jail (although he did later remortgage the house), and Malik had already claimed in court during his bail hearing that he was worth $10 million clear of debts. Yet all three men received legal aid. They successfully argued that in such an immense case, where the Crown had years to prepare its case at taxpayers' expense, it would not be fair to allow the accused to shoulder the costs of defending themselves.

Reyat was not the only defendant to use public funding to hire a relative. Bagri's team obtained permission to hire his son-in-law, Jaswinder Parmar, to develop a computer program that could manage the massive number of documents in the case. The young man was now working for the legal team that later blamed his late father for the bombing during the trial. Jaswinder was paid about $250,000 for his expertise in computer programming.

Rani called me occasionally in the year after the Air-India arrests. She had really struggled to build a new life in witness protection. I think she just wanted contact with someone who understood her predicament. She told me that I was the only person other than police who would know if something ever happened to her.

We never spoke about her evidence or the upcoming trial. She would ask me about my kids, I would ask about hers. I had never known where she was, but at one point, she ran into a former

Khalsa School teacher in her new hometown. The news quickly circulated back to the Lower Mainland, and I made sure she knew so that she could move to another town in order to protect herself and her child. She moved.

A few months after the charges were laid, defence lawyers were told by the Crown that Rani had once confided in me about Malik's confession to her. They wanted to know if I had notes of our conversations from 1997 and 1998. The RCMP delivered a letter, written by lead prosecutor Bob Wright, to our newsroom. I was alarmed. I felt like I was going to get drawn into the case as a witness whether I liked it or not.

I also had a visit around this time from Cpl. Doug Best, the task-force member who had been dealing with Rani. He asked me if I had been talking to her and I refused to tell him. He tried to interview me about what I knew regarding her Air-India evidence. He was surprisingly aggressive and I was instantly defensive. I said I would not confirm or deny anything. He also asked for my notes and I told him the newspaper's policy was never to turn over anything without a court order. He left empty-handed.

I talked to managing editor Patricia Graham and our lawyer, Rob Anderson. I told them that I didn't think I had written any notes about what she had said in connection with Air-India. I wouldn't have wanted a record of that because I could never have used it in an article. Nor would I have wanted to scare Rani off by making notes in front of her.

In Canada, when a jury trial is in the offing and a source is already known to be a police witness, a journalist can be charged with contempt of court if she publishes information that could give rise to a real risk of prejudicing a fair trial for the accused.

Anderson called Bellows, the Crown prosecutor, to see what was going on. Bellows said that he did not intend to call me as a witness, but that the defence might want to. I was horrified. I had resisted the Crown's attempts to get me to co-operate for almost three years and now I was worried the defence might call me.

I was concerned not because I had done anything wrong, but because no reporter likes to find herself in someone else's story. Our job is to scrutinize, not to become the object of scrutiny. I knew that if I were subpoenaed as a witness, I would not be able to cover the case I had spent seventeen years working on. The prospect was depressing.

After Best's visit to my newsroom, I didn't hear from Rani for more than three years. I didn't know what they had told her. I had a pain in the pit of my stomach that lasted for months.

Pre-trial motions got underway in the spring of 2002, a year before the trial was set to begin. Most of the material was banned from publication, so reporters did not spend much time in the courtroom, despite the fact that some of the most interesting material came out during this phase of the case.

The Crown tried to get Justice Josephson to allow the evidence against Bagri for the 1988 Hayer shooting to be used at the Air-India trial. The key piece of evidence was Hayer's statements about overhearing Bagri's alleged confession to the bombings. The Crown also offered statements from Sukhminder Cheema, the journalist who had also been threatened. He said that Bagri had told a July 1992 meeting in Surrey that he had convinced the shooter to come to Canada from Pakistan to assist the Sikh community by killing Hayer.

But Josephson wasn't buying. He called the Hayer case against Bagri weak, said Cheema was unreliable, and that the evidence was too "highly prejudicial" to use in the Air-India case.

"The attempted murder is a chilling crime which would tend to show a disposition towards extreme violence," Josephson said in a decision that sent an early signal about which way he was going to go.

Maybe the evidence would have been prejudicial had there been a jury, but there was no jury when the trial got underway. Josephson alone would preside over the trial and he already knew about Hayer's statements to police.

Josephson also claimed in his ruling that the Crown's theory was flawed. He said prosecutors believed that Harkirat Bagga worked with Bagri to silence Hayer in 1988 because of an article Hayer had written that stated Bagri had confessed to a role in the bombings.

"The Crown theory is that Mr. Bagri was involved in the attempted murder of Mr. Hayer in an effort to silence him as a witness," Josephson wrote. "The basis of that theory is an article written on August 19, 1988, three days before the shooting. However the alleged conspiracy or plan formulated by Mr. Bagri and Mr. Bagga was initiated many months prior to that article being published. There is no other evidence to support the Crown's theory. As well, there is no evidence either that Mr. Hayer was a witness or that Mr. Bagri believed that he was a witness in relation to Air India/Narita at the time Mr. Bagga shot him in August 1988."

That portion of the ruling contained two errors. The August 19 article was published a full week before the August 26 shooting – not three days, as Josephson said. And there was other evidence that Bagri had known Hayer was going public with the confession – Hayer had first written about Bagri's alleged confession in September 1987 in his *New Horizons* magazine – almost a year before he was shot and just before Bagga and Bagri met in Pakistan. That article, in which Hayer declared war on Bagri by mentioning a confession heard by "at least four others," was among the court documents before Josephson.

While Hayer may not have been a witness in the legal sense back in 1988, Bagri knew then of the open and ongoing contempt

Hayer had displayed in his newspaper for him and the other Babbar Khalsa members. Hayer's public reference to the alleged confession would have been a shock – a potentially fatal breach in the wall of silence. The news would have spread like wildfire among the conspirators. All of them would have known at once that Hayer had to be silenced. And yet, when it came to court, Hayer's account of Bagri's alleged confession – a sworn and videotaped account, from a former separatist sympathizer, that dovetailed perfectly with the other evidence – was ruled out.

The judge also decided that the attempted murder of an Air-India witness would take up too much of the Air-India proceeding "with the potential of significantly diverting the trial." I was extremely disappointed. Hayer had lost his life for nothing. His evidence would not count in the final analysis.

Just a month later, in June 2002, Josephson again sided with Bagri's defence team when he ruled that Bagri's Charter rights had been violated by the long-ago erasures of the CSIS tapes of Parmar's calls. It didn't matter that the Crown and RCMP believed the tapes would have made their case much easier against both Bagri and Malik. It didn't matter that, when Reyat's lawyers tried the same line during his 1991 trial, another B.C. Supreme Court Judge, Raymond Paris, concluded that the erasures did not negatively impact on the Crown's case at all. But Josephson declared that those same erasures made Bagri, the man who had called for the murder of fifty thousand Hindus, a victim of "unacceptable negligence."

In September 2002, a source told me that Hardial Johal, one of the unindicted suspects, was critically ill. I thought about doing a story and called the RCMP to see if the task force was able to get anything out of Johal. Or were deathbed confessions something that happened only in the movies? John Schneider told me they would go to see him.

Within two months, Johal was on life support at Vancouver
General Hospital, suffering from liver failure. I got a call from
Schneider, asking if I thought he should talk to Johal.

"You mean you didn't talk to him before?" I asked. "He's in
a coma. It's too late."

The RCMP had missed a golden opportunity. Johal was
unplugged from life support on November 15, with about thirty
relatives and supporters in the room. Even though he had been
an Air-India suspect for seventeen years, members of the legislative assembly, a provincial cabinet minister, and other politicians
crowded into his funeral, where they vied for the microphone.

Johal, the man seen at Vancouver International Airport the day
the bombs were sent, the man who met Talwinder Parmar repeatedly in the days before the murders, the man whose old phone
number had been given when the tickets were booked, had no
shortage of high-profile friends willing to praise him in death.
Some had even spoken earlier the same day at a memorial service
for Tara Hayer. Herb Dhaliwal, then a federal Liberal minister,
was unable to make Johal's funeral, but he sent a letter of con-
dolence, in which he described the suspected terrorist as a friend.
A second service for Johal was held the same day at the Khalsa
School in Surrey.

I was desperate to return to India before the trial, which was
slated to open in March 2003. I wanted to track the roots of the
story and see how life in Punjab had changed since I was there
in the late 1980s. The first week of February 2003 was abuzz with
Air-India rumours. A police contact told me to wait before
getting a ticket – something big was about to break.

On Thursday, February 6, Dave Hayer called me. He didn't want
to talk on the phone but asked me to drive out to Surrey immediately. Behind the closed door of his MLA office, he told me that
he had received a call from the RCMP. Investigators had reached

a deal with Reyat. He was going to plead guilty on Monday to manslaughter. I told him I had heard from sources that something was up. I felt pure joy. "Yes!" I exclaimed. "I can't believe it."

But Hayer quickly cautioned that the deal was not fantastic, that Reyat had not agreed to testify against the other two, and would likely be released from prison very soon.

"Then what is the point?" I asked.

Police had explained to Hayer that the plea would mean the Crown would not have to prove at Malik and Bagri's trial that a bomb brought down Air-India Flight 182, something that would have taken months of expert testimony in court to demonstrate. I was eager to publish the story of Reyat's plea bargain and I pestered his lawyers. But they warned that even a hint of the deal getting out could kill it. It would not be official until it was announced in court on February 10.

The courtroom was packed hours before Reyat was due to arrive and enter his new plea. He walked in smiling and shook hands with his lawyers and the sheriffs. A brief statement of his guilt was read by lead prosecutor Bob Wright. In it, Reyat agreed that in May and June, 1985, he purchased materials that were then used to build the bomb that destroyed the Air-India flight. But he claimed not to know that the bomb was going to be placed in an aircraft, or that human beings were going to be targeted.

"Mr. Reyat was told and believed that the explosive devices would be transported to India in order to blow up property such as a car, a bridge or something heavy," Wright said. "Although Mr. Reyat acquired the materials for this purpose, he did not make or arm an explosive device, nor did he place an explosive device on an airplane, nor does he know who did or did not do so."

The statement of fact also claimed that Reyat did not "intend by his actions to cause death to any person or believe that such consequences were likely to occur. However, unbeknownst to

Mr. Reyat, the items that he acquired were used by another person or persons to help make an explosive device that, on and about June 23, 1985, destroyed Air-India Flight 182, killing all 329 aboard."

Chief Justice Donald Brenner sentenced Reyat to five years, which I quickly calculated to be five and a half days per victim. Some family members were outraged. Some were resigned and sad. Few had had advance warning of the controversial plea bargain.

Perviz Madon and her children, Natasha and Eddie, now both adults, came to court to hear Reyat admit his guilt in person. They wanted to be there in memory of Sam. The Madons had so often been the face of the victims for us. But this was a hard day for them. Natasha broke down in tears as the proceedings concluded. Eddie comforted her in the courtroom.

While political commentators across the country attacked the Reyat plea, Malik and Bagri re-elected to be tried by judge alone. Reyat had been holding out for a jury trial – having been convicted by a judge in 1991. The other two preferred a judge to preside over their fate – especially in a post–9/11 world where many North Americans were suspicious of religions they did not understand. Some now unfairly equated beards and turbans with terrorism.

Hundreds of people who had received jury notices for the Air-India trial were relieved at the change. So were the lawyers on both sides involved in the case. They knew that a jury trial would have been unmanageable. There would have been much risk of a mistrial.

Suddenly journalists could get their hands on all kinds of material from two and a half years of court hearings outlining much of the Crown's case. They ran no risk of publishing material that would prejudice a jury, and the law deems that a judge cannot be influenced by news stories.

In late February, headlines across the country screamed that both Malik and Bagri had "confessed" their involvement to various friends and associates over the years. But we also published disturbing details about witnesses being paid and about the lack of any direct evidence. Never before in Canadian jurisprudence had so much evidence been published before a trial. Even the Crown prosecutors seemed startled by the volume of material coming out. Their concern led them swiftly back to court, where they got everything sealed again just ten days after it was opened.

Unable to publish much in Canada, I persuaded my editors to send me back to India for the first time since 1989, when I'd undertaken my second futile search for Talwinder Parmar. Before leaving, I visited the Surrey home of Narinder Gill, one of the Crown witnesses, to tell him about my trip. He said his house had been targeted by a shooting just days earlier and that the task force was looking into it. He took me down to the basement where the RCMP had installed thirteen monitors and VCRs connected to thirteen cameras. Even with all that hardware, a gunman had been able to get near enough undetected to shoot out the windows of Gill's family car.

It felt good to return to India on the eve of the trial. I was sure people there would speak more frankly about events, now that it was almost twenty years since they happened.

In New Delhi, I was able to meet Jagdish Sharma, who had been the consul general in Vancouver through the most tumultuous stretch of the investigation from 1984 to 1988. Of all the postings he had in his diplomatic career, he had been most at risk in Vancouver. His children had been escorted to school daily by the RCMP. He had faced threats, sit-ins, an office attack, and protests at his home and at the consulate. And he had watched in frustration as the Canadian police seriously investigated charges that the Indian government had blown up its own plane.

"I knew that this was a movement of misguided people with a lot of violence, and they were able to hijack the community and feed them propaganda that was not correct," he told me. "In the garb of human rights, you had plain and simple terrorist organizations, militant and separatist organizations. They abused the forum of human rights, and they were very successful in it."

I travelled next to Punjab. Outside the Golden Temple complex in Amritsar, I saw no sign of the separatist movement that had once flourished here. Pilgrims held up fists of rupees, ready to barter at one of the many shops for velvet-covered ceremonial swords or brightly back-lit electric photos of the stunning gilt-domed complex. Worshippers mingled with tourists crowding through marble entrances to get a glimpse of the temple itself and the shimmering pools of water that surround it. Inside, it was so serene that it was hard to picture how it must have been, nineteen years earlier, when a rising Sikh separatist movement headed by Jarnail Bhindranwale – a martyr to some and terrorist to others – took over this complex. Inside its walls, he and his automatic-weapon-toting supporters had amassed an arsenal.

A short distance from the temple, I found the multi-storey building the size of a city block that was owned by Malik's Satnam Trust, according to the staff members there. Rani had told me about the building. She had never visited Punjab or seen the building, but Malik had described it to her perfectly. The staff at Satnam Trust took me to meet Bhai Jiwan Singh, the Akhand Kirtani Jatha leader who had baptized Malik and remained his spiritual leader. He was living in a comfortable multi-level home a short walk away from the Golden Temple down ancient, narrow streets. A brand-new Jeep was parked outside the house.

I wanted to ask Singh hard questions about his long association with Malik, but he could barely speak, still ailing from a
stroke that had made him bedridden. His wife, Bibiji, would only
say, "Malik never did anything. All he did was *sewa* [service],
nothing else."

When I asked about the Air–India case, she replied, "We heard
about it. But we don't know anything about it."

It was hard to find anyone still committed to the separate
country of Khalistan in the Punjab of 2003. In the lush agricul-
tural state where I had gained so much insight into the separatist
movement on my trips as a rookie reporter in 1986, 1988, and
1989, I was now the expert.

People questioned me about the Air–India case and the groups
that had wreaked so much havoc: the Babbar Khalsa, the Khalistan
Commando Force, and the International Sikh Youth Federation.
Many of the separatist leaders who had been in exile or in jail were
now back in Punjab living openly and peacefully, including Dr,
Chohan, who first preached separation thirty years earlier and who
had helped a young Talwinder Parmar when he needed to escape
India in 1982.

Chohan warmly welcomed me to his humble house in the
town of Tanda, where he had run his own hospital when he was
forced into exile in 1980. He had finally returned to India shortly
after I saw him in London in 2001. He founded a new separatist
political party, but it did not seem to have much zeal. Chohan
openly admitted the movement had been ruined by the violence
of some of the groups, including Parmar's. "You can't build a
country with violence. It should be done with logic, by constitutional means," Chohan said.

He remained close to Simranjit Singh Mann – the last elected
Khalistani politician, who also admitted the movement no longer

had support in the countryside because of the violence of some of its leaders in the 1980s,

"They started raping girls, abducting the girls, looting the people. Once a militant movement loses its high moral ground, it is going to fail," Mann told me.

Jasbir Singh Rode, Bhindranwale's nephew, echoed Mann's sentiments when I visited him in his large, comfortable home in Jalandhar. He had also returned from England, where he co-founded the International Sikh Youth Federation with Vancouver resident Harpal Nagra.

"The movement was fore-doomed because we were not well organized, we had no country to back us," he said. "There was no public opinion in our favour. We were taken full advantage of by the Indian intelligence agencies who infiltrated our ranks, manipulated our members. Killings and counter-killings were organized and the blame was put at the door of the Sikh movement in all cases."

These few remaining Khalistani leaders blamed former Punjab police chief K.P.S. Gill for the brutality with which he crushed their movement between 1988 and 1992 without regard for human rights.

Gill agreed to meet me at the Punjab Armed Police officers' mess in Jalandhar. There, junior officers bowed before the retired chief in reverence, touching his feet. Later that evening, they danced the bhangra for him as he sipped scotch under a tent on the manicured lawns of the mess. Gill told old war stories – impatient at the questions about human-rights violations from a Canadian journalist.

"When we were fighting terrorism, the British government would come and lecture me about human rights. The Americans would come and lecture me about human rights," Gill complained as his entourage nodded in agreement. When a general is at war, he doesn't go off and check the manual to see what to do, Gill explained. When terrorism was at its height here, it was a war. He said his police had fought it all on their own. The courts had not helped, the magistrates had not helped.

The police force also suffered immensely. More than eighteen hundred members were killed by terrorists, Gill said. So many died that he opened a special school for their children.

"What would happen in Canada if eighteen hundred policemen were killed?" he asked.

It helped in dealing with the separatists that he was a proud Punjabi, a Sikh. "I could understand the Sikh mind better," he said. "Being a Sikh, it was easier to crush this movement."

I told him bluntly that the RCMP had information that his police force had tortured and killed Parmar. He acted surprised, but I don't think he was. He claimed to have been sitting in police headquarters in Jalandhar when he got the news Parmar had been killed in an encounter with police. He had visited the site of the attack.

"To me it looked very genuine. There was no sign of torture. The body was lying there. He was wearing clothes," he said. "The Canadians made a big fuss about Parmar. He was totally insignificant as a leader here."

A few days later, I returned to Parmar's village, Panshta, where many still admire his leadership. Someone was being allowed to live rent-free in his old house, as his family did not want to charge rent and profit from Parmar's sacrifices.

Bagri's village, Chak Kalan, is not far away. I travelled there by rented car and asked around for his family home. Within minutes I was led there and introduced to Bagri's younger brother, the village leader Piara, and Bagri's elderly parents. They spoke of how weak the case against Bagri was and their hope that he would be acquitted. They said that he called them regularly from jail and always seemed optimistic.

It was harder to find the Malik family home in the city of Ferozpur. A friend of Malik in Vancouver said that it had long since been sold. But Rani once told me that Malik had described to her the beautiful mansion near the Pakistani border that had a swimming pool and gardens. I was determined to find it.

With the help of several contacts, I was taken to the gas station and pharmacy where Malik had worked as a youth. The new owner mentioned that the Malik family still had a house nearby by and pointed me in the right direction. Within an hour, I was at the gate of the estate introducing myself to Malik's aunts. The property was exactly as Rani had described it – stunning gardens, a pool, and a large home. I was grinning as I stood at the wall to the grounds, with "Malik's" clearly marked in black ink. I wished I could have told her that I had followed her tip to the other side of the world and it checked out.

Malik's two elderly aunts invited me in for tea and told me how Malik had always been a good boy. They said that they prayed every day for his release from jail.

When I was in India, I also visited some of the families of the victims. Many of them, including Amarjit Bhinder, the co-pilot's wife, had been kept in the dark about developments in the case. They knew there had been arrests, but details about the upcoming trial were scarce in Punjab. They lived in isolation from each other and from the victims' families in Canada.

It occurred to me as I travelled from village to village that the story I had so associated with the conflict in Punjab was no longer an Indian story. The answers to what had happened were not in the lush wheat fields of Punjab. They were back home in places like Surrey and Vancouver and Mississauga.

CHAPTER 10

Trial of the Century

T HE MOST ANTICIPATED TRIAL in Canadian history began
April 28, 2003, in a specially built $7.3-million high-security
room in the Vancouver Law Courts at 800 Smithe Street. The win-
dowless underground courtroom was a stark contrast to the all-glass
building designed by renowned architect Arthur Erickson.
Courtroom 20 was packed with families of the bombing victims,
supporters of the two accused men, media from around the world,
and a few high-profile members of the Indo-Canadian community who felt they had to be there. One veteran journalist observed
that the courtroom was like a bad basement renovation – low ceil-
ings, red wall-to-wall carpeting, and too much wood panelling.

Reporters wore special photo identification and everyone had
to pass through metal detectors and other security checks before
being allowed into the courtroom. Seats were colour-coded for
different groups. The courtroom, which had 143 seats in three
sections, had space enough to keep those who believed the
accused killed their relatives far away from those who believed
Malik and Bagri were innocents being persecuted by the

Canadian government, just as they had been by the Indian government.

The two accused wore traditional Punjabi clothes. They waved and smiled at supporters as they were led into their bulletproof prisoners' box by a small army of gun-toting sheriffs.

About a dozen senior RCMP investigators were also present, including Assistant Commissioner Gary Bass and Staff Sgt. Doug Henderson, who first interviewed Inderjit Reyat in 1985. Family members of the victims shook hands with victorious-looking police officers.

Eddie Madon, the young accountant who was just a boy when his father, Sam, was killed, said he was glad the day had finally come. Malik's lawyer son, Jaspreet, optimistically predicted to reporters that his father would be vindicated and freed within the year.

Malik and Bagri each repeated the words *not guilty* eight times as the indictment was read aloud. It was the only time we would hear their voices at the trial, as neither man spoke in his own defence.

With pomp and ceremony and not an empty seat in the house, the trial got underway. Lead prosecutor Bob Wright was the first to stand up. He is larger than life – an imposing, wide-shouldered man, who has to be six-foot-four. He told Justice Josephson that Inderjit Reyat and his wife, Satnam, would both be called to testify. Satnam Reyat was then brought into the courtroom and the judge ordered her to appear again in September to take the stand. My journalist colleagues and I were all surprised. Did that mean there was a deal with the Reyats to co-operate, to tell the truth at last?

Wright then laid out the Crown's case against Malik and Bagri, which he said had been broken into five chapters for ease of presentation. There were few surprises in what he told the court, since we in the media had successfully fought to get access to pretrial documents in the wake of Reyat's guilty plea. What was dramatic was that the trial was happening at all. So many pundits had predicted the case would never make it to trial. Others had claimed that charges would never be laid. Yet there we were. There was a sense of the historical significance of the moment.

In his summary, Wright said that the Crown would show that Malik and Bagri conspired with the late Babbar Khalsa leader Talwinder Parmar and "others unknown" to bomb planes from the national airline of India in retaliation for the Indian Army's attack a year earlier on the Golden Temple.

Although Parmar had been killed by Indian police in 1992, his involvement in the conspiracy would still be part of the Crown's case. Wright promised that one witness would describe how Parmar threatened to kill him if he did not change statements he had given to the police about driving him to Duncan in 1985 to do test blasts. He called Rani the "lynchpin" of the Crown's case and described the confessions she said Malik had made to her.

As for Bagri, Wright said, "the evidence will show that Mr. Bagri was a militant Sikh terrorist. Mr. Bagri was intent on the violent overthrow of the Indian government." He referred to Bagri's videotaped statements calling for revenge made in the months before the bombings. And he paid tribute to the heroic men and women who participated in the recovery efforts off the coast of Ireland.

In an unusual move, after Wright had finished, the defence teams also chose to make brief opening remarks, given the unprecedented nature of the case and the horrific act that had led to it.

Malik's counsel, David Crossin, began. The slim, balding mid-fifties lawyer with slightly hunched shoulders calmly suggested that the massive media interest in the Air-India bombings for almost two decades was one reason the testimony of witnesses was suspect. All of the information being provided by witnesses against his client was available on the public record, both in book form and in newspaper articles, he claimed. But I and the other reporters had already heard in pretrial hearings of the alleged confessions of both Malik and Bagri described to police by key witnesses. Crossin was wrong. Most of the details of those confessions were never published in any form prior to the arrests of the two men in 2000, with the exception of Hayer's 1987 and 1988 articles.

Crossin's next comment hit a little close to home.

"The evidence will show that various people in the media were in close contact with the police," Crossin said.

I was the only journalist he named. He then suggested, as my cheeks burned and I stared down at my notebook, that he might call me as a witness to explain my relationship with police and with Rani. He quickly added he would not ask me to leave the courtroom as witnesses are normally required to do. Not just yet anyway.

I felt that I had been slimed. The innuendo was that I had not acted professionally, even though he knew from prosecutors that I had refused to co-operate with them or to be interviewed by the RCMP. Yet court procedures did not permit me to defend myself. And I had the spectre hanging over me that I could be subpoenaed at any moment and lose my chance to cover the story I had been on since 1985. I thought it was very dirty.

Crossin described Rani as a disgruntled ex-employee who was so hostile to Malik that she had filed a human-rights complaint as well as a civil suit. "She expressed bitterness, anger, and hatred towards Mr. Malik," Crossin said.

He also took time to acknowledge the magnitude of the Air-India disaster: "The most difficult challenge that we have faced —

and will continue to face throughout – is the constant presence of the palpable horror of this alleged crime."

Then Richard Peck, lead counsel for Bagri, got up to speak. The veteran trial lawyer said his client was not present at any of the main events leading up to the twin bombings. There is "no scintilla of evidence that Bagri was involved," Peck claimed. He said the two main witnesses against Bagri – a man called John, who went home with a cheque worth $460,000, and Premika, the woman who was now denying what she had told investigators – could not be believed.

Known for his sharp wit and skilful cross-examination, the bald, round-faced lawyer previewed the tack his team would take in the months ahead. The brightest legal minds in the province, if not the country, were assembled in the courtroom on opening day. The all-star teams would not disappoint in the historic trial.

That opening day gave journalists a taste of the drama and hyperbole that was yet to come. There were many fewer of us in court by day two of the trial. But I was there, in the seat directly behind Malik that would become my regular spot.

From intriguing hints of the tales of love, betrayal, and confessions we'd heard on the first day, on day two the trial took a sudden turn and delved into the mundane details of airline ticket purchases, baggage check-ins, and airport security. One by one, an array of employees who had worked for the now-defunct CP Air took the stand. Among them was the delightful Martine Donahue, looking much younger than her seventy-seven years. She testified about getting the original call from a man named Mr. Singh on June 19, 1985, at 5:52 p.m. He sounded like a mature man with an East Indian accent and he was booking tickets for two friends heading in opposite directions around the globe. Their names were Mohinderbel Singh and Jaswant Singh, he

had told her. But the man was concerned about the connection
Donahue found him through Montreal. The CP Air flight arrived
at Dorval, while Air-India Flight 182 left from Mirabel, an hour's
drive away. That would have meant the man had to pick up his
luggage in Montreal, Donahue explained.

Airline computer reservations expert Paul Downs testified
about the records he reviewed regarding the two tickets. Someone
had called on June 20 and changed the names on the tickets from
Mohinderbel to L. Singh and Jaswant to M. Singh. The destinations were also changed, Downs said. The CP Air ticket to
Montreal was instead booked through Toronto. The ticket to Asia
was changed from a Hong Kong connection to Tokyo. The
contact number was also changed, he said.

Jeanne Bakermans, who had gone to work at the Vancouver
airport on her day off, testified that she argued with "an East
Indian man" with shaggy hair and a medium build. He had bright,
sparkly eyes and his English was quite good, she said. He wanted
to check his bag through to the Air-India flight out of Toronto,
without a confirmed reservation. She said she finally relented and
allowed him to "inter-line" his suitcase because he was holding
up a queue of thirty and kept insisting he had paid business class
to get the confirmation.

The evidence painted a picture of air travel in pre-terrorism
Canada, where ticket agents allowed third-party callers to book
international tickets over the phone, using incomplete names.
Changes to the tickets, including the names on them, did not raise
suspicions. And a traveller needed to arrive at the airport only an
hour before an international flight to pick up a ticket and check
in bags without showing any identification. There were no
quizzes about whether you packed your own suitcase.

While much of the evidence was long known by most of us
who had been on the story, it was frustrating to hear how easily

things could have gone differently. Because Air-India had faced threats, an X-ray machine was used by the airline to check bags in Toronto, including luggage on connecting flights. But fate would have it that it broke down on June 22, not long before the bomb-laden suitcase was loaded. A hand-held sniffer device was brought in to replace it, but it was later learned the machine was more likely to have been triggered by curry powder than dynamite.

The Air-India bombing had been the biggest story for years for journalists like me. As excited as I was to cover the trial, it was soon bogged down by minutia to the point where my colleagues and I wondered if we could really stick it out for more than a year. All the hype of the first few days evaporated. Editors were less interested in the stories we were filing. On some days, even the families of the victims and the accused found it too boring to stay. And then there were the breaks. Court would start at 10:00 a.m. By 11:15, the morning break would begin. Every day, Justice Josephson said, "Fifteen minutes" as we stood up. Every day, the breaks lasted at least half an hour. On the fullest of days, court would be in session for four and a half hours total.

But there was also an unusual sense of camaraderie among the regular journalists: me, Terry Milewski of CBC's *The National*, Robert Matas of the *Globe and Mail*, and Camille Bains from Canadian Press. We went for coffee together. We debated and discussed the evidence we had heard. And we banded together to fight for access to documents and exhibits, hiring lawyers when necessary.

We soon developed a routine. All the sheriffs knew us by name as we passed through the metal detector every morning and every afternoon. We'd greet the lawyers from both sides as they arrived. We'd see which family members from the victims or the suspects were there each day.

One of the touching moments of the early weeks was when the British and Irish rescue crews encountered the victims' relatives in the courtroom lobby. They began by shaking hands, but soon they were hugging each other.

I was surprised by how emotional the rescue workers were on the witness stand when talking about events from almost two decades earlier. Michael Quinn, the Irish air traffic controller who last communicated with the ill-fated flight, broke down as the tape was played of his conversation with the pilot minutes before the deadly blast.

British seaman Daniel Brown also wept as he testified about holding some of the victims' bodies in his arms but being unable to pull them from the water into the boat. Sean Murphy, the Irish lifeboat captain, testified about leaving mass and spending six hours racing to the scene. And how the boat had run low on fuel as he and his crew recovered the remains of three women, a man, and a little girl.

James Robinson, second-in-command of the Irish Navy, recalled how emotions were running high on his vessel as he and his crew surveyed the waters where the plane had dived into the Atlantic and they saw bodies everywhere. And winch man Mark Tait, of Britain's Royal Air Force, described in painful detail how he was lowered from a helicopter on a cable into the ocean and grasped the bloody and oil-covered corpses with his legs in an attempt to recover them.

So grateful were the relatives that they asked Victims' Services to arrange a more substantial meeting the third week of May, just before the rescuers returned home. Over tea, the relatives thanked the men they considered heroes for their efforts on June 23, 1985. Until that point, nobody had ever thanked Daniel Brown. Nor had he known about the memorial in Ireland that was attended yearly by the relatives. He pledged to make the journey to west Cork and to return to Canada for the verdict.

The gripping testimony was the most dramatic in the first month of the trial. It was also devastating for the relatives who sat through it. But the graphic details did not appear to affect either Malik or Bagri. Malik could be seen dosing off repeatedly. While witnesses spoke, he often read from a Punjabi-language prayer book that he carefully wrapped in cloth after each use. Sometimes he would finger loose strands of hair that had fallen from his turban and tuck them back. Bagri appeared to pay more attention. He sat there beside a Punjabi interpreter and listened to the evidence. But he expressed no emotion and would sometimes cast his eyes downward for long stretches.

The horror of the bombing was apparent, but there was very little in the evidence presented in the opening weeks of the trial that linked Malik and Bagri to the terrorist plot. Their lawyers did acknowledge that both men had been photographed by CSIS meeting together in the days before and after the murders. The defence also acknowledged a flurry of phone calls, some of which seemed suspicious in nature, that had been made in the same period among Malik, Bagri, Reyat, Parmar, and others believed to be involved in the plot. But there was no smoking gun, no single piece of forensic evidence that pointed unwaveringly at the two men in the prisoner's box.

The Crown may have made a fatal error in the way it presented the part of its case that linked the two men with Parmar and Reyat. Instead of bringing in witnesses to testify about the phone calls and reports by CSIS, the prosecution reached an agreement with the defence to admit certain facts about the calls and the CSIS surveillance photos. Wright read the admissions into the court record on Friday, May 23 – less than a month into the trial.

He said Malik had been photographed by CSIS at Parmar's Burnaby house on June 18, 1985 – four days before the bomb-laden suitcases were checked in at the airport. Bagri, long known as a Parmar associate, was seen by CSIS with Parmar at Vancouver International Airport on June 9, 1985, after both men arrived on a flight from Toronto. Parmar's wife, Surinder, picked the pair up, dropping Bagri at the Vancouver home of Premika, the woman who would later testify for the Crown.

In addition to the sightings of Malik and Bagri with Parmar, the vehicles of both accused men were also seen at Parmar's house on other occasions in the weeks before the bombings, Wright said. On May 21, 1985, at 8:20 p.m., Malik's beige Volvo station wagon, bearing a vanity plate in the name of his company, Papillon Eastern Imports Ltd., was parked unoccupied directly in front of Parmar's Burnaby house.

Malik drove the same car back to the house on the evening of June 18, and another car belonging to the late Hardial Johal also arrived at Parmar's home. CSIS couldn't say for sure if it was Johal driving, so they called him an "unknown male." A witness at trial later looked at the picture and positively identified Johal for Josephson.

Bagri's yellow Pontiac was seen at Parmar's house again on June 21. CSIS referred to the driver as an "unknown male," but the defence had got the Crown to describe the driver in the admissions as "an unknown East Indian male who was not Mr. Bagri and who has not been subsequently identified." This admission would come back to haunt the Crown later in the trial, preventing them from corroborating other evidence that strongly suggested Bagri was in Vancouver on the eve of the deadly terrorist attack.

Justice Josephson sent signals from day one of the trial that he appreciated every effort on the part of both the Crown and the defence to reduce the number of witnesses and simplify the enormous case. The prosecution took his words to heart and repeatedly removed names from the witness list. In place of testimony, the court heard admissions – all agreed to by the defence and the Crown in meetings held away from court and away from the scrutiny of regular Air-India watchers like me.

Witnesses are more powerful than written admissions. Things come out during testimony that are not always clear when evidence is reduced to a few lines or a few paragraphs agreed to by both sides. Crown witnesses, like the CSIS agents who watched Parmar's house on June 21, 1985, might have been able to clarify any confusion about exactly what they saw. All lengthy criminal cases are streamlined to keep the proceedings on track, but in the Air-India trial, we would later suspect enough evidence was edited out of the Crown's case to have swayed the verdict.

The removal of witnesses left large gaps in the trial schedule. So instead of continuing through that first summer, the trial broke for what turned out to be three months.

We fed the appetite for Air-India stories that summer by fighting to get access to more of the restricted material that had been sealed until the beginning of the trial. We ended up getting partial transcripts of the first interviews with Malik, Bagri, and Johal after their 2000 arrests and one held with Reyat when he was charged for the second time in June 2001. We also got a flurry of newly released memos in which RCMP officials were accusing CSIS of hampering the investigation from day one.

But the most explosive detail came from the interrogations of Malik and Bagri when the veteran RCMP interviewers – Don Adam and Jim Hunter – each suggested that Surjan Gill had been a CSIS mole. They went on to suggest that he had pulled out of the plot at the last minute because the spy agency could not have been seen to have allowed the bombings to happen.

It was a bombshell. When I called them to get their response to his allegation, both the RCMP and CSIS immediately denied having an inside informant. My RCMP sources told me that the interrogators were merely using a common technique: trying to elicit a response from the suspects by suggesting they had been duped by a government agent.

When news of this was broadcast, there was a new round of calls by politicians and family members for a public inquiry. There were angry denials from Solicitor General Wayne Easter that CSIS might have had an agent in the middle of the terrorist conspiracy. But the denial left many unanswered questions about the role of the mysterious Mr. Gill. How was he able to leave Canada right before the arrests of his former associates? Did he have advance knowledge that charges were imminent? Why was he never charged? And why did so many RCMP officers with years of experience on the Air-India case still have suspicions that he was an agent for some country, if not CSIS.

All the Air-India reporters were scrambling to get to the truth. It was already apparent after the first month of the trial that much of the material gathered during the RCMP investigation would not come out in public. But the problem with this round of released documents, as it was on other occasions, was the lack of context. Reporters, me included, would focus on the one recently released memo written fifteen years earlier and not even get a chance to look at another thousand or so memos that might have contradicted the one.

We did find information in the documents that CSIS had been talking to Ujjal Dosanjh. When I spoke with him, Dosanjh explained that CSIS approached him after he had provided information to the Vancouver police about two militant Sikhs from India having been in the B.C. area just before the bombings. Dosanjh said it was no secret that he had expressed his concerns to government about the potential violence of Sikh militants.

Ironically, while CBC journalist Terry Milewski was at Dosanjh's law office interviewing him about the latest revelations, Surjan Gill – the man everyone was looking for – phoned from England to talk to another lawyer in the office about some documents that needed signing in Vancouver. He was still a client of Dosanjh's law firm.

RCMP Assistant Commissioner Gary Bass later told me adamantly that Gill was not a CSIS agent. But that didn't rule out the possibility that Gill was working for the Indian government, Bass said.

Despite the media fascination with the CSIS memos and interrogations of the accused, the defence lawyers never suggested when the trial resumed months later that Canada's spy agency or the government of India had anything to do with the bombings, even though it had been a common refrain from some Sikh separatists over the years. The defence teams accepted, while denying the involvement of their clients, that the bombings had been carried out by militant Canadian Sikh separatists associated with the Babbar Khalsa.

Just as the furor over the CSIS memos calmed down, the federal government announced that it was, at long last, placing the Babbar Khalsa and International Sikh Youth Federation on the list of organizations banned in Canada. This was eighteen years after the Air-India bombing and seventeen years after members of the ISYF plotted the assassination of a visiting Punjabi cabinet minister. It was so Canadian.

The Air-India trial adjourned in the third week of June for a long summer recess. Or so we thought. By accident, I discovered a secret hearing was continuing under Canada's new anti-terrorism law that was indelibly linked to the bombing case.

On June 27, 2003, I made a routine stop at the courthouse to pick up some documents from the registry and paused to chat with my colleague Neal Hall in the building's lobby when Bob Wright walked by. I knew he was working exclusively on the Air-India case, so I asked him why he was there.

"Is there something going on?"

"Nothing for you," he replied as he headed for the elevator.

A couple of minutes later, Malik's lawyer, Bill Smart, wandered in. He was quickly followed by Michael Code, the Toronto lawyer from Bagri's team. If that wasn't enough to signal that something was up, seconds later in walked Hans Van Iperen, legal counsel to CSIS. None of the lawyers would comment on what was going on or why they were in court on a Friday afternoon days after the Air-India trial had adjourned. Neal urged me to follow them. And so I did.

As we all got into the elevator together, I said that they had better push the button. "I'm not sure where we are going," I said.

They seemed uncomfortable with my presence. Without saying a word, the three lawyers got off on the third floor and walked down the hall to Courtroom 33 – on a different floor than the Air-India courtroom. That also struck me as weird.

When I tried to follow them into court, I was told by a sheriff that it was a closed hearing. She would not provide any information about what was going on.

I called my editors, who instructed me to get our lawyer, Rob Anderson, down there. He arrived within minutes. Anderson also tried to enter the courtroom and was also denied access. When he asked for his business card to be handed to the judge, a number of additional sheriffs were called. I thought he was going to get arrested, so I moved away from him and hid around the corner.

No point in both of us being taken in, I thought. Besides, I needed to write the story.

But Anderson was not detained. He was advised by a sheriff that Madam Justice Heather Holmes would not hear him that day. Holmes was not the Air-India trial judge, which raised our already high level of curiosity about the unusual proceeding even higher. Nobody at the court's criminal registry desk could provide insight into what was going on.

The *Sun* decided to challenge the secret hearing. Within a month, Justice Holmes released a few details, though she denied the *Sun*'s request for transcripts and documents of what we were told was a five-day proceeding. She had ordered a mystery witness believed to have information about the Air-India bombing to testify at an in-camera investigative hearing under the new anti-terrorism law. The witness had refused.

My sources in the Sikh community told me that the witness was Satnam Reyat, the wife of the man convicted for both bombings. But we were not allowed to publish her name or any other details we might have gleaned about what was going on until all her court challenges of the anti-terrorism law were over.

The woman, despite being on welfare for years, had hired a team of lawyers to fight the order to testify all the way to the Supreme Court of Canada. It was the first case of its kind in the country. She was backed by both Malik and Bagri, whose lawyers also didn't want her to be forced to answer questions about Air-India at the anti-terrorism judicial hearing.

I strongly believed that the secrecy of the hearing was an affront to democracy and the principle of the open courtroom. It was a great issue for the *Sun* to challenge. If Canada was going to force people to answer questions in court about terrorism cases under our new law, it should not be done behind closed

doors. It would be months before either Mrs. Reyat or my newspaper got an answer.

After such a huge buildup to the start of the trial, and after
years of volatility in the Sikh community, the summer of 2003
was remarkably quiet. Sikhs of all persuasions seemed to be allowing the trial to take its course. No one was speaking out too
strongly one way or another. Everyone knew the key Crown
witnesses – the ones who would allegedly link the pair to the
conspiracy – were all due to testify in the fall. It was as if the whole
community was holding its breath and waiting.

The magnitude of the Air-India case meant there was always
something going on, even when the trial was officially adjourned.
Whether it was Mrs. Reyat's Supreme Court of Canada challenge,
or one of the many media applications to get access to information, lulls in the case didn't last long.

So I wasn't surprised when the summer break was interrupted
by yet another court application. Malik, the man who had told a
judge he was worth $10 million when he wanted to get bail, was
claiming he was broke and that the government would have to
pay for his lawyers. In his funding application, he declared that
he owed his brothers and children more than $1 million and
couldn't continue to pay for his defence, which he estimated
might cost $6 million for the duration of the trial. Without money
from the taxpayers, the charges against him would have to be
stayed, he argued.

But the B.C. government played hardball. It said it believed
Malik was still a multimillionaire who was attempting to dimin-
ish his assets by claiming to owe money to family members.
Government lawyer John Waddell suggested Malik should have
put a little cash aside, knowing for so many years that he was
a suspect.

"It is fair to say that from '85 onwards I was suspected," Malik testified before Madame Justice Sunni Stromberg-Stein. "I believed even until several months after my arrest that I had enough funds to defend myself."

Malik was surprisingly relaxed, making quips throughout his cross-examination. His family members did not appear worried either, and often chuckled in the public gallery. He admitted to having lied on the records he submitted to the government, when he stated that he had spent $26,000 alone on the jail canteen. In fact, the bill was $7,800. He claimed as part of his legal expenses a $2,000-a month-retainer to his son, Jaspreet, who was not working on the Air-India case, as well as bills for an unrelated court case.

He also gave a little insight into when and why he had started to fear arrest. In 1997, he said, the suspicion around him increased so much that he hired Terry LaLiberte in case he was arrested. This was about the same time that Rani began providing information to the RCMP and CSIS. My stories in the *Sun* started shortly afterwards. He held his hand low to show the judge the level of suspicion up until 1997 and then he raised it high above his head to indicate the shift.

Malik boasted about providing everything for his children, including his sons in their twenties who did not need to support themselves.

"It may be difficult for Canadian-Canadians to understand, but as an East Indian-Canadian, that's how we do things. They all keep their good habits and they keep their religion. All of my children wear turbans."

But Malik couldn't really explain how, if they were so broke, his wife and children had paid off three luxury cars – a Mercedes, a Lexus, and a Chevy Blazer – while he was in jail.

I was surprised when his wife, Raminder, and his three eldest sons took the stand to say how much they were owed by their father and to admit that they didn't want to spend their own money on his legal troubles. The whole family had always been so proud of its wealth and status in the Sikh community and this seemed like a humiliating exercise. The adult sons also admitted that they never contributed a penny to live in the family home and that their father provided them with cars and spending money.

Jaspreet Malik, the lawyer, said he had done the paperwork to get his uncle to sue his father for more than $600,000. He found his uncle another lawyer, then advised that lawyer about the right time to sue in order to help his father's legal-aid application.

Stromberg-Stein didn't buy any of their claims. In September, she issued a scathing judgment against Malik, saying that he had "submitted erroneous, contradictory and unreliable evidence" about his finances. She went on to say that the family's claims of poverty were "unbelievable" and that Malik remained "a multi-millionaire despite leading evidence to suggest his net worth is zero." In other words, the man who was proclaiming his innocence in the mass murder of 331 people had lied under oath at his funding hearing.

Stromberg-Stein's ruling threw a wrench into the Air-India trial, which had to be delayed for several weeks until a deal over how his lawyers would be paid could be worked out. The B.C. government demanded guarantees in the form of liens against some of the Maliks' properties in order to continue financing Malik through a loan that would have to be repaid.

But the trial did continue. In the fall of 2003, the Crown finally got to the heart of its case. First it called an American academic, Dr. Paul Wallace, who likened the attack on the Golden Temple to the storming of the Vatican. Sikhs around the world were outraged. There were many calls for revenge. It was obvious stuff, but still a necessary component to the Crown's conspiracy case. Wallace appeared delighted to be giving evidence. He punctuated every sentence with a little laugh.

The courtroom was packed on September 10 when Inderjit Reyat was brought into the witness box. Spectators thought he might shed some light on the unanswered questions about his cohorts in the dastardly terrorist attacks. We all held out hope that this man who claimed to be so religious might finally tell the truth as his religion's founder, Guru Nanak, mandated when he preached that "truth is the highest virtue."

As soon as I saw him bow in greeting to Malik and Bagri, a slight smile on his face, I knew Reyat would protect the two accused. But it was still frustrating to watch him do it. He claimed he had no idea who he provided bomb components to back in June 1985. He claimed he had tried to build a bomb at Parmar's request that was to be used back in India "to do a big job." He claimed the tests had failed and instead he had passed the supplies to a mystery man whom Parmar had brought to stay with Reyat on June 4, 1985.

"I called him Bhaiji," Reyat said, explaining the word means brother.

Throughout several hours of tough questioning by prosecutor Len Doust, Reyat skilfully avoided giving meaningful answers. He said he never realized the bombs he was trying to build would be used to down airplanes filled with people. He stuck to the story he told so long before to Doug Henderson after his first arrest in November 1985.

He had only agreed to assist Parmar in bomb building "to help people in India," he explained.

"How was sending a bomb to India going to help people in India?" asked Doust, sarcasm dripping from his tongue.

"The bomb won't help," Reyat replied.

The exchange between Doust and Reyat may not have helped the Crown's case, but it was riveting to watch. People in the gallery even burst out laughing when Doust caught Reyat contradicting things he had said earlier in the day. He admitted he took a phone number for the mystery man, who he said might have been a teacher from Toronto.

"Who were you going to ask for if you called?" Doust said.

Reyat couldn't answer.

He testified that he couldn't recall whether Malik, a Khalsa School director named Kewal Singh Nagra, and the men's spiritual leader, Bhai Jiwan Singh, had come to see him in Duncan months before the bombings to urge him to participate in the plot.

Reyat told the court that phone calls between his house and Malik's both before and after the bombing were made because Malik was trying to get him to contribute money to start a credit union. He also said he did not know why Malik had supported Reyat's wife and children with monthly contributions after Reyat was convicted in 1991. During the year he had been incarcerated with Malik before he made his guilty plea, he had never asked Malik about the financial aid, he claimed.

"Weren't you curious to know why he would do that?" Doust asked.

Reyat replied, "He doesn't help only my wife. He helps lots of people."

Records submitted to the court showed that Malik appeared to favour aiding those suspected or convicted of terrorism. He gave more than $100,000 to Reyat's family. He financially supported Parmar and the Babbar Khalsa. He helped Tejinder Pal Singh, the convicted hijacker, when he lived in the school basement. He had supported Gurbax Kaur, the Babbar Khalsa terrorist killed in India in the summer of 1999.

Doust was able to show that Reyat's inability to remember certain facts was unlikely. For instance, Reyat claimed not to remember seeing Parmar, Bagri, Surjan Gill, or Malik at a Vancouver demonstration after the attack on Golden Temple. He was then shown CBC footage of the protest, which showed him holding a large sword standing right beside Gill. Bagri was a speaker.

While he continued to say he did not know what Parmar had in store for the bombs he wanted made, Reyat was forced to admit that he had travelled from Duncan to Vancouver on June 22, 1985, the day the bomb-laden suitcases were checked in at the airport. But he suggested it was just a big coincidence. He was only visiting his brother in Surrey and his father in Richmond and did not make contact with any of the other Air-India suspects despite being seen near Parmar's Burnaby home, he said.

Doust confronted him again with records of phone calls made between his house and the Vancouver residence of suspect Hardial Johal on the evening of June 21 and the afternoon of June 22.

"I was not at his house," Reyat said.

Reyat refused to use the word *bomb* in his testimony, prompting a flippant Doust to call the explosive device "that thing you made." Nor could he explain why he never confronted Parmar when he realized the bombs he said he had provided supplies for were used to kill hundreds of innocent people.

"Did you not want to know in your own mind whether what you had done had contributed to causing these disasters?" Doust asked. "Why didn't you just ask Mr. Parmar so you knew?"

"I should have asked him," he said unconvincingly.

The prosecution was so frustrated by Reyat's evasions that it applied to have him declared a hostile witness so that he could be cross-examined even more forcibly than Doust had already done. Just as he had done on almost every Crown motion to that point, Justice Josephson denied the request. The judge based his ruling on his observation that Reyat had been remarkably consistent in his story since 1985, even if it contained lies. He hadn't contradicted his earlier statements at this trial, and so he should not be pressed harder to explain any of them.

Families of the victims felt a renewed sense of outrage over the five-year sentence Reyat had received for his part in the bombing. It did seem ridiculous in light of Reyat's solidarity with the two accused men. There was no remorse. The families could have accepted the deal if Reyat had convinced them he had told the truth. But, according to Doust, Reyat's testimony was just "a pack of lies."

With the Reyat testimony a bust for the case, the Crown moved on to present its most compelling evidence against Malik and Bagri. It was the part of the trial that everyone had been anticipating.

The courtroom was appropriately packed for the expected drama in the trial, and the tension was at its peak. Victims' relatives from around the world were sitting in the same rows as Air-India suspects, supporters of Malik and Bagri, and some of their relatives. Sometimes the opposing sides seemed to vie for the seats closest to the prisoners' glass box so witnesses would see the two men's faces if they glanced over. Sheriffs kept a close watch on the partisan groupings of people that gathered outside the courtroom during the morning and afternoon breaks. Security cameras were positioned behind transparent purple bubbles in the public gallery and lobby. Sheriffs – well aware of who was in the crowd – monitored everyone via closed-circuit televisions.

As Malik and Bagri entered court each day with sheriffs in tow, they would turn to the public gallery to see their supporters. Bagri usually waved, while Malik, with hands clasped together, would bow and smile.

Malik's son Jaspreet and his wife, Raminder, were there almost daily. His sons Darshan and Hardeep were there regularly. And his two youngest children, teenaged daughter Kirat and son Japnaam, attended occasionally. Kirat, a girl of sixteen at the time, with a passion for soccer, amused herself by making faces at me and other reporters.

Bagri's four adult daughters were regulars, sometimes with their husbands tagging along, including Jaswinder Parmar. Two of Bagri's toddler granddaughters, clearly born after he was arrested on terrorism charges, played quietly throughout riveting testimony or sucked on bottles as they lay on the courtroom floor.

First up was the Malik evidence and a former friend of his who alleged Malik asked him to carry a suitcase aboard an Air-India flight. The short round man, a farmer who had been embroiled in a financial dispute with Malik for years, had lived in the Witness Protection Program since the fall of 2001, when his south Surrey house was shot up in the middle of the night. One bullet flew past him, barely missing his head as he lay in bed.

A turbaned Sikh dressed in a suit, who testified in Punjabi using an interpreter, the mid-sixties man said he had once been sympathetic to the Babbar Khalsa. The farmer, whose identity is also shielded by court order because of threats and the shooting, testified that Malik wanted him to carry the bag "to teach the Indian government a lesson." When the farmer had expressed concern, he alleged, Malik told him that if anything happened, the farmer would be considered a martyr and the community would look after his children. The man refused to carry the bag and said he was later warned by Malik and others never to discuss the original conversation.

But the farmer contradicted himself during cross-examination. He testified he had never asked Malik what would be in the suitcase, but was confronted by a police statement in which he claimed he did ask. Some of the contradictions were more minor – whether he first approached Malik at a Sikh temple about a loan or asked him over he phone. The farmer also claimed never to have told anyone about his exchanges with Malik – something that was contradicted by Rani and Narinder Gill, two other Crown witnesses.

Something the farmer did not disclose at the trial was that he had approached me years earlier and told me about his conversation with Malik. He told me he had heart troubles when the bombings happened and realized he might have died if he had done what Malik asked.

The defence pointed to inconsistencies in the farmer's statements to police and the fact that he never told anyone about Malik's request until April 7, 1997 – the same day he first argued with the accused bomber about their money dispute.

Next on the stand was Joginder Singh Gill, a Nanaimo man who didn't really know Malik and had testified at Reyat's earlier trial. He told the court he had driven Parmar and a Mr. X from the Nanaimo ferry terminal to Duncan at the request of a friend back in early June 1985. But his testimony focused on what happened a couple of years later when he was approached on separate occasions, first by Parmar and then by Malik. Parmar had summoned him to the home of a mutual friend and urged him to change his statement to the police. When Gill refused, Parmar was furious and, according to Gill, had said, "We are going to kill you."

"Go ahead," Gill said and left the house.

A short time later, the friend who originally asked for the favour told Gill to go to the Nanaimo home of Karnail Singh Manhas, a long-time Malik ally who later became a director of the Khalsa Credit Union. Several others were at the house, Gill said, including Air-India suspect Daljit Sandhu and Parmar's brother Kulwarn.

Malik took Gill aside and again urged him to claim to police that he had earlier been mistaken, that it was just Mr. X and not Parmar in the car. Malik wanted the evidence changed before Gill testified at Reyat's trial. For a second time, Gill refused to be coerced.

Prosecutor Joe Bellows next called Raghbir Singh Grewal to the stand. Grewal had lost his brother-in-law, Daljit Grewal, in the bombing. Raghbir said he was with his brother at the Vancouver International Airport on June 22, 1985, waiting for the connecting flight to Air-India. He saw Hardial Johal, the community leader and Air-India suspect, rushing around the terminal. Johal greeted the Grewals and said he would be back in a few minutes to see them. He returned with an envelope he said contained money for his mother in India. He asked Daljit Grewal to deliver it for him, and the man who was hours away from his death obliged. He stuffed the envelope in his shirt pocket. Johal told them he was at the airport to meet somebody.

The small detail about the envelope was chilling. If Johal was involved in the plot, as police believed, how callous he must have been to create a cover story suggesting his innocence while chatting casually with a man he knew was fated to die.

Jagdev Dhillon's testimony was brief but powerful. Dhillon and his wife had met Malik when he first came to Canada and was living in a basement suite in East Vancouver. They became close friends and eventually business associates, though the friendship cooled a little after Malik embraced his religion with zeal.

Sometime in the months before the bombing, the Dhillons were at a religious gathering at Malik's home. Dhillon was in the kitchen area with several guests when Malik came in and made a comment about a meeting in one of the other rooms in the house. Dhillon couldn't remember Malik's exact words, but it was something like: "They say to crash the planes." Dhillon earlier told police: "I heard him saying, 'They are saying they should blow up an Air-India plane.'"

Dhillon said that he told Malik it would be wiser to organize a boycott of Air-India and the State Bank of India if they were upset with the Indian government. When the defence rose and suggested to Dhillon that Malik had only been stating the view of others in his house who advocated violence and didn't necessarily agree with it, Dhillon couldn't disagree.

Narinder Gill, whom I had come to know so well over several years, testified next. He said he had been at a meeting in Calgary in early 1985 and had heard Talwinder Parmar say that there was a violent plan in the works to take revenge against the Indian government. Balwant Bhandher, who would later move to British Columbia and become one of Malik's closest associates, was also at the meeting.

Gill was the treasurer of the Calgary temple at the time, and Parmar asked him for money to send to India to buy arms. Gill refused.

He also told Justice Josephson about going to a meeting in Seattle with Bhandher in either June or July 1985. En route they stopped and picked up Bhai Jiwan Singh, the Amritsar-based AKJ leader who was so close to Malik. Once they reached the temple in Seattle, Gill met Malik for the first time. He said the Reyats were both there, as was Mr. Reyat's cousin Parmjit Singh Panesar. Bagri was also there and so was Kewal Nagra, another man who would become closely associated with Malik and his school. Gill said he was pretty sure the meeting was before the Air-India bombing. But human frailty meant his memory was not perfect, he said.

That doubt gave the defence an opening. They spent days introducing records to show Gill had to have been in Calgary in the days just before the bombing, meaning the meeting had to have taken place later.

Gill later told me how frustrated he was about the defence's attack. Both he and his wife were sure he travelled with Bhandher in mid-June to Seattle. But in the end, there was reasonable doubt about the timing of the meeting.

Gill, a successful businessman, had later moved to Vancouver from Calgary and had become involved in Malik's school as a volunteer treasurer. There he got to know Rani, the star witness. He testified that she had revealed to him details of the bombing plot that she said she had been told by Malik in the summer of 1997, just before she was forced from the school.

Gill also testified that Malik came to his house after Rani's departure. He said he feared there was a bug in his car and asked Gill to take a drive in his own vehicle.

"He said, "Do not talk to the police. I can give you a lawyer. Tell the police to talk to the lawyer and that I did not want to talk,'" Gill said. "I said, I haven't done anything criminal. I am ready to talk."

Gill said he had asked Malik why so much money had been paid from the school's accounts to the Reyat family, and Malik told him that Reyat had been working for the community and deserved support.

"He said if I ever did something like this, they would support me as well," Gill said. He explained that Malik was referring to the Narita bombing, for which Reyat had already been convicted.

Gill testified about the close relationship Malik had with Parmar. When Parmar secretly visited Vancouver in 1992, he stayed at Malik's house. And he described how Parmar and Bagri did not appear to have had any falling out, despite what Bagri's lawyers had argued. To the contrary, Parmar had arranged for his eldest son, Jaswinder, to marry Bagri's daughter. Several of

Parmar's relatives worked for Malik at the school, the credit union, and his private business, Gill said.

After Gill finished his testimony, he met with victims' family members in the lobby. It was touching to watch someone who was once part of Malik's inner circle reaching out his hand in acknowledgement of the families' great losses. He said simply, "I am very sorry."

Sometimes I found it very frustrating to be sitting in court, knowing how many of the witnesses had been threatened and warned and hearing so little of it come out.

I knew the farmer had had his house shot up, but that was not part of his evidence. I knew Jagdev Dhillon had been pressured by a friend of Malik's not to testify against his old friend. That was not raised during his testimony. I knew Narinder Gill had suffered a number of vandal attacks, a shooting, and an intimidating phone call from the Malik household, yet none of that came out during the Crown's case.

I asked Doug Best during one of the breaks one day why the Crown was not introducing evidence of threats and intimidation. He said it was their call and they just didn't see fit to make it part of the case, with the exception of the attacks and threats against Rani.

When Rani began her testimony on October 31, 2003, the courtroom was full to bursting. Sikh community leaders sympathetic to the prosecution joined the victims' families. Relatives of Malik and Bagri and their supporters filled row after row. Aniljit Uppal, who had once faced a criminal harassment charge for an incident with Rani, was sitting with Malik's wife, Raminder. The charge was stayed when Rani went into the Witness Protection Program.

I was eager to see Rani again after so many years. But I was also worried. I didn't want my name to come out during her evidence. I thought Malik's lawyers would ask her about the stories I had written and the conversations I had had with her over several months. I remembered Crossin's comments on day one of the trial when he suggested I might get called to testify.

She looked straight at me when she entered the courtroom and batted her eyelids, which I took as a friendly signal. She also pressed her hands together and bowed slightly to Malik as I had seen her do before. Then, as prosecutor Joe Bellows led her testimony, she described the intense feelings she still had for Malik,

"I still love him. I still respect him. I miss him and I hate being here. I wish I wasn't here," Rani said.

She looked right at Malik and told him she was not testifying for revenge and would not be doing it at all if she could have avoided it. "You don't know how horrible I feel. If there was any way, anything I could do not to be here. It's a betrayal and it is so insulting to me."

Some of the men sitting near me expressed surprise at her declaration of love. The women said they understood. I also suggested that she probably still feared Malik and wanted him to know she was forced to testify.

Rani was soft-spoken, but confident and polite, dressed in a dark suit, her hair shorter than it had been. She described the great joy and pride she had in the Khalsa daycare from the moment Malik hired her in September 1992.

"We worked really well. We were very good friends. We were very happy together. We shared a love and friendship that is very hard to find," she said. "We had great times. He was a workaholic. . . . We both had great dreams for Khalsa School."

Malik cast his eyes downwards as Rani spoke. She had tears in her eyes at several points but also smiled at fond memories.

She described her friendship with Satnam Reyat, who worked beside her from day one on the job. She said Malik told her he was supporting Mrs. Reyat to keep a promise made to her husband because he had done a great *sewa* for Sikhism.

The first time Malik told her he had fallen in love with her was in January 1995 – three years after she was hired by the Satnam Education Society, which Malik headed. "He told me how special I was and gave me a big hug and told me he had a lot of feelings for me." She was too afraid to express her feelings. "I said, 'I admire you a lot.'"

But while they fell in love, they never had a sexual relationship or even kissed. "We held hands, we hugged each other," she said, as Malik looked downwards. Malik told her that he was having difficulties in his relationship with wife. "He said that he wasn't attracted to her. She's not the kind of person he likes to go out with, he doesn't enjoy a sexual nature with her and he doesn't like her ideas," Rani said, pointing out how embarrassed she was to disclose that information in court.

Malik told her he wanted a sexual relationship "but it would be dangerous . . . for us to do that because of the Sikh guidelines."

She said she wrote down much of what Malik confided to her about the activities of militant Sikh leaders, including Bhai Jiwan Singh, Parmar, and school directors Balwant Bhandher, Kewal Nagra, Aniljit Uppal, and Gurdev Gill. She also destroyed a lot of her papers after she was forced from her job in the fall of 1997 because she didn't want to be a witness in any trial.

So far, there had been no mention of Air-India. Bellows was building up to the most critical point of his case. The crowd would have to come back the following week for more.

And they did. When Rani took the stand again the following Monday, Bellows got her to recount what she said were Malik's first admissions to her. Despite their love, she often challenged

Malik about the way he ran the school. He didn't seem to mind her straightforwardness, especially when so many others feared him. She resisted signing any documents related to the government grants the school was getting because she felt that they were sometimes misused.

She testified that one of her worst conflicts with Malik arose after a young student, Preethi Cudail, attempted suicide in May 1996. The girl was distraught after religious teachers at the school ridiculed her for shaving her hair against Sikh doctrine. In fact, Cudail was on medication that had made her hair fall out.

Rani thought Malik was very cruel because he had not visited the girl in the hospital or made amends to the family. She confronted her boss and platonic lover, she testified.

"'If one child dies for Sikhism, so what? Others will learn not to break the rules. And we will not be bending our rules for anyone,'" Rani quoted Malik as saying. "'1982 – 328 people died. What did anyone do?' I didn't say anything and he said, 'People still remember Khalistan.'"

Malik would often forget names and dates, she said. So she wasn't surprised that he was wrong about some details of the airline bombing.

As Rani spoke, sobs and gasps broke out in the public gallery. She continued repeating Malik's comments to her. "'We had Air-India crash,'" she quoted Malik. "And then he goes, 'Nobody, nobody can do anything. It is all for Sikhism.'"

No one spoke in the gallery. It was so quiet you could not even hear people breathing. Spectators – including family members of the victims and the suspects – were literally sitting on the edge of their seats or leaning forward to get a better view.

Rani said Malik firmly shook his finger at her at one point in the conversation, which took place at the daycare centre next door to Malik's school. Malik told her he was like a Hindu god who spins the world on his fingertip, controlling everyone and everything.

Rani said Malik then invited her out for coffee, rubbing her back and saying, "Always remember, I love you." After he left, she was so upset that she was crying uncontrollably. She was in shock, so she started to write, over and over, the stunning comments he made to her: "If one child dies, so what? 1982 – 328 dead, so what? We had Air-India crash, so what?"

The incriminating notes were left on her desk, but Mrs. Reyat helped her rip them up the next morning. Rani said she also documented the conversation in her journal with a simple note, abbreviated because she was writing fast: "We'd Air-India crash."

She considered leaving the school several times after that, but Malik always made up with her and drew her back in. It was like a cult, she explained. "It's like there's this power that grabs and when I would hear about the Air-India task force I asked [them] 'leave him. It's a long time ago, just go away.' I can't explain [to] you but it's like a magnet. It's like I can't let it go."

She started seeing things from Malik's perspective and not through normal, clear eyes, she said. So she stayed.

The packed public gallery was clearly splitting into camps. The Malik supporters mocked Rani and muttered expletives during the breaks in the lobby. Many of the woman who didn't know her – including journalists – said they could understand falling for a jerk. Some had first-hand experience. The men in the press corps said they couldn't understand how she could have found Malik attractive. I tried to give some perspective based on my many conversations with her about what happened.

But the idle relationship gossip stopped when Rani took the stand for a third day. She launched into the most chilling testimony of the entire trial. There was absolute silence in Courtroom

20 as she recounted the day in late March or early April 1997 that she would come to regret for the rest of her life.

It was a normal morning at the Khalsa daycare when she arrived for work. Some of the staff were already there, sitting together reading an article in a Punjabi-language newspaper called *Awaaz*, or Voice. She asked them what the story was about. They hesitated before answering, but said it was about the Air-India bombing. She did not read Punjabi, but was curious, especially when no one would tell her what was in it. She phoned Mrs. Reyat to come down and help her out.

Satnam Reyat obliged and explained to her that the story said that arrests were imminent in the bombing case. The article alluded to the identities of several suspects including Inderjit Reyat, Parmar, Bagri, Malik, Hardial Johal, and Surjan Gill.

Rani said she was shocked. "I just thought, No way, you are wrong. I did not have the energy to move. I just sat there and cried."

But then she became angry. She went to Malik's office in the school next door and confronted him. She said that she pushed him until he finally told her that he had booked the tickets by telephone that were used to load the bomb-laden suitcases at Vancouver International Airport. Malik told her that he gave the money for the tickets to Daljit Sandhu, the former Ross Street Sikh temple president, who went to pick them up. He explained that a group of people went to the airport with the bombs including Bagri, Johal, and Balwant Bhandher. Later, the group gathered at Parmar's Burnaby home to await news of their plot's success.

Rani said that when she asked him to explain the motive, Malik told her that many more people were supposed to have died in the plot, which he called "the project."

"'If only things were going right. If things were going on time and if there were not that many glitches and if the plane had landed on time, there would have been far greater impact. There would have been far more, more deaths,'" Rani quoted Malik as saying. "'They would have known what we are all about. They would have understood. They would have understood Khalistan. They would have known what we were fighting for.'"

There were more gasps from the public gallery. So, the deaths of 331 were not enough for Malik? He would have liked more?

Rani tried to explain to Justice Josephson that even as Malik was confessing his role in Canada's worst mass murder, she wanted to protect him.

"Malik is part of me. If something affects him, it affects me. I have protected him. I have stood up for him on many occasions," she said. "He was like my hero. If Mr. Malik would tell me to go do something, even though I knew it was wrong, I would do it."

She said she asked Malik how he could have blown up a plane when Sikhs were also killed, and that he had replied that the Sikhs who took the flight were not "real" Sikhs.

Malik told her on another occasion that the conspirators had all been at the Kamloops home of one Babbar Khalsa member. They had the plans of a Boeing 747 laid out on the table when the young son of one of the men, Avtar Narwal, walked in on them.

She was asked to respond to suggestions that she had really just gleaned all her knowledge of the Air-India bombing from books and media reports. She said she had never seen any of the books on the case and knew only what she did because Malik told it to her.

She testified that her loving friendship with Malik deteriorated toward the end of 1997 after his supporters, Balwant Bhandher and Aniljit Uppal, continually suggested to Malik and to her that she was an agent for CSIS and had taped conversations with her boss.

By that time, CSIS had its eye on Malik and his Surrey school. Some parents of children at the Khalsa School had already spoken to a CSIS agent about its links to terrorism and were happy to give Rani his number to call when her situation got desperate. She made the call to Nick Rowe in October 1997 and asked for a meeting.

"I wanted to find out who was spreading the rumour that I am a CSIS spy," she explained. "In [the] Sikh community, you never ever [should] be called a CSIS spy. You can be really in trouble."

She explained how CSIS soon led her to the RCMP, and that the Air-India Task Force pressed her for more and more information about Malik and his associates. But she said she had been reluctant to say anything about Air-India, although she provided details of some of the other criminal activities going on at the school.

Prosecution lawyer Joe Bellows never asked Rani about her discussions with me or any other journalist. She explained that she had waited five months before telling police about the main Malik disclosures, dubbed the "newspaper confession" by Malik, because she never appreciated the value of it. How could she prove what he had told her, given that there were no witnesses or documentation?

Rani's dramatic testimony was news around the world. The court went to extraordinary measures to protect her identity. Not only was her real name and photograph banned from publication and broadcast, even court illustrations that blurred her features were seized by the police because they were deemed too revealing.

So it was particularly outrageous when a U.S.-based Sikh Web site with separatist leanings published articles cribbed from my newspaper, the *Globe and Mail*, and the *Toronto Star*, but substituted Rani's real name in them. The site, Waheguroo, also changed my byline slightly, by adding the words *panthic dusht*, or enemy of the Sikh nation, under my name.

The RCMP called my editors about the Web site and immediately raised the issue in court. The police contacted Waheguroo's
Web masters, who agreed to remove the offending articles. They
did, but the site's chat room continued to post banned material,
as well as threats against certain individuals, including me.

Rani held up amazingly well under weeks of vigourous cross-
examination, though her motives were constantly challenged by
Malik's team of experienced lawyers, David Crossin and Bill Smart.

I kept waiting for Crossin to follow up on his opening day
threat to raise my professionalism and relationship with Rani
during her testimony. But he never asked her a thing about me.

Crossin began his cross-examination by attacking Rani's
motives, suggesting she was desperate to get back at Malik after
losing the job that was so important to her. He pointed to an entry
in her journal from the summer of 1996 saying Malik was "in
fact a thief hiding behind religion." Another journal entry from
November 1996 – six months before she said Malik confessed in
detail to her - said she was planning to "break her ties" with him.
He suggested she never shared a loving relationship with Malik
and only went to CSIS and later to the RCMP to get back at
her employer.

Crossin asked her why she would stick around, given her concerns over financial irregularities and Malik's treatment of the
Cudail girl.

"It was not easy to walk away," she explained. "Emotionally
it was just tearing me apart."

She also said Malik could always convince her he was sorry
and that she should stay with him. She had wanted to believe him.
She loved him and cared for him.

Crossin again turned to her journal to discredit Rani. The entry
date was ambiguous. It said: February 28–16 March '97. "Mrs.
Reyat told me some stuffs that came in the paper and it shocked

me. I confronted Malik and he confirmed but told me not to worry. But I am worried. I care about him and Mrs. Reyat."

Crossin said that the entry must have referred to the so-called "newspaper confession," in which Rani claimed she had confronted Malik after the *Voice* article. The problem, the defence said, was that the article came out after the entry, meaning she must have fabricated the journal to corroborate her story. But Rani was adamant that she had never written about the detailed Malik confession in her journal, despite the Crown having once mistaken the same entry as a reference to Malik's admissions. "I never put it down in my journal," she said. "I have never written about Air-India in my journal." But she could not provide a specific incident that did lead to the journal entry.

Malik's team also suggested that Rani could have gleaned details used in the alleged Malik confession from two books that had been published in the 1980s: *Soft Target* and *The Death of Air India Flight 182*. She claimed she had not read either.

The lawyers argued that some of the details she provided to police were identical to those in the books – including some errors. She called CP Air "Canadian Airlines." So did one of the books. She said that Daljit Sandhu had been short of money went he went to get the tickets. So did the books, even though the ticket agent did not give that information in his police statement or testimony.

Some of the most difficult cross-examination for me to hear was Crossin grilling Rani on the reason for her five-month delay in reporting the main confession to police. I kept waiting nervously for any reference to my bad legal advice to her. It never came.

"I said, 'I don't think it is important. I have no proof of it. It was just a conversation between Mr. Malik and me.' He got excited," she said of the conversation she had with Doug Best in the spring of 1998.

She was also asked about small inconsistencies in her numerous statements to police and Crown prosecutors over almost
seven years. She originally quoted Malik's 1996 confession as, "We
had Air-India crash." But in one late-night police interview she
quoted him as saying, "We finished Air-India."

Rani's explanation made sense to me: No one told her she had
to use the exact words. She was tired and was using her own
description of what he had told her, she said.

Malik's lawyers scored the biggest points when they repeatedly asked Rani why she hadn't run screaming from the school
after hearing her boss, whom she said she loved, admit to hundreds of murders.

"And was it clear to you then that he participated in this horrible event?" Crossin asked.

"Yes, sir," she said.

"That must have been shocking for you."

"It was, but I looked at it as all he did was bought the tickets,"
Rani said.

She was firm in her resolve. On the last day of her testimony,
November 29, 2003, she reiterated what she had said all along –
that she had come forth reluctantly and would pay the price for
the rest of her life.

"Whatever your feelings were toward Malik over the years, it
was not a relationship that gave rise to any intimate discussions,"
Crossin argued.

Rani adamantly replied, "I was there, sir. You were not. I
remember what he said."

Crossin also said that although she claimed not to be bitter,
the witness had taken several actions against Malik and the school,
including filing a human-rights complaint, a lawsuit, and talking
to CSIS, police, and journalists.

"I suggest to you, Madam, that you probably are of the view that Malik ought to be punished, but not as a result of any information he gave, but as a result of the information you received over the years," he said. "That's why you feel he deserves punishment, not only for Air-India, but for a number of things."

"No, sir," Rani replied again.

The most emotional part of Rani's testimony was when she described the ordeal she has lived for years as a result of her relationship with Malik. She described the threats, the attacks on her house, the time an acquaintance at the mall said he was going to finish her and her children with an AK-47.

"You don't know, Mr. Crossin, how many times I have regretted ever knowing this information," she said. "Everything is lost, Mr. Crossin. I don't know how safe I am. I know one thing – I can never come back and live here. I know one thing – that I lost my family, that I have to live on my own. I grew up very protected, very loved by my family. There is nothing, nothing that can bring that back."

Doug Best of the RCMP and Nick Rowe of CSIS were both called to describe their interactions with Rani. Crossin asked Best several times about references to me that he had in his police notes, apparently about information Rani had told me. He tried to suggest through innuendo that there was something untoward about a witness talking to a reporter.

Rowe, a tall, lanky man who looked like he belonged on a British television comedy, was asked all kinds of questions about the mindset of the woman he met briefly on a few occasions in October 1997. Defence counsel Bill Smart wanted to portray Rani as having been all too eager to pass on any dirt about Malik and the school to the spy agency and later police. Rowe admitted she had provided him with a lot of information, although none of it was about Air-India. But, he said, "the salient point here is that this woman was at risk."

He pointed to a report of one of their meetings, in which he wrote: "The source is pragmatic enough and wise enough however to realize that Malik is a powerful individual with resources and the possible motivation to harm her."

Rowe also took on the defence suggestion that it was somehow inappropriate for Rani to have contacted CSIS, that citizens only contact law enforcement agencies because they have grudges or want to pay back their enemies.

"What is she supposed to do if not seek help?" Rowe said. "Was she supposed to sit back and continue to live in that environment? Continue to get threats from thugs? Was she supposed to wait perhaps for a bullet through the living-room window?"

CHAPTER 11

Reasonable Doubt?

L OOMING LARGE over the entire Air-India proceeding was the murder of publisher Tara Hayer. Prosecutors said that they had no doubt he would have testified against Ajaib Bagri if he had not been so mercilessly slain on November 18, 1998. Yet, Justice Josephson had ruled that details of Hayer's police statements implicating Bagri were too prejudicial to include at the Air-India trial.

So it was particularly ironic that, just as the Crown's case against Bagri got underway in December 2003, unsettling details linking Hayer's unsolved murder to Bagri's own organization, the Babbar Khalsa, were revealed in an unrelated trial taking place a few floors above the Air-India courtroom.

Journalists were not focused on the other trial – an Indo-Canadian gangland slaying in which a friend of the dead man was charged with having set him up. No reporter was in the courtroom when a senior investigator from the Vancouver suburb of Delta testified that the accused had told police one of the Hayer shooters had confessed to him.

When sources told me about this testimony, I persuaded my editors to pay almost $2,000 to get a transcript of it. What the documents revealed was startling, even to those of us who had long suspected a link between the Babbar Khalsa and the assassination of Hayer.

The young man on trial, Hardip Singh Uppal, was trying to work out a deal to save his own skin when he told police that the Babbar Khalsa had put up $50,000 to kill Hayer. Uppal passed a polygraph test during which he laid out how and why the Punjabi newspaper publisher was gunned down in cold blood.

Uppal, a brilliant student and a community volunteer, had got caught up in the seedy criminal underworld of drug trafficking and gangland murders. He claimed to police that he was too afraid to do much to stop the murder of his buddy, Gurpreet Singh Sohi, by a gangster named Robbie Soomel.

The reason he feared Soomel was because Soomel had boasted about his role in a series of hits, including that of Hayer. Uppal said that Soomel had told him that he drove the getaway car between Vancouver and Surrey the night Hayer was killed. Soomel had said that another gangster named Daljit Singh "Umboo" Basran had pulled the trigger.

"You should have seen Umboo," Uppal quoted Soomel as saying. "He was almost crying. Umboo said it was like watching his grandfather get shot."

The two hired guns did not have anything personally against the *Indo-Canadian Times* publisher, but agreed to do the job on behalf of another gangster from a prominent Khalistani family, Ranjit Singh "Doc" Bahia. Police were told that Bahia, whose father was a leader of the International Sikh Youth Federation, had been approached to kill Hayer by a contact with the Babbar Khalsa in Kamloops.

Uppal claimed that Bahia had considered doing the job, but decided he faced too much police scrutiny for unrelated crimes at the time, so he had hired Soomel and Basran. The hit was so successful that the two young men were then approached about killing Sikh moderate leader Balwant Gill for another "50 grand," according to Uppal's police statement.

Delta police Staff Sgt. John Robin did not identify the Babbar Khalsa contact during his testimony at the Uppal trial, but my sources confirmed that Uppal named Jethinder Singh "Roman" Narwal. Narwal, who had a long history of involvement with Indo-Canadian gangs and marijuana trafficking, was the son of Avtar Narwal. The elder Narwal was a listed director of the Babbar Khalsa and one of Bagri's closest allies in Kamloops when he drove into a lake and drowned in October 1998. He was also an Air-India suspect.

Roman Narwal's name had surfaced at the Air-India trial during Rani's testimony. She claimed Malik had told her about the younger Narwal walking in on the Air-India conspirators as a child while they had the plans of a Boeing 747 laid out on the table before them.

An old friend of Narwal had told me about this same incident years earlier, though I had never discussed it with Rani and was surprised when she mentioned it at the trial.

After his father's death, Roman Narwal viewed Bagri as a surrogate father, some of his close friends told me. Both Narwal and his mother, Gurmej, visited Bagri in jail, and Narwal attended the Air-India trial regularly to show support for the man he affectionately called "uncle."

The transcripts we had paid thousands to get were a journalistic gold mine. All the shocking details about who allegedly killed Hayer could be splashed across page one because the information had been raised at another trial. It was privileged, meaning we could not be sued for reporting it. And it depicted exactly the scenario we had long since speculated upon.

Staff Sergeant Robin had also testified that Uppal told him that "the Kamloops connection was a weapons specialist and strict orthodox Sikh family and that connection, both he and his 'uncle,' were directly related to the Babbar Khalsa." Uppal was talking about Narwal and Bagri.

Uppal also provided dramatic details about how the hit went down. He said Doc Bahia, the young man whom Roman approached, had met the two young gangsters at a gas station in south Vancouver and said, "It doesn't really matter how it's done, [just] done quick."

The killers were promised not only cash, but drugs, guns, and serious protection. The Babbar Khalsa contact knew Hayer's schedule, his house layout – "everything about him, down perfectly." The young men were given a black folder with Hayer's address and the house layout. Afterwards they had thrown the gun into the Fraser River off the Knight Street Bridge connecting Vancouver and Richmond.

Police were told by Uppal that the money for the Hayer hit was from "high up."

Both Delta police and the RCMP had wanted to offer a deal to Hardip Uppal in exchange for his testimony in a prosecution for Hayer's murder, something the Hayer family supported when they were finally told about Uppal's information in December 2003. The police called them to a hastily organized meeting in response to my application to get access to the court documents. But there was a disagreement between prosecutors in the gang case and police and no deal was ever reached. In February 2004, as the Crown's case against Bagri was gearing up a couple of floors below, Uppal was found guilty of manslaughter in the gangland murder and sentenced to five years.

Richard Cairns, the lead prosecutor for the Bagri portion of the Air-India trial, did the best he could without Hayer as a witness. But he was also without another controversial journalist who had been on the witness list, Sukhminder Cheema. Cheema had told police that during a 1992 meeting he had attended, Bagri admitted that he had played a role in the 1988 attempt on Hayer's life in order to silence him about Air-India.

After co-operating with the RCMP, Cheema had received help with his immigration status and was given a $2,000-a-month retainer from the police that lasted about three years. He had been caught lying in a related court case, but the RCMP had corroboration of his crucial meeting with Bagri and others. Unbeknownst to Cheema, surveillance photos had been taken of the 1992 meeting, which included several people from the International Sikh Youth Federation – Cheema's old group – and Malik.

Before the Air-India trial began, Cheema said he would no longer co-operate with the prosecution. He told me he did not want to end up like Hayer and was facing pressure from within the Sikh community and from his employer, the owner of a Punjabi radio station who was once aligned with Malik.

He was not the only witness to raise the spectre of the Hayer murder. Rani had testified that she was terrified of being murdered like the late publisher. And in December 2003, the Air-India trial was told that Premika, the reluctant witness against Bagri, had told the RCMP after Hayer was gunned down that it would be their fault if she were also killed.

Her feelings of fear were among the few things from her statements to investigators that Premika did confirm during the trial.
Between 1987 and 1990, Premika told a CSIS agent and the
RCMP six times that Bagri had come to her house on the eve of
the bombings and asked to borrow her car to leave some bags at
the airport, But at the trial, she repeatedly said that she did not
remember or recall any of the incriminating information she once
provided about Bagri. Even so, she still managed to win a permanent ban on the publication of her real name, as well as any
details of her family and profession.

The attractive, divorced mother had known Bagri's family
when she was a girl in Punjab. She said they had reconnected in
Vancouver in the early 1980s and that Bagri had offered to help
her after her volatile separation from her abusive husband.

Many police investigators believed that Premika, as I call her,
was having an affair with Bagri in the mid-1980s, though she
denied it at his trial, calling him an old family friend.

Premika was first visited by CSIS agent Willy Laurie in
September 1987. Laurie was a skilled investigator who was able to
make her feel completely at ease. Laurie said that he explained
to her at their first meeting that he was not a police officer, but
was gathering intelligence to be used by the Canadian government. He offered her confidentiality, which seemed to relax her
immensely. Laurie, who returned to the RCMP after years with
CSIS, was one of the Crown's best witnesses. He explained how
he gently built trust with the Punjabi woman by bringing Indian
sweets to their meetings and sharing chai. He never took notes
until afterwards, as he didn't want to make her feel nervous.

She spoke generally about Bagri at first, Laurie said, providing information about his links to the Babbar Khalsa and other
militants. When he raised the Air-India bombing, she became
very emotional and spoke of losing three of her cousins.

Laurie said he was shocked when she then disclosed that Bagri had visited her the night before the bombing and asked to borrow her car to go to the airport. He hinted he could get caught and was doing something very important. She refused to give him the car.

"He indicated he wasn't going anywhere, that only the luggage was going," Laurie quoted Premika as saying. "I was a little bit startled by the revelations she came out with."

Laurie read from one of his reports, in which he had written: "She said she was 100 per cent certain that the night he came to borrow her car was the night before the plane exploded."

Laurie confirmed that she always said she would never co-operate with police, but that she had agreed to provide information to CSIS. She repeated the same information about Bagri's late-night visit when Laurie visited again a short time later. She was very emotional, Laurie said, and slumped on the floor and wept after she told him about Bagri's complicity in the Air-India bombing.

But when Premika first took the stand in December 2003, she claimed that both CSIS and the RCMP had forced her to make false statements over the years and that she needed the help of a psychiatrist because of the stress.

"I was really mentally tortured for years, and both statements were signed under very, very bad pressure," Premika testified.

Crown prosecutors were so frustrated by her claim of memory loss that they applied to have Premika declared a hostile witness. Josephson said no.

But the judge accepted another prosecution argument to have some of Premika's statements to Laurie and the RCMP admitted over her sworn testimony. Josephson said he believed she was feigning memory loss, and he ruled that her lack of recall was directly related to the fact she believed her life would be in danger if she testified against Bagri.

"I accept the evidence of Laurie with respect to what he was told by the witness," Josephson ruled. "The witness described to Laurie what she interpreted as a serious threat to the lives of herself and her family should she reveal this information. Her actions then and now are consistent with a belief that the threat was and remains real. She was prepared to reveal her story only when she believed she could do so without risk to herself and her family.

"The core incident related by the witness is a simple, brief, and unusual encounter with Mr. Bagri, a person well known to her. It was not the kind of evidence fraught with the risk of inherent unreliability, such as with eyewitness identification. Her story is internally consistent. For example, his request for her vehicle at that time of evening was unusual and would reasonably have elicited her request for further information. That further information was also unusual as it suggested that he was about to become involved in unlawful activity. . . . This was followed by what she believed to be a serious threat to herself and her family if she revealed her 'secret,' which she believed to be that late-night visit. Memory of such an event would be deeply embedded and slow to erode, if ever. . . . A motive to falsely implicate Mr. Bagri is inconsistent with her not revealing the information until she felt assured that it would not find its way to the police. No other motive to fabricate is suggested or reveals itself. . . . The witness did testify that, while she does not remember the conversations, she told Laurie the truth."

The Crown was understandably optimistic. It seemed as if Josephson was working hard to get the truth out under difficult circumstances.

Premika was called back to the witness box several times over the course of three months at the trial. Each appearance was as frustrating as the last, especially for her cousin, who sat in the gallery. "She said she cared about my sister and the children, but she won't tell the truth," he told me. "I know she is afraid, but she should do the right thing." I can't name the man now even though he lost three relatives in the bombing because to do so would violate the court order protecting Premika.

Another major part of the Crown's case was the infamous Madison Square Gardens speech made by Bagri in July 1984. While Bagri did not target Air-India specifically in the speech, he called for the retaliatory murder of fifty thousand Hindus and said that traitors to the Sikh cause and their children would be "crushed in crushers." He stirred up the crowd, who called for Indira Gandhi's murder. It was shocking, even considering how recent the Golden Temple attack had been. The young, angry Sikh on the videotape proclaiming his hatred of Hindus was a stark contrast to the mid-fifties man with the rounded belly, greying beard, and grey cardigan who sat day after day in the prisoners' box. As he entered court, Bagri smiled at his loyal daughters, and would wave at his little granddaughters on the days they were in court. They giggled or called out the word *grandpa* in Punjabi.

The Crown called the conference organizer, Amarjit Ahluwalia, who agreed to testify because he thought he could help Bagri. He rationalized the violence in Bagri's speech by saying that Sikhs were justified in doing whatever they had to do in revenge against the Indian government.

"When you are angry, you are allowed to do what you want, say what you want," Ahluwalia said. "Sikhism is about standing up for your rights. Sikhism is about catching hold of the oppressor. Don't let him [go] scot-free. We know how to get even. That is the philosophy."

There were other frenzied calls for revenge in the months before the bombing. The Crown played a video of a September 1984 speech by Bagri in which he described Air-India as a legitimate

target. In a third video played at trial, Bagri stood beside Talwinder
Parmar as Sikhs raised swords and shouted, "Death to Indira
Gandhi" and "traitors of the nation." Bombing suspect Surjan Gill
was there too.

Sometimes the legal arguments bordered on the absurd. For
days, Bagri's lawyers harassed the Crown translator who had prepared the English version of the three videotaped speeches about
one of her translations. Couldn't the expression "*Murtabad* Indira
Gandhi," which literally means "Death to Indira Gandhi," really
mean "Down with Indira Gandhi"? lawyer Michael Tammen asked
repeatedly. Translator Surjeet Kaur Kalsey stuck to her guns and
said the chanters were cursing Gandhi to die. But Tammen would
not let it go. He asked her over and over again to the point where
the journalists were sarcastically muttering to each other in the
gallery: "Gee, I guess Gandhi's assassins misinterpreted the slogans."

In the *Sun's* archives, there are pictures of a 1984 protest that
show Bagri, Reyat, and Gill. Gill was wearing a black T-shirt with
white printing on it. "DEATH TO INDIRA GANDHI," it said in plain
English. Not "DOWN WITH INDIRA."

A former Sikh temple priest from Hamilton, Ontario, testified
that Bagri and Parmar had both been regular visitors before the
Air-India bombing. He said he had heard Bagri urge people "to
get their weapons ready" to take revenge against the Indian government. Money was always collected and donated to the men
when they visited, the priest said.

Bagri had also justified violence for the separatist cause in an
interview he gave to Scotland Yard in the fall of 1985, the trial
was told. Chief Supt. Keith Weston said Bagri had described terrorist attacks in India as "executive action."

"He claimed that he was a holy man and a man of peace who
would not indulge in activities against Indian government inter-
ests or personnel which would bring him in conflict with Canadian

or British authorities," Weston told Justice Josephson. "But he did say he was prepared to fight for Khalistan in India."

Bagri had also described himself as second-in-command of the Babbar Khalsa, behind Parmar, Weston said. Bagri had named the other leaders of the group back in Kamloops: Avtar Narwal, Gurmit Gill, and Dalbir Gill.

He told Weston he was trying to unite the Canadian group with the British group on his trip. The British Babbar Khalsa had evolved from the Akhand Kirtani Jatha, Bagri said, referring to Malik's organization.

As dramatic as the violent imagery of Bagri's speeches were, the Crown had less to link him directly to the bombing plot than it did for Malik. There were Premika's statements to CSIS and the RCMP – which she denied on the stand.

Then there was John, the former villagemate of Bagri's who was, without a doubt, the most controversial witness at the trial. By the time the elderly, turbaned Sikh took the stand in March 2004, reporters had already learned that he had demanded and received a payment of U.S.$300,000 in exchange for agreeing to testify. We knew he had killed his own brother during a family dispute in India. And we knew that he had admitted to being a member of a U.S.–based Sikh militant group called Dashmesh Regiment that was linked to an assassination plot against a visiting Punjabi politician.

John's real name was also banned permanently at the trial at the request of the New York man and of the FBI. He had called himself John when he first began to make anonymous calls to the FBI to inform on hard-liners in his own group whom he feared would commit acts of violence and ruin the reputation of the Sikh separatist movement.

John's evidence about Bagri's alleged confession was simple. Bagri had visited him a few weeks after the bombing. They had gone with another man to visit a friend who owned a New Jersey gas station. Outside the building, John expressed his concern to Bagri that his group, the Dashmesh Regiment, had been linked to the Air-India attack.

John said that Bagri had replied, "Why the fuck are they bothering you? We did this."

The elderly Sikh testified that he hadn't said too much in response to Bagri because he was "so stunned and shocked about this."

He was vague on exactly when the conversation took place, but he did recall reporting the comments to his FBI handler, Ron Parrish, within a few days.

John's first encounter with the FBI was like something out of a spy thriller. He began making anonymous calls in late spring 1985 when some members of his group were suspected of plotting to kill the visiting Punjabi politician. He passed on information anonymously to an agent on several occasions. The apartment he shared with several others was then raided in the summer of 1985. He asked one of the agents during the raid if he knew who had been talking to "John." Ron Parrish was standing there in John's apartment and said that he had taken the calls.

"I am John," the informant told Parrish.

John testified that he reconnected with Bagri at the July 1984 convention in New York. Bagri agreed to come to his apartment and speak to about twenty members of the regiment. John claimed that Bagri had bragged about having enough explosives to take out a city block.

At the FBI's request, in conjunction with the RCMP, John met Bagri on several occasions over the years to try to get more incriminating statements out of the Kamloops millworker. John claimed that while Bagri made more cryptic references to the bombing plot, he never again took direct responsibility for it.

Richard Cairns knew that John would be the subject of rigorous cross-examination, so he launched a pre-emptive strike, asking the colourful man to explain a few of the controversies in his own life, including the death of his brother in a family sword fight in the early 1970s. John testified that he had faced a murder charge and had initially been convicted, but eventually won on appeal, when a judge ruled he had killed his drunken brother in self-defence.

Cairns then asked John about the most sensitive of subjects – the money he was paid by the RCMP. John said he wanted to make sure his family would be looked after in the event that something happened to him after he testified. He pointed out that he first told the FBI about Bagri's alleged confession back in 1985 for no money, and had always said he did not want to be a witness. It was only after years of approaches by the RCMP, who could not subpoena the U.S. resident, that John agreed to come to Canada and repeat what he told Ron Parrish in September 1985. For a price.

"I will have some hard time after the testimony," John explained. "I know that difficulties are coming on."

John also admitted to submitting false work records in the United States to try to get his permanent resident's status. And he had lied on other government documents over the years, he said. John explained that he believed lying to help one's family was a small thing that didn't hurt anyone. He never would have lied about Bagri.

John faced a grilling in cross-examination. Defence counsel Richard Peck accused him of minimizing the death of his brother and downplaying his own role in violent militant activities. He called him an opportunist who was willing to do anything or say anything for his own economic gain. Peck noted that John had tried unsuccessfully to get another U.S.$200,000 from the RCMP on the eve of the trial.

The record spoke for itself, but John's demeanour was better than I had expected. He admitted to his own shortcomings and seemed humble and reflective. And John had a big booster in the form of Parrish, the now retired FBI agent, who said the Sikh immigrant was a reliable informant who had provided accurate information over the years. Parrish recalled meeting with John on September 25, 1985, when the informant said Bagri had claimed responsibility for the Air-India and Narita bombings.

"He was very surprised that Bagri was claiming credit for both these explosions. He had no idea [the Babbar Khalsa] had anything to do with it," Parrish said.

He also said that John had never asked for a specific amount of money or for immigration help, although the FBI provided both because John was seen as a valuable asset. It was he who tried to keep John on the hook, Parrish said. The FBI needed people like him to avert U.S. terrorist strikes or assassination plots.

Parrish was asked to authenticate telexes he had prepared for his superiors regarding information that John had provided him between 1985 and 1989. He explained that he sometimes altered what he'd learned slightly to protect John's identity. When he first reported the information about Air-India, he did not attribute it to Bagri, fearing that would identify his source. Instead, he said a number of Canadian members of the Babbar Khalsa, including Bagri, Parmar, Surjan Gill, and Gurmit Gill, were taking credit for the terrorist attack.

The defence then levelled an attack of its own – a direct hit on Parrish's professionalism. Bagri lawyer Michael Code got the FBI agent to admit that he had not told any of his bosses about the alleged Bagri confession.

"If it is a potential confession of a suspect in the most serious crime imaginable, you don't have to alert them to that?" Code asked in astonishment.

Parrish said he felt he had conveyed the information generally in his telex, though he had attributed the confession to more people than just Bagri.

The Bagri legal team went on to have a field day with the lack of information sharing between the FBI and the RCMP on critical information about Air-India. An FBI lawyer sat at the trial, objecting when he thought it necessary to the release of some of the FBI telexes. Several times the questioning of both John and Parrish went in-camera at the FBI's request and we were all forced to leave the courtroom. The *Sun* hired a lawyer to fight the courtroom closure. It did not seem right that the Americans could shut Canadian journalists out of the biggest case in our history, even for a few days.

Parrish was in the witness box off and on for weeks in March and April 2004. At one point the prosecutors had to make an emergency trip to New York to go through additional FBI material at the request of Bagri's lawyers. They came back with a surveillance photo showing John and Bagri meeting at one of the conferences that John had described in his evidence.

The Crown knew it faced great challenges with its case against Bagri, despite his being the documented leader of a terrorist organization banned in Canada. One witness was dead. Others had been threatened. And John was difficult to believe because of the fat wad of cash he was paid by the RCMP, albeit years after first disclosing Bagri's admissions to him.

Joe Bellows first mentioned in December 2003 that a surprise witness had come forward with information about Malik's role in the bombing plot. The prosecution would need time to prepare for his evidence, Bellows said, suggesting the man be brought in to testify in March 2004. It was an intriguing tidbit. I wondered who the man was and began to make some calls around the Sikh community. I didn't have to look far. I learned from Dave Hayer that the seventy-three-year-old retired millworker had visited his constituency office to say he had information about Air-India. Hayer called the police to talk to the man.

When he took the stand, the soft-spoken, fragile gentleman, with his turban and suit, testified that twenty years earlier, between July and October 1984, Malik had asked him to help take an attaché case to the airport.

The millworker, who also won a permanent ban on his name, claimed he barely knew Malik when the businessman approached him on a plaza in front of the Ross Street temple where Malik sold religious artifacts from a table. But, the man said, Malik told him that Parmar had suggested the approach. The millworker had attended separatist meetings with Parmar. He had contributed $100 at one meeting toward a plan to murder Indira Gandhi.

"You are to drop the attaché case at the airport. . . . There is a time-bomb in that. When the plane will go, then the plane will be destroyed," the millworker quoted Malik as saying to him one Sunday in front of the famous South Vancouver temple.

Malik's lawyer, Bill Smart, expressed disbelief that the millworker was only coming forward eighteen years after the bombing. He suggested the man wanted to make a claim on the reward money, and he said the plaza where the man claimed the conversation occurred did not exist in 1984.

But the old man stuck with his story. He was not lying, he said. He described in intimate detail the exact location of the plaza. He was not trying to gain financially, he said. He did not want the reward and had never applied for it.

The Crown closed its case with the forensic evidence in both the Air-India and Narita bombings. The prosecution had a bit of a shocker up its sleeve. It had secretly reconstructed parts of the downed aircraft in an undisclosed Vancouver-area warehouse. The trial would move to the secret location so that Justice Josephson could understand what the forensic experts were saying.

Reporters would be allowed to watch this testimony only on a television monitor. That did not strike me as reasonable, and I launched yet another court challenge demanding public access to this portion of the trial. I didn't win, but the prosecution and the RCMP did agree to give us a tour of the facility after the evidence was presented.

We knew that very little wreckage had been recovered from the ocean's floor – less than 5 per cent of the plane. What we didn't know was that other large pieces had been recreated. Using photographs and film images from the ocean's floor, Prof. Christopher Peel, a British scientist, had been able to pinpoint the exact location of the bomb.

Peel was a very effective witness for the Crown. He explained complex science and metallurgical physics in a way that everyone in the courtroom could understand what he was saying. From looking at the recovered pieces, Peel said he could see where the crack ran forward and aft from a point on the rear left side of the plane. He had analyzed the tortured and twisted bits of metal to determine the force and location of the bomb. In chilling testimony, he described the order in which the pieces had ripped off the fuselage, throwing everyone out. He said that the bomb had been in cargo hold 52. This was where the Crown said it would have been if it had originated in Vancouver and been transferred to Air-India Flight 182 in Toronto.

"What I was looking for was a hole blown in the fuselage structure, surrounded by deformed, damaged material in a reasonably symmetrical way," Peel explained. "If the bomb is of sufficient size to blow a hole in the fuselage, a hole will appear.

Around the hole will be this very twisted, curled, deformed metal in very much a symmetrical pattern, and from that hole will escape critical cracks." The cracks break apart the plane, he said, splitting it "as if clamshell is opening."

To back up his theory, Peel showed a dramatic video of a test explosion he had done aboard another Boeing 747 under controlled conditions in England in 1997. Victims' relatives in the gallery gasped in horror as they watched a fireball bursting from the plane's side one-hundredth of a second after the bomb was set off. By six one-hundredths of a second, cracks in the plane's fuselage could be seen racing away from the flames and large panels of metal began to peel off. They could imagine the deaths of their loved ones.

Peel said the bomb aboard the Air-India flight was five times more powerful than the one that brought down Pan Am Flight 101 over Lockerbie, Scotland, in 1988. Both Peel and the defence expert, Dr. Edward Trimble, had worked together on the Lockerbie case. But in Canada, they presented duelling views of where the bomb had been located. Trimble, who admitted he was a generalist in the field of air disaster investigation, claimed his analysis showed the bomb was located about two metres away from where Peel said it was. That placed it smack dab in the middle of cargo hold 51, meaning it had to have been inside a suitcase that originated in Toronto.

When the press corps finally got inside the secret warehouse to see the remnants of the plane close up, I found the sight haunting and eerie. Some of the pieces, looking grey and corroded, were clearly the ones I'd seen floating in the ocean in news photos at the time. A large part of the outer shell towered above us, suspended by cables, its red-and-white Air-India markings and part of the corporate logo intact.

The most striking thing was how little of the plane had been put back together. The majority of the recovered pieces, including large segments of the wing and the landing gear, as well as passenger seats, tray tables, and the outer shell carrying the Air-India logo, sat off to the sides of the partial reconstruction. When I saw the seats, with fabric torn and foam hanging out, I could picture the people sitting in them. The window holes, which we looked at from the outside in, made me think of the people looking out at the view as the plane flew smoothly toward London.

We all zeroed in on the spot underneath a piece of passenger floor where Peel said the bomb had been placed. We stood there trying to imagine the instant when it exploded. As overwhelming as it was to see the wreckage, what was really eerie was the absence of anything related to the victims – no suitcases, no clothing, no personal effects. Terry Milewski commented that it was "bloodless," like a graveyard without any bodies.

I was filled with sadness as I stood there. I wished that all Canadians could have seen the absolute devastation wreaked by the bombing. Maybe then, they would have understood the magnitude of the calamity.

After a short break in the trial, the defence began its case. We thought the two lead counsels might argue that the defence did not need to call witnesses, that the Crown had not met its burden of proof. That was the tactic the defence used in the earlier Reyat trial. But it had not been successful.

I was anxious to learn whether the defendants would testify, something I had been looking forward to covering for years. But neither defence team would tip its hand.

Because Malik's name appeared first on the indictment, his team was the first to present its arguments.

The first two Malik witnesses cast doubt on the timing of a meeting in Seattle that the Crown had suggested was where the final Air-India planning had taken place. A Calgary school board official and a doctor testified that bombing suspect Balwant Bhandher and his family appeared to be in Calgary in the days before the bombing, according to records on file. That contradicted testimony from Narinder Gill, who had earlier told the trial that he had travelled with Bhandher and his family to Seattle.

It seemed obvious to me that Malik's lawyers would be reluctant to call Bhandher to testify about the Seattle meeting. In my dealing with him, I'd found him to be cocky and mouthy, and he had admitted to reporters that he was an Air-India suspect. At one point he had faced a criminal harassment charge for his treatment of Rani. The charge was stayed only after she entered the Witness Protection Program.

I was not the only journalist who was surprised when Bhandher's son, Raminder Singh "Mindy" Bhandher, was brought in as a witness for Malik, despite his admitted criminal history of gangsterism.

Mindy had been a presence in Courtroom 20 on and off since the trial began, as had his father. The younger Bhandher would come with other admitted gangsters. He was there once with Roman Narwal, the son of the late Kamloops Babbar Khalsa leader and Air-India suspect. Roman had been fingered by other gangsters as being involved in the Hayer murder plot. The sons of the two Air-India suspects had shared a place in Calgary in the months before Mindy was called to testify for Malik.

It was the friendship between Mindy and Roman that led Malik's lawyers to call the gangster to testify. They wanted him to refute Rani's evidence about a conversation the two young men had had years earlier regarding the bombing. Rani had testified that Mindy told Malik he was concerned that Roman was mouthing off to friends about Air-India. Roman had apparently told some buddies in a bar that he had walked in on his father, Malik, Bagri, and Parmar when he was just a boy of ten. They had had the plans of the plane laid out on the table.

Sporting a flashy jacket and unbuttoned dress shirt with a flared '70s collar, Mindy testified that he had had no conversation about Air-India – either with Malik or with Roman. He said he was in India in April 1997 when the conversation with Malik was alleged to have occurred. He brought a passport and airline ticket stubs to court to prove his whereabouts at the time, and denied a prosecution suggestion that he and his family had often sold or loaned their passports for others to use to get illegal entry to Canada. I wasn't surprised by his denial, several of my community sources had told me that others often used Bhandher family passports. Balwant Bhandher, they alleged, had loaned his to Talwinder Parmar to flee to Pakistan.

Mindy denied it all. He claimed he was in India for a sham marriage for which he had received $10,000. But he did admit to Justice Josephson that he had repeatedly lied under oath at other trials.

Laughter erupted in the packed courtroom several times during Mindy's testimony. He claimed he had made more than $350,000 from drug smuggling, trafficking, and fraud and that he still had a machine to illegally copy credit cards, but had had to get out of the business because he couldn't find reliable help.

A graduate of Malik's Khalsa School, Mindy said Malik was a father figure to him and that he had lived with the Malik family after a falling out with his own parents. He said Malik had given his family a Land Rover and paid for him to go to India.

He laughed when Bellows asked him if he dealt heroin. He denied it, but admitted to selling marijuana, cocaine, and ecstasy. He said he carried a loaded handgun for protection and had threatened to kill at least two people. He admitted that he had threatened Crown witness Narinder Gill and had thrown rocks through the man's living-room window in 1997 after I first quoted Gill in an article critical of practices at the Khalsa School.

It was hard to imagine a more unreliable witness. Yet, in the end, Josephson believed him.

Right after Mindy, Malik's lawyers called Daljit Sandhu, the former Vancouver temple president, who was also an Air-India suspect.

Sandhu angrily denied Rani's claim that Malik had identified him as the man who had gone to pick up the tickets used in the bombings. Humility was not Sandhu's strong point.

"You are telling me I would go to pick up the tickets at the request of Mr. Malik? I am a community leader. He is just a business leader. You want the prime minister to ask the governor general to pick up something for him? It's not possible," Sandhu said.

He yelled "bullshit" when the prosecutor accused him of being involved in the bombing and forcefully denied ever supporting violence in the name of the Sikh separatist cause. But he was quickly contradicted in cross-examination on his evidence by archived news reports from my newspaper and the CBC that showed him publicly and passionately promoting violence, time and time again. He had praised the assassins of Indira Gandhi as martyrs. He was quoted as saying he wished he had killed Gandhi himself. He had organized a memorial service for Gandhi's assassins. He even presented the Air-India trial with a photograph of himself with one of the assassin's wives, taken when she visited the Ross Street temple.

Sandhu also testified that the evidence of the anonymous millworker implicating Malik had to be false because there was no plaza outside the Ross Street temple until 1986. The man had earlier testified that Malik approached him on the plaza and asked him to take a bomb-laden attaché case to the airport. Sandhu said Malik did not have a booth in front of the temple as the millworker had claimed in his evidence. But the prosecution was able to confront Sandhu with photographs published that day in my newspaper showing that a plaza had existed from the time the temple opened in 1970. It had just been enlarged in 1986. Despite the photographs sitting in front of him, Sandhu insisted he was right.

It was clear that the prosecutors were starting to feel confident. The first two main Malik witnesses had not done well on the stand. And now came Satwant Sandhu, another close Malik associate, who was alleged to have been involved in the bombing plot.

While less angry that Daljit Sandhu on the witness stand, Satwant also got caught in a web of his own making. He denied any involvement in the bombing plot, contrary to Rani's testimony, but he was forced to admit that he had lied to police years earlier about knowing bombing mastermind Talwinder Parmar. He had claimed to police that he had no dealings with Parmar in 1985, when he had in fact given Parmar advice on how to check his house for listening devices.

Satwant also admitted that Parmar gave him thousands of dollars to travel to India in 1986. He had been a director of both Malik's Khalsa School and Khalsa Credit Union, Sandhu said. He admitted he had made an on-air death threat against me in

February 1998, though he claimed he did it only because I had written a story against him. In fact, I did not even know who he was at the time.

It was a disastrous beginning to the Malik defence. Three witnesses in a row were proven by the Crown to have a history of lying. Two were terrorist suspects and the third a drug-dealing gangster. Many of us in the public gallery were left shaking our heads and even feeling a little sorry for Malik's lawyers. But they bounced back, convincing Josephson to allow into evidence a day-planner from the late Hardial Johal. It contained a note from the week before the bombing, suggesting that a meeting at Parmar's house was to discuss an ongoing lawsuit against Tara Hayer and his newspaper. Justice Josephson agreed to let in the daybook, although he had earlier disallowed the evidence of another dead man – Hayer himself.

The last Malik witness was a religious teacher at the Khalsa School named Inderjit Singh Arora, who is married to a cousin of Malik's wife, though the relationship was never revealed during his evidence. Arora testified that he had seen Rani taking a copy of *Soft Target* from the school's bookstore. The controversial 1989 book provided some details of the Air-India bombing and a link to Malik. Rani had earlier denied reading any books about the bombing.

Arora claimed that Rani had never returned the book. He admitted he had once shared a close friendship with the daycare supervisor, as had Malik. He confirmed what Rani said about Malik hosting a birthday party for her at his house and their attending religious camps together.

Up until Malik's team closed its case in the third week of June 2004, I was left wondering whether he would testify in his own defence. Knowing Malik as I do, he would have wanted to testify. Knowing his lawyers, they would have advised him against it. At the time, I really wanted to go to Ireland to attend the annual memorial service in the small Irish hamlet of Ahakista, near where the plane went down. I gambled that Malik would not be called to the stand and took a few days off the trial, leaving on June 20. Malik's lawyers informed the court the next day that he would not be testifying.

Hours after the memorial service finished in Ireland, I got word that the Supreme Court of Canada had finally ruled in the case of Mrs. Reyat and the anti-terrorism hearing. Canada's highest court ruled that it was constitutional to force her to answer questions about her knowledge of the Air-India bombing, but it shouldn't be done behind closed doors. The parallel application by my newspaper, which we'd started when I stumbled across the secret hearing a year earlier, had been successful, the court also said.

As happy I was to be part of legal history, it was clear to me that the historic twin judgments had come too late to affect the Air-India trial. The prosecution had already rested its case. And Crown lawyers had already told Mrs. Reyat that she would not be called to testify.

Her decision to fight this to the Supreme Court, which had been backed by the lawyers for both Malik and Bagri, had succeeded in keeping out of the trial what could have been some of the most critical evidence. Rani had said Satnam Reyat had disclosed all the details of the plot to her. Satnam – whose name means truth in Punjabi – had been there the day that Rani confronted Malik. Now, none of this would come out at the trial, despite the Supreme Court's ruling. Satnam's secrets about what she had told Rani would stay with her and her family. Once again, clever legal manoeuvring had triumphed over the truth.

Even in the midst of this high-profile trial, some of the more militant supporters of Malik and Bagri did not shy away from showing their true colours. The Waheguroo Web site, which had violated the publication ban on Rani's identity, allowed a posting on its message board by a Surrey youth claiming to be forming a new Babbar Khalsa organization in the name of Talwinder Parmar. I did a page-one story on the posting, which included quotes from other users of the Web site criticizing the young man. That elicited a barrage of attacks against me, including pages and pages of postings under the heading "Death Threats to Kim Bolan."

I showed the material to my editors, who suggested I contact the Air-India Task Force. I passed on everything to the RCMP. They contacted the Web master, but claimed they could not do much more because the site originated in California. But the site also hosted links to Canadian sites run by relatives of both Malik and Bagri. One of those sites was for the group Sikh Vision, which was founded by Bagri's son-in-law Jaswinder Parmar and his friend Pary Dulai, who was working as an investigator for Bagri's lawyers. The Web site had pictures of both Parmar and Dulai wearing vests with Babbar Khalsa logos. It also featured photographs of Talwinder Parmar posing with automatic rifles, and called him a *shaheed*, or martyr.

Bagri's lawyers pulled out all the stops in defence of their client. The accused man didn't have some of the legal woes Malik faced – his defence was 100 per cent government-funded, meaning almost limitless resources. And his lawyers were passionate.

Michael Code, thespian in his presentation, argued forcefully on Charter issues and made compelling legal arguments that seemed to captivate Justice Josephson. Michael Tammen, the youngest of the trio of lead lawyers, was the pitbull who ripped into Crown witnesses with such vigour that he sometimes turned red-faced. Richard Peck, the veteran defence lawyer, was always impeccably prepared and could pick off witnesses with precision.

The Bagri team had successfully mounted Charter challenges throughout the case – first over the CSIS tape erasures, then over late disclosure by the prosecution, and finally over the erasure of interview tapes with Premika and CSIS agent Willy Laurie. Josephson agreed with them each time.

But the Bagri team also brought in a few dubious witnesses of its own.

Amarjit Singh Buttar, a Connecticut lawyer with connections to the Democrats, travelled to Vancouver to defend Bagri's violent rhetoric, saying that every Sikh back in 1984 was talking that way. Nobody really meant it. But Buttar went a little far on cross-examination when he refused to describe hijackings as necessarily being terrorist in nature. He said he would need to know the motive of the hijackers. He also helped the prosecution by confirming that the slogan "*murtabad*" meant "death to" someone, which contradicted what the defence translator had claimed.

Next up was Dr. Gurmit Aulakh, the colourful separatist leader based in Washington, D.C., who once told me he did not support either Malik or Bagri. But there he was, on behalf of the former Babbar Khalsa leader, testifying, as Buttar had, that many Sikhs had preached violence in the emotional aftermath of the Golden Temple attack. Aulakh blamed the government of India for the Air-India bombing, as well as Talwinder Parmar, who he said was an Indian agent. Aulakh also justified murder if it was done in defence of Sikhism.

But it was a soft-spoken Sikh woman who gave Bagri his best alibi. Jagdish Kaur Johal, sister of the late bombing suspect Avtar Narwal, aunt of Hayer murder suspect Roman Narwal, and long-time friend of both the Bagris and the Parmars, came to court and testified that she and her brother were using Bagri's car the weekend of the bombing.

She said they had borrowed the Bagris' only car to drive from Kamloops to Vancouver to do some shopping prior to her wedding that fall. So, although the Johals had two cars of their own, Johal asked the court to believe that, for some unstated reason, they had had to use Bagri's only car, leaving Bagri's large family carless. Johal claimed that after reaching the Lower Mainland, she and her brother stopped by Parmar's Burnaby home for "a bite to eat" – just as he would have been putting the final touches on his terrorist plot.

She claimed that she had not seen Bagri in the Vancouver area at all during the weekend of the bombing. This threw a wrench into the Crown's contention that he was an active participant in the plot and that he was at Parmar's house that weekend and had asked his girlfriend, Premika, to borrow her car.

The young investigator working for the Bagri defence, Pary Dulai, had found the perfect witness. Johal said Dulai had approached her to testify in 2003. How Dulai would have known that Johal could testify about who drove the Bagri car to Vancouver did not come out in court. But she surfaced as a convenient witness given that the Crown agreed in the first two weeks of the trial to a controversial admission that said Bagri was not the man CSIS saw driving his own car to Parmar's house on the eve of the bombings. The CSIS report had been less definitive than the admission read into evidence in May 2003. Johal's brother Avtar Narwal wore the same Babbar Khalsa uniform that Bagri did – a long dusky blue tunic and tall orange turban. They were about the same age and both had long dark beards. Jagdish Johal agreed that her Kamloops home had at least two vehicles and a motorcycle, but she and her brother still took the Bagris' sole car for a weekend of shopping.

She said her brother Avtar was just a member of the Babbar Khalsa, nothing more. In fact, he was listed on corporate documents as a director of the group. She said she knew that her sister-in-law, as well as her nephew, had visited Bagri throughout his incarceration.

Bagri's lawyers also contended that he was working at the mill during all the key periods of the bombing conspiracy, including on the Friday before the bombs were taken to the airport. In his cross-examination, Cairns was able to demonstrate the mill's 1985 work records were full of errors and omissions.

Having refuted the statements that Premika made to CSIS about Bagri being in town for the bombing, Bagri's lawyers then called to the stand a number of U.S. witnesses to discredit John, the FBI informant. They had hired a former FBI agent named Jack Cloonan to attack the credibility of Ron Parrish, John's handler so many years earlier.

Cloonan was a typical hired gun. He did commentary for a U.S. news network and he had been featured in the hit documentary *Fahrenheit 9/11*, where he empathized with the victims of the World Trade Center attack. At the Air-India trial, several victims' families watched anxiously as he discredited Parrish.

With the appropriate level of outrage, he ripped into Parrish's professionalism, accusing him of breaching FBI protocol by doing little to follow up on Bagri's alleged confession to his informant. "It would appear that Ron Parrish did not report all this information to his superiors," Cloonan said.

The implication was that there could not have possibly been a confession passed on to Parrish because if there had been, he would have done more with it. But Cairns got quite ticked at the slick American commentator. In his cross-examination of the witness, he suggested it was Cloonan who was breaking FBI protocol by trashing a fellow agent in a Canadian courtroom. "You are really anxious to find something wrong with what Mr. Parrish had done, despite evidence to the contrary," Cairns said.

Cloonan was also used by the Bagri defence team to round up some New York friends of John to attack him in court. First on the stand was Kamal Jit, whose son Bagri had once saved from kidnappers and who also knew John. Jit claimed John had told him he was making up the story about Bagri and would be willing to change it if Bagri's family came up with some money. But Jit was an odd fellow. He had already done several interviews with investigators in English, but claimed not to understand it while in the witness box. He also lied in court about having a meeting with Bagri's lawyers in Vancouver, perhaps not knowing that the lawyers had already described it to the judge.

Next up was Balbir Singh, who had lived with John at the time of Bagri's alleged confession. He said he could not recall John's mentioning anything about it. Nor did he loan his car to John, he said. But he also denied things he had earlier told the prosecution and contradicted some of his own testimony.

The final witness was said to be another former roommate of John whom Cloonan had approached to testify. But once Gurmit Singh Kalotia arrived from New Jersey to dispute John's earlier testimony, it became apparent that he had not lived with John in 1985. Another man called Gurmit Singh was the roommate at the time. "It can be a different Gurmit," Kalotia conceded on the stand.

Bagri's lawyers finished off their case by saying the charges against Bagri should be stayed because the tapes erased by CSIS could have proven Bagri's innocence.

One of the things that surprised me most about the Bagri defence was that his lawyers implicated Bagri's closest associate in the bombing, Talwinder Parmar, as well as other Kamloops Babbar Khalsa members, such as Avtar Narwal. They also suggested that Hardial Johal was involved. It struck me that the strategy was to blame the dead men and not to bother explaining the years-long association Bagri had with each of them after the bombing. Bagri's lawyers did not once suggest that the Indian government blew up the plane, nor did they try to justify Bagri's close relationship with Parmar, a man they were saying was a mass murderer.

The closing arguments in the Air-India case lasted for weeks. The trial did not end dramatically. It just petered out. In early December, as everyone associated with the case neared exhaustion, Justice Josephson thanked all for their unprecedented co-operation – defence and prosecution lawyers, court staff, sheriffs, and the two young lawyers who had been working with him for months. He also announced, much to everyone's surprise, that he would present an executive summary of his historic decision on March 16, 2005.

As the trial closed on December 3, 2004, after more than nineteen months and 115 witnesses, Ian Bruce Josephson gave no hint of which way he was leaning.

For the victims' optimistic families, it was the beginning of 102 days of hope.

CHAPTER 12

Loss of Faith

O N MARCH 16, 2005, I stood in the rain for two hours waiting to get into the courtroom to hear the historic judgment. It was a heavy, relentless rain – not the kind Vancouver usually gets in March.

I had got up at 3:00 a.m. to do a spot on Canada AM, so I was tired. But pumped. More than eighty victims' relatives from around the world had travelled to Vancouver to hear the verdict first-hand. As they waited to go inside the courtroom, they greeted and hugged people they had not seen in a long time, including reporters like me who had known some of them for twenty years. We all hoped that today the story would be over, that maybe the families would finally have some measure of peace. There was so much hope.

Television stations had set up satellite trucks on the street outside the courthouse so they could cut into broadcasting and tell Canadians the verdict as soon as it was known. I kept getting asked for interviews as I waited with other journalists for our media passes into the courtroom. For the first time since the trial began, I dared to make an on-air prediction.

"I think there will be at least one conviction," I boldly proclaimed on both the CBC and CTV. I quickly qualified: "Of course, only Justice Josephson knows for sure for about another hour."

Mine was the first name called by the court staff handing out media passes. I joined the crowd in the courthouse lobby waiting to go through security and found myself within a few feet of the relatives and supporters of the two accused men. I was surprised how many of them had come and how confident they appeared. Several muttered comments to me – some in English, some in Punjabi.

Bagri's daughters were there, dressed in traditional Punjabi clothes for the first time since the trial began. Bagri's son-in-law Jaswinder Parmar was there – not looking at all disturbed that Bagri's lawyers had tried to pin the bombing on his late father, Talwinder, and had repeatedly suggested there had been a falling out between Bagri and Parmar before the bombing. Bagri's brothers were there too. Malik's family was present, including his elder brother Gurdip from California and his younger brother Jasjeet from India.

What impressed me though was not the number of relatives there, but the array of supporters, from other Air-India suspects and long-time friends to a number of young men known to be linked to Indo-Canadian gangs.

Balwant Bhandher was there – the man named in Rani's testimony as having taken the bombs to the airport. Satwant Sandhu, another alleged conspirator was there, smiling and comfortable as he entered the same courtroom in which he had admitted a few months earlier to making a threat against me.

Malik's close friend Narinder Singh Bhullar was there, urging me to accept whatever the judge said. "I will if you will," I shot back. Bhullar was standing with his buddy Balbir Singh Hara, who almost lost his son on the ill-fated flight before the teenager's ticket was mysteriously switched by Amarjit Pawa, the travel agent who was part of the plot. Hara had remained loyal to Malik ever since. He had refused to co-operate with the RCMP.

I wondered why they would all show up unless they already sensed an acquittal. I remembered a sheriff telling me two days earlier that both men had confidently cleared out their jail cells, sending everything they had accumulated over four and a half years home with relatives.

It was almost an hour before everyone was seated in Courtroom 20. I was in my usual front-row seat directly behind the bulletproof glass protecting Malik. Terry Milewski was right beside me and the Robert Matas was beside him. In the section to our right were more journalists, with the friends and supporters of the two accused men behind them.

In the centre section, behind the journalists, were more relatives and friends of the defendants, some of them next to relatives of the victims. The two courtroom sections were filled with more victims' family members – some were regulars, like Perviz Madon and her children, Eddie and Natasha. Others, like Banu Saklikar, who lost her sister and brother-in-law, had previously come to court only on a couple of occasions.

It was not just the relatives who had travelled great distances to hear the verdict. Others whom fate had dragged into the tragedy were at the courthouse too. Daniel Brown, the British seaman who had pulled bodies from the sea for hours two decades earlier, had come from northern England with his wife, Louise. Martine Donahue, the delightful senior who had taken the original call at CP Air's booking office from the terrorist ticket purchaser, was there also. So was Jeannie Bakermans, the CP Air clerk who was working at the counter when the bomb-laden suitcases were checked in.

There were almost as many police officers as civilian spectators – dozens of sheriffs and members of the Vancouver Police Department, as well as RCMP officers from the Air-India Task Force and at least one CSIS employee who had sat through most of the trial. Even some retirees had returned to witness the outcome of the biggest case of their careers.

When Justice Josephson began reading the summary of his ruling, I quickly started my tape recorder. His opening comments were about the events of June 23, 1985. "Words are incapable of adequately conveying the senseless horror of these crimes," he said. "These hundreds of men, women and children were entirely innocent victims of a diabolical act of terrorism unparalleled until recently in aviation history and finding its roots in fanaticism at its basest and most inhumane level."

At first, he seemed to be siding with the Crown. He accepted the evidence of the prosecution expert Prof. Christopher Peel when he testified the bomb was in a cargo hold containing a bag that had originated in Vancouver. He accepted that Talwinder Parmar had masterminded the bombings according to both the Crown and the defence. And he attacked the credibility of Inderjit Reyat, who had pleaded guilty to supplying some bomb components, but claimed at the trial not to know key elements of the terrorist plot. He called Reyat "an unmitigated liar under oath" who crafted a story that was "improbable in the extreme."

I was encouraged in thinking that he was going to convict someone.

Josephson then began his assessment of the Crown's case against Malik. After nineteen months of testimony and arguments, it all came down to the evidence of three witnesses, he said. Then he proceeded to attack the first two – the farmer and the millworker – who had both testified that Malik had asked them to carry suitcases to the airport as part of a plot against the government of India.

Josephson said the farmer was not believable because of inconsistencies in his story and a financial dispute he had with Malik that had gone on for years. He then said he did not believe the millworker either, because the elderly man only came forward in December 2003 and by then had had access to news reports detailing evidence from the other witness. Josephson also said the man was lying because a plaza in front of the Ross Street temple where he claimed to have talked to Malik about the plot did not exist in 1984.

That comment startled me.

"What?" I whispered to Terry Milewski, who was sitting beside me. Photographs from my newspaper showing the plaza in both 1970 and 1984 had been entered into evidence. Had Josephson forgotten? The CBC had footage of the plaza as well, showing Sikh militants dancing and setting off fireworks on it as they celebrated the murder of Indira Gandhi in November 1984.

I calmed myself with the thought that he could still convict Malik on the strength of Rani's evidence alone. But, without a doubt, I was not the only one perturbed by Josephson's comment. I could feel the tension rising in the courtroom.

Josephson began his assessment of Rani – the star witness – by saying positive things about her demeanour: "She appeared energetic, intelligent, outgoing and had a pleasant manner, while exhibiting a strong will and determination. She revealed an excellent memory, relating vivid details surrounding certain events."

So far, so good, I thought. Maybe his flawed dismissal of the millworker wouldn't matter.

Then he did a 180: "Surprising, however, were her adamant protestations of ongoing love, respect, and longing for Mr. Malik, a man whom she claims admitted his complicity in the senseless mass murder of hundreds of complete innocents," he said. We all suddenly realized where he was going. "When one adds to that her evidence of his treatment of the student [Preethi] Cudail, his countless acts of fraud and, ultimately, his cruel treatment and firing of her from a position that was a central part of her life, that surprise edges towards incredulity."

He said he found too many inconsistencies in her testimony. He said she repeated information that had been in the public domain and must have been lying about reading books that contained it. And he said he didn't believe her explanation for waiting months to tell police about the key confession – that she didn't appreciate the value of the evidence.

Before he got to the not-guilty proclamation, I ran from the courtroom. I called the newsroom, interrupted the morning story meeting, and yelped, "Malik is getting out. Malik is getting out. Malik is getting out."

I raced back into court, squeezing past the scribbling reporters as Josephson continued: "There is simply no evidence tending to point to the role that Mr. Malik may have played in the conspiracy to place bombs on Air-India planes." I saw several victims' relatives burst into tears.

"It follows that the Crown has not proved its case against Mr. Malik beyond a reasonable doubt with respect to his being a member of the alleged conspiracy."

Like the wails I had heard in the Cheemas' home on the night of the bombings, the gasps and sobs in the courtroom that day were anguishing, unforgettable.

I ran from the courtroom a second time, as did several other reporters, as Josephson launched into the case against Bagri. I had to tell the news desk the official verdict, and I figured that if Malik was getting off, then Bagri would be also. The case against him had always been weaker.

When I tried to take my courtroom seat a second time, I accidentally caught a heel in the metal tray containing dozens of coloured pencils belonging to courtroom artist Jane Wolsak, who was there for the CBC. She was furious. As I desperately tried to pick them up, I missed several of Josephson's initial points lambasting the Crown's case against Bagri. But I heard him throw out everything said by John, the FBI informant, declaring the man was "an individual driven by self-interest" who was willing "to engage in deception and lies, even under penalty of perjury, whenever he believed it would advance his self-interest." There had been much controversy over the RCMP agreement in 1997 to pay John to testify.

Josephson surprised me, though, when he also discounted the evidence of retired FBI special agent Ron Parrish, who testified that John told him details of the Bagri confession back in September 1985, before any payments were made to him.

Josephson was then left with Premika, the close female friend of Bagri who had implicated him to CSIS, but never in court. He said, "Proof of Mr. Bagri's guilt beyond a reasonable doubt rests upon hearsay statements for which there is no reliable confirmatory evidence. These statements were provided on a confidential basis and not under oath by a person who falsely claimed loss of memory when testifying. When one adds to this the inability of the defence to conduct an effective cross-examination on significant issues surrounding those hearsay statements, I conclude that . . . a reasonable doubt arises with respect to the ultimate reliability of [Premika's] hearsay statements."

In other words, while he believed Premika was feigning memory loss, presumably because she feared she might be killed, he thought Bagri was placed at a disadvantage because his lawyers couldn't cross-examine the woman.

As I twisted in my seat at the perverse logic of a defendant benefiting from a witness's fear, Josephson dismissed all the charges against Bagri. His family members cheered. Those who had lost loved ones sunk deeper into their chairs. Some held their faces in their hands.

Josephson's final comment was strange, as if he was somehow trying to convince the shell-shocked family members he had done the right thing: "I began by describing the horrific nature of these cruel acts of terrorism, acts which cry out for justice. Justice is not achieved, however, if persons are convicted on anything less than the requisite standard of proof beyond a reasonable doubt. Despite what appear to have been the best and most earnest of efforts by the police and the Crown, the evidence has fallen markedly short of that standard."

I saw RCMP members who had worked on the case for most of their careers break into tears on hearing this judgment. Some victims' relatives had to be helped from the courtroom. Reporters, me among them, ran to file their stories.

In the courthouse lobby, Malik and Bagri supporters laughed, joked, and embraced. Some muttered negative comments to me. A couple of the gangsters started mouthing off to Doug Best. It was tense and surreal.

My first reaction to the verdict was selfish. I was afraid. I thought I would be in danger when the two men got out. Their supporters had already threatened me in person, on the phone, and on-line. I had pushed the story more than any other journalist both before they were charged and throughout the trial. Now I was sure I had made the right decision in sending my two children out of the country for the duration.

And then I thought about Rani. She was already living in fear, her life completely ruined. Now it was all for nothing. I thought back to when I had told her that if it were me who had information about the bombing, as a citizen I would feel obligated to do the right thing – to tell police what I knew.

I no longer think that way. Tara Hayer tried to do the right thing and was killed. So many of the witnesses risked their families and themselves. Yet they were not believed.

Then I thought about the victims' families. They had come to the trial week after week, their sorrow so evident even years after their losses. They had come again to hear the verdict, only to be devastated, absolutely devastated. I had never seen anything like their pain. I couldn't even speak to people I had known for two decades. It was as if the plane had only just come crashing down, as if they were reliving the catastrophe all over again.

They said they felt betrayed. They had fought for justice with such dignity and grace, for almost twenty years. And it meant nothing. They said they felt like second-class citizens. They said they felt sure that if the victims had been white Canadians, the whole case would have been handled differently from the beginning. They were right.

I had to scramble to cover the news conferences, to do television and radio commentary. I had stories to file. I had stories to rewrite, given the outcome. And I think I was in shock the whole time. Every journalist who had sat regularly in the trial had believed that there would be at least one conviction that day. We were completely wrong.

During an interview on CBC *Newsworld Today*, I was asked how we could have been so wrong. I tried to explain that the judge obviously understood the law better than journalists, who are lay people after all. Reasonable doubt to me meant something different than it did to Justice Josephson.

To me, it wasn't reasonable that Rani would have made up a confession from Malik only to have her own life completely ruined. It wasn't reasonable that Premika would have been so fearful that she feigned memory loss in the witness box if Bagri had been innocent. It wasn't reasonable that John would have told the FBI about Bagri's confession back in 1985 for a little expense money, only to be accused of being an opportunistic liar for negotiating the RCMP payment twelve years later. It wasn't reasonable that both Malik and Bagri had an ongoing close association with both Parmar and Reyat before and after the bombings, but were not involved in the conspiracy.

Bagri and Malik were released within an hour of the verdict. Bagri was the first to appear at a makeshift podium under a dripping tarp on the fourth-floor plaza of the courthouse. His daughter read a prepared statement to the media as he stood beside her, his lawyers behind him.

"I want to repeat publicly today what I have told the authorities numerous times since 1985 – that I had absolutely no involvement in any of these criminal activities," the statement read. "The loss of so many innocent lives resulting from these events is an enormous tragedy . . . It has brought unspeakable suffering to the families and friends of those who died."

I asked Bagri if he regretted his 1984 statement demanding the retaliatory murder of fifty thousand Hindus. He didn't answer. He didn't answer any questions. His lawyers quickly hustled him off.

Word circulated through the animated crowd that Malik would be leaving the building soon at street level, two floors below. It was amazing that no one got hurt in the throng of journalists, cameras, sheriffs, police, and spectators that rushed downstairs.

Malik had a gleam in his eye and a bemused little grin as he exited the courthouse to an awaiting Mercedes. He was with his brothers and sons, and the sheriffs pushed us reporters aside to

clear a pathway. He refused to make any statement. The crowd
was so unruly that some of us got shoved out onto the street into
the traffic. Malik chatted to someone on a cellphone as the sedan
raced off.

He was greeted back at his Shaughnessy mansion by dozens
of well-wishers shouting the Sikh war cry, "Bole So Nihal. Sat
Sri Akal." Reporters shouted questions from the sidewalk, but
Malik did not answer. He took off his shoes and walked inside.

He later issued a statement on a Web site his son had
confidently registered a few days before the verdict under the
URL notguilty.org. "Our family deeply sympathizes with
the families of those that died in this horrific tragedy. The anger
and sadness that the families are going through because of
today's decision should be directed towards the RCMP and
Crown. They had given these families a false hope of justice by
proceeding with a case without merit."

But the anger of the victims' families was not directed at the
RCMP or the prosecutors. At an emotional news conference, relatives with tear-stained faces said they felt betrayed by the justice
system and by their country. They were confounded by the verdict.

Eddie Madon again addressed the reporters who had watched
him grow up. "Let me start out by saying how devastated I am
and we all are that the true perpetrators of this crime are free
men," he said. "They have made yet another mockery of the
Canadian justice system."

Mary Lougheed, a Manitoba woman who had lost her brother
Don, said bluntly, "I feel this is a victory today, a victory for terrorism in Canada."

Sanjay Lazar, orphaned as a teen and now a lawyer, had lost
his entire family – his pregnant mother, his father, and his baby
sister. He had travelled all the way from Mumbai, India, to hear

the verdict, assuming there would be justice. But it left him, as he said, feeling "totally hollow."

"Today once again we have lost our families all over again, this time to the Canadian justice system," he told reporters.

Rattan Kalsi's voice cracked as he pushed forward to the cameras a small photograph of his beautiful twenty-one-year-old daughter Indira. "I accept the judge's decision, but this is a small court. There is another, higher court – God's court. They will be punished a little later," he said.

Speaker after speaker called for a public inquiry into the terrorism plot and failed twenty-year criminal investigation. And they expressed anger at comments made earlier that day by federal Public Safety Minister Anne McLellan dismissing their demand for an inquiry.

"I would have to be convinced that after a year of evidence, and over one hundred and twenty witnesses, that there is anything to be gained, that could be learned," a callous-sounding McLellan said. "I would have to be convinced that there is anything further after twenty years, and this trial, that is not on the public record, that we would learn."

Lata Pada, the gracious dancer who had lost her husband and daughters, said McLellan was pouring salt into their wounds: "That's a totally irresponsible and premature decision on her part when she hasn't even taken the time to review the judge's decision."

Pada said she felt betrayed by the verdict, just as she had felt betrayed by the government's response to the bombing twenty years earlier. "Had this been a tragedy that affected mainstream white Anglo-Saxon Canadians, I think the response would have been very different," she said with fire in her eyes. "I think we all believe this and today, again, we've been let down."

As I rode in a cab back to the newsroom to write more stories, I felt completely drained. But I also wondered if the RCMP thought there might be retaliation against people, me included. I paged Doug Best, who called me back on my cellphone while I was still in the taxi.

"I think I am hooped," I said. "Malik is going to feel like he can do anything now. You know he blames Rani and me for getting arrested."

Best said the RCMP investigators were absolutely devastated. "We prepared for a lot of different outcomes – but not this one," he said. "None of us imagined that there would have been two acquittals."

He said they were going to do threat assessments on their witnesses and others, including me, and that he would call me back later in the day after talking to the new head of the task force.

Three task-force members suggested that I stay at a downtown hotel for a few days until they had had time to assess the volatility of the situation. My editors agreed.

I was given a police escort to the CBC, where I was to do a show at 6:30 p.m. with Milewski. As I was driving in a van with two RCMP corporals, my cellphone rang. It was Bal Buttar, a blind quadriplegic former gangster who had confessed to me a few months earlier about several murders he had committed. Even he thought the verdict was an outrage. "All those innocent people," he said. "It's a travesty of justice."

Later that night, a few of us journalists gathered for drinks in the lobby of the hotel in which I was staying. It was a strange evening. At one point I just broke down and cried. "I feel like the last seven years, all that I went through, all that Rani went through, Tara getting murdered – it was all for nothing," I said.

Patricia Graham, now the *Sun*'s editor-in-chief, who had supported me all the way, tried to reassure me that it had not been for nothing, that we had exposed so much over the years that the public really understood. But I was not persuaded.

I finally crashed near midnight, only to be awakened a short time later by the BBC on my cellphone wanting an interview. I woke up early to do a CBC Radio interview as well. The story was big news, ironically, because of the verdict.

I later learned that the next night, March 18, Justice Josephson had attended a reception at a lawyer's office. He seemed relaxed. He seemed to enjoy the party. He left a couple of days later for a week on the beach in Cuba with his wife.

That same night, the RCMP installed video cameras at my house. They measured for bulletproof film on my windows. They gave me a panic button and told me to watch my back. I declined to be escorted around or to tell them my schedule. "I'm a reporter. How can I do my job?" I said.

Prosecution witnesses in the case were also concerned for their security. When I contacted them, they maintained they had been telling the truth and now felt frustrated the judge did not believe them. The RCMP revealed that all of them had passed lie-detector tests that the defence witnesses had not had to take.

The Canadian public also reacted with shock. Sixty-eight per cent of those polled in British Columbia said they disagreed with Josephson. Many said his verdict had made them lose faith in the justice system.

Bagri quietly returned to Kamloops but did not make any public statements. Malik kept promising to do interviews for the Indo-Canadian media, only to renege a little later. He was being followed around town by television cameras and he seemed to enjoy the celebrity. As he placed an insurance decal on another new Mercedes the day after the verdict, he joked to journalists that he was going to the CBC. He wasn't. But he did give an exclusive interview to the *Globe and Mail* two days after his release.

In it, Malik said he was not a devil and not a saint. He denied all responsibility for the bombing, as he had done to me before his arrest. He was not asked about his link to terrorists through the school or his financial support of Parmar and Reyat. He spent his first weekend out of jail visiting a number of fundamentalist temples around Vancouver.

Some media commentators started pronouncing that the Crown's case should never have been brought, that it was extremely weak from day one. But none of the columnists and broadcasters who took that position had spent any time in the courtroom, listening to the witnesses, assessing their demeanour. Several Indo-Canadian news outlets suggested that Malik had been unfairly persecuted not just by the RCMP and the Crown, but also by media companies like my newspaper and the CBC. Again, most of the journalists making that claim had not spent a day at the trial.

Within a week of the verdict, I was again receiving threatening comments, as were some of the witnesses. Dave Hayer also received word about potential threats to him for being such a forceful spokesman against Sikh terrorism. Careless talk at a union hiring hall by someone linked to the International Sikh Youth Federation revealed a plan to retaliate against several people, including Hayer and me. Cryptic comments posted on Waheguroo and other Web sites suggested I would get what was coming to me.

Everything was passed on to police. But as always, it was hard for them to chase down a concrete lead or a specific plot to harm someone. As RCMP Sgt. Grant Learned had said after Tara Hayer's murder, "It is like trying to arm wrestle with a shadow. It is there, but you can't get at it."

I made sure I pored carefully over the full six-hundred-page verdict. I thought I might be convinced of Josephson's viewpoint if only I read more of his reasoning. But I was left with even more questions. I also realized that some of the evidence the Crown and RCMP had in their possession was not led at trial. Maybe the case had been so simplified to keep it on the rails, that crucial details had been left out. Maybe it was impossible for someone without years of background knowledge to understand the big picture.

Even some of the victims' families didn't know the whole story. They didn't know how many of the Crown witnesses were approached to change their testimony or withdraw it all together. They didn't know about the threats that some journalists and some Sikh moderates endured for years. They didn't know about the connection between Sikh terrorists and Indo-Canadian gangsters.

Josephson didn't seem to appreciate how a small group of extremists within the Sikh community had for years used violence and intimidation against anyone who opposed it. The Air-India and Narita bombings were the worst incidents of retribution by this militant group, but there have been many other victims of the same extremist violence.

Sometimes the extremist violence had been directed at moderate Sikhs who dared question the separatists, people like federal Health Minister Ujjal Dosanjh, who was brutally beaten and repeatedly threatened. Sometimes the threats had been directed at those, like Tara Hayer, who believed they could implicate the Air-India suspects. And sometimes even journalists like me had been threatened.

That volatile political climate is something Air-India journalists had seen and understood. It had influenced our analysis of the 115 witnesses who testified at the trial. And it enabled some of us to reach a different conclusion than Josephson's about the credibility of some of those witnesses.

I took context into the courtroom that Josephson didn't have, a context that was not fully conveyed by the evidence brought forward by prosecutors and the RCMP. There was just one U.S. academic called to explain to Josephson the reaction of some Sikhs to the Indian Army's June 1984 assault on the Golden Temple. This was the singular event the Crown said had inspired the bombing plot.

Former *Vancouver Sun* reporter Terry Glavin had been prepared to testify and had given numerous interviews to the RCMP about his coverage of the Sikh separatist movement and the Air-India suspects before the bombing. Now an author of several non-fiction books, it was easier for him to co-operate with the Crown because he no longer wrote about Air-India. Glavin could have explained what he was told in May 1984 in the Golden Temple when he interviewed Babbar Khalsa leader Sukhdev Babbar, who pledged his allegiance to Talwinder Parmar. Glavin could have described how Jarnail Bhindranwale and his men were carrying AK-47s and had a cache of weapons just weeks before the raid at the temple. And they were boasting about all the enemies they had killed.

The motive for the bombing put forward by the Crown was not hard for journalists to grasp. I had seen the consequences of separatist violence up close during my four trips to India to cover the conflict in Punjab. It is a motive attested to by those B.C. Sikh leaders I interviewed who called for the assassination of Indira Gandhi before she was gunned down. I have covered Sikh separatist rallies in which Punjabi chants claimed that Hindus "sucked the blood of Sikh children." I have seen the bloody imagery on posters hung in dining halls of some local temples, calling Canadian Sikhs photographed in Punjab with assault rifles and rocket-launchers *shaheeds*, or martyrs.

But that crucial context was missing in Courtroom 20, where

lawyers in black robes on both sides politely presented their arguments and cited case law to make their points.

Josephson seemed bewildered by the prospect of an attractive woman like Rani still claiming to love a man who had confessed his role in a mass murder to her. Many women, including some victims' relatives, found Josephson's logic sexist.

Lata Pada travelled from her Toronto home to hear Rani testify: "How many women visit their husbands, their lovers in prison knowing that they have committed a crime?" she said. "You can see the evil in a person and yet love them despite that, and her declarations of love for Mr. Malik were completely misread. But every person that was there, who witnessed this, knew that this was a woman speaking the truth."

Rani had often told me how she felt she was betraying Malik by talking to the police. She told me how reluctant she was to discuss their private relationship and expressed frustration at the amount of personal information both the investigators and prosecutors tried to get out of her.

On the stand, she did her best to explain that she was caught up in Malik's spell, that it was like being in a cult, that after five years together she did not want to see him go to jail or the school negatively affected by the Air-India investigation.

Josephson did not apply the same reasoning to others involved in the Air-India case who maintained loyal and loving relationships with those who he accepted were involved in the bombings. Inderjit Reyat's wife, Satnam, had stood beside her husband from the beginning, even though Josephson found he was deeply involved in the terrorism plot and "an unmitigated liar."

Parmar's family had stood behind him, setting up the Sikh Vision Web site on which long after the trial they still called him a martyr and showed a photograph of him with the Sikh holy book and crossed AK-47s. Bagri, while blaming Parmar for the bombings at trial, maintained close ties with him. Bagri served as Parmar's spokesman. He arranged the marriage of his eldest daughter to Parmar's eldest son in 1992 – even after Parmar made public statements saying that anyone who flew Air-India was "suicidal."

Malik continued to support the Reyat family to the tune of $109,000 while they illegally collected welfare. Josephson said the payments were not proof of Malik's involvement in the plot. Malik could have paid all that money because of "sympathy for Mr. Reyat's perceived cause," the judge said.

So it was okay for Malik to be sympathetic with and supportive of a mass murderer, but the fact that Rani professed her love for Malik made her testimony incredible. Others could remain devoted and loyal to Parmar and Reyat despite knowing their role in what Josephson himself called "the senseless mass murder of hundreds of complete innocents."

One CBC viewer was so offended by the notion that it was impossible to love a killer that he sent an e-mail to *The National* reminding people about Eva Braun, Adolf Hitler's long-time mistress who married the mass murderer long after he ordered the execution of six million Jews.

Sheila Isenberg, who wrote the book *Women Who Love Men Who Kill*, says it is not unknown for normal, intelligent, attractive women like Rani to fall in love with killers: "They are likely to be attractive and intelligent, often successful in their profession and almost always unacquainted with the world of crime and criminals," Isenberg told me. "In the eyes of these women, these men are a magnetic mix of evil and vulnerability, extreme danger and reassuring safety."

Rani had a less-than-satisfying arranged marriage with a much older man. She fell for Malik long before he told her of his link to the Air-India case. He was powerful, charming, quick-witted, and hard working – all qualities that she admired. But Josephson could not accept that she was ever close enough to Malik for him to confess to her.

In his ruling the judge expressed difficulty understanding the reason for Rani's "delay" in reporting to police the main confession she said Malik made to her. She first told Doug Best about the so-called "newspaper confession" on March 23, 1998, five months after she began talking to police. "She explained this delay by saying that: Because I didn't know that my statement had any value," a troubled Josephson said in his ruling.

He quoted Rani trying to explain that she didn't have any proof of what Malik told her and that she didn't want to be an Air-India witness.

Josephson concluded that her "explanation for the delay in reporting the Newspaper Confession lacks credulity." Josephson was not only mistaken in his logic, but in his choice of words. Credulity means being gullible. He meant to say that Rani's explanation for the delay in reporting lacked credibility.

But I know exactly why she didn't tell police earlier about the confession. So did the RCMP and the Crown, but no one raised it in court. Rani had told Joe Bellows in her first meeting with him in July 1999 that she stayed silent about the critical Air-India information after getting bad legal advice. She told him I had suggested that what Malik had said to her was hearsay and would be inadmissible in court.

My reporter's instincts had forced me to resist all attempts by the Crown and the RCMP to get me to tell them what I knew about Air-India or what Rani had told me. But I could have provided an explanation for why she waited for months before telling police about the critical confession. She didn't lie about why she waited. Her explanation of not appreciating the value of it was true, thanks to me. I believe that she didn't pin it on me while she was in the witness box because she respected me as a journalist and did not want me to be forced to testify. Or to look like a fool.

The Crown notes were disclosed to defence lawyers. So they knew about her logical explanation, but did not raise it at trial either. Nor did Bellows subpoena me to testify. "I am doing everything I can to keep you off the stand," he told me at one point during the trial.

Josephson accepted the defence suggestion that Rani was a disgruntled former employee and that Malik did not have a loving relationship with her. But I was standing beside her the last time she saw Malik on April 19, 1998, outside a Khalsa Credit Union branch in Surrey. I was covering the election for the institution's board of directors when she offered Malik some tea. Air-India suspect Hardial Johal was standing with us too.

Rani accurately recounted the day during her testimony – "[Malik] greeted me. And then he smiled and said, 'She's still not talking to me. I haven't seen her in so many days, so many hours, so many months.'"

Johal had turned to me and made a quip about Malik's weakness for the woman.

I could have vouched for this part of Rani's story had I testified. I could have told Josephson that several Malik supporters approached me repeatedly between the time Rani fled into witness protection in late summer 1998 and the Air-India arrests in 2000. Whenever they saw me covering an event, they would raise the issue of Rani.

"Where is your friend? We want to talk to her," one Khalsa School volunteer asked me at a Vaisakhi parade in the spring of 1999.

"I don't know," I replied. "She moved away."

I could have corroborated the numerous threats that were directed both at me and Rani in the months before she left for good. I had never received death threats in all my years as a journalist until December 1997 when I began my series on the Khalsa School.

I still believe Rani was telling the truth, despite Josephson's ruling on her credibility. Everything she had ever told me about the school or the credit union I was able to verify. I followed some of her tips all the way to India and they all proved to be accurate.

Should the Crown have forced me to testify? In retrospect, yes, they should have. And I am not the only one. There were other journalists with information about the case. There were other people who had given statements to police but were not called to testify.

But there is a lot that hindsight is now telling us about Air-India.

The Crown did not bring forward other important evidence that might have changed the outcome. Josephson believed Inderjit Singh Arora, who testified that Rani had taken a copy of the book *Soft Target* from a bookstore in the school's basement. The Crown failed to point out to the judge that Arora is related to Malik's wife and is beholden to the family for his immigration status. In 1998, Arora had provided me with information that corroborated several things Rani told me about the school. He was her ally then, even after she left British Columbia.

The Crown did not ask the anonymous millworker to explain that he came forward in late 2003 with evidence against Malik only because he was battling cancer and wanted to tell the truth before he died. Instead the man explained simply that he saw others testifying and thought he should tell as well. Josephson discounted his testimony that Malik had asked him to take a bomb-laden

attaché case to the airport because he did not understand why the
man would have kept this a secret for almost two decades. But,
given the threats, attacks, and Hayer murder, I find it a wonder
that he came forward at all. Many others have still not had the
courage to tell the truth, even after twenty years.

The judge said the plaza in front of the Vancouver Sikh temple
where the millworker claimed the conversation took place did
not exist. The plaza did exist. Malik did have a table there in 1984
from which he sold religious artifacts. I saw the table. Thousands
of others saw the table.

The Crown also did not introduce documentation the RCMP
possessed of payments Malik made in 1985 into the Babbar
Khalsa's bank account, one of which was corroborated by
Parmar's call to the bank captured on one of the tapes that was
later erased. It did not get into evidence the fact that the Babbar
Khalsa had regular meetings at Malik's school for years. Nor did
the prosecution introduce evidence of Malik assisting Parmar
and Bagri in opening a Babbar Khalsa bank account in the
Bank of Credit and Commerce Canada in 1985. And the Crown
did not have the information from Kulwarn Parmar about
overhearing Malik's commitment to his brother to finance the
terrorist group.

Malik later facilitated the transfer of the Babbar Khalsa funds
via money draft to the Khalsa Credit Union when it first opened.
The signing authorities on the Babbar Khalsa account at Malik's
credit union were Parmar's eldest son, Jaswinder, his brother
Kulwarn, and another Babbar Khalsa supporter. The prosecution
had evidence of this, but none of this entwined financial relationship came out during the trial.

Very little evidence was presented about the other terrorist
connections at the school – the convicted hijacker living in the
basement, the fact that the family of Babbar Khalsa leader

Sukhdev Babbar hid in Malik's school before making a success-ful refugee claim in Calgary.

And the judge never heard from Satnam Reyat – the woman who could have shed light on so many elements of the Air-India mystery. Police did not introduce wiretap records of calls between Reyat and her imprisoned husband in which she expressed concern about imminent Air-India arrests and made numerous references to Malik.

Maybe Mrs. Reyat would have explained on the stand how she managed to arrange a marriage between one of her daugh-ters and the son of the former Ontario leader of the Babbar Khalsa – Tejinder Kaloe – if she had no association with the group. The marriage happened in the summer of 2003, just weeks before Inderjit Reyat testified that he did not know anything about the Babbar Khalsa's militant ideology.

Mrs. Reyat was prepared to co-operate with the RCMP on more than one occasion, according to police documents, but she backed out after being threatened. Rani had told the RCMP that Mrs. Reyat said that both Malik and Bagri were involved in the bomb-ings. She'd said that Bagri and Parmar had recruited her husband into the plot and that he had promised never to expose the others.

Critical evidence was either left out or ruled out of the trial, not least of which were Hayer's statements to the RCMP alleging that he overheard Bagri confessing to a role in Air-India, which Josephson deemed were too "prejudicial" to include. Incriminating statements to CSIS by Premika could not be used to convict him because she feigned memory loss and therefore could not be cross-examined by Bagri's lawyers, Josephson ruled, despite his earlier decision stating clearly that she told CSIS the truth about Bagri's involvement in Air-India.

In the media commentary after the verdict, much was made of CSIS's erasure of taped phone calls between Parmar and other suspects around the time of the bombing. But journalists who covered Reyat's earlier trial for the Narita bombing knew that another B.C. Supreme Court judge, Raymond Paris, had ruled that the erasures did not hurt the Crown's case against Reyat at all.

"I'm not at all satisfied that there has been anything reprehensible in the conduct of the CSIS agents," Paris said during the 1991 trial. "I do not see any reasonable possibility that the information sought is required for a full answer and defence." But Josephson ruled those same erasures were "unacceptable negligence" that violated Bagri's Charter right to have access to all the evidence in the case.

If anything, the erasures punched holes in the Crown's case against both men. The logs of one of the erased tapes indicates that Parmar told Bagri to travel to New York to meet with a man named Avtar Singh the third week in September. That would have placed him in the Big Apple the weekend that John says his conversation with Bagri took place outside a gas station owned by a man named Avtar Singh. But the tape no longer exists, so neither does evidence that could have corroborated what John told his FBI handler about Bagri's alleged confession.

Aside from the threats that Rani faced, and the police statements that Premika also had been threatened, very little came out at the trial about threats or attempts to influence other Crown witnesses, including Narinder Gill, Jagdev Dhillon, and the farmer.

Justice Josephson obviously made a judgment call on key Crown witnesses long before the close of the Air-India trial. His ruling will have ramifications that many others will have to live with long after he has moved on to other trials.

Two weeks after the verdict, I was reviewing some documents at B.C. Supreme Court with Terry Milewski when we ran into Josephson in the courthouse lobby. We took the opportunity to talk to the judge, who was waiting to go to lunch with some colleagues. Milewski gingerly raised the issue of the ruling.

"The problem now is that the whole Air-India thing is still open for us," Milewski said.

Josephson nodded in agreement. Milewski commented that the local Sikh separatists were feeling pretty cocky again and that tensions were running very high.

"That is most regrettable," Josephson said. "Let's hope it is just sabre-rattling."

"Let's hope it is just that," Milewski said.

I piped in, "But people are already getting threats."

Josephson repeated again, "That is most regrettable."

Then off he went for his lunch.

I reached Malik on his cellphone in July 2005 to ask him for an interview for this book. I wanted to ask if he regretted any of his earlier associations with and financing of Parmar and Reyat – the two men even Josephson said were among those responsible for the mass murder of 331 people. But Malik refused my interview request. "What a daydreamer," he said.

Without convictions in the biggest murder trial in Canadian history, the families were left once again to depend on the Canadian government for some form of justice, some answers to their twenty-year-old questions. They would have to turn to the same politicians who for years have accepted contributions and political support from Sikh separatists sympathetic to the bombers, if not from the suspects themselves.

It was perverse, but very Canadian. To quell the growing criticism of the justice system and flawed police investigation, Public Safety Minister Anne McLellan appointed former Ontario premier Bob Rae to review the Air-India case and figure out if a public inquiry was warranted into Canada's worst mass murder and the subsequent investigation.

The verdict clearly was a political embarrassment. Suddenly, victims' relatives, who for years could not get the attention of the country's politicians, had people lining up to meet with them, including Prime Minister Paul Martin, Anne McLellan, and the heads of CSIS and the RCMP. Martin pledged to attend the twentieth Air-India memorial service in Ahakista, Ireland – the first time a prime minister would ever have participated in the event.

At the same time, more than a dozen men suspected by police of being involved in planning or executing the bombing continued to live normally. Bagri returned to his job at the Kamloops sawmill and began preaching at Sikh temples in the B.C. interior. He welcomed Malik and all his old Babbar Khalsa directors to a three-day religious program at the Kamloops Sikh temple two weeks after the verdict. Parmar's widow attended, so did his son. They appeared undaunted by Bagri's strategy to implicate Parmar during the trial.

Almost immediately after the trial, Malik was appointed to fill a vacancy on the board of the Khalsa Credit Union created when his son Jaspreet was forced to resign because the government regulators raised concerns over his testimony at his father's legal-aid hearing. But for the first time, he was not put in the president's chair. That job went to Satwant Sandhu, the Malik ally who testified in his defence and who admitted lying to police and threatening journalists. And Malik maintained his influence at the Khalsa School with two of his sons and a team of supporters making up the board of directors. Despite all its documented links to terrorists and welfare fraud, the school's annual provincial grant has increased to about $4 million.

After the verdict, Sikh separatist slogans were chanted again – both in Surrey and in Punjab – for the first time in years. At the Vaisakhi parade in Surrey three weeks after the acquittals, an organizer praised the man who started it all, Jarnail Bhindranwale, as a

martyr and yelled, "Long live Khalistan." Standing on the stage
behind the Khalistani booster was B.C. premier Gordon Campbell
and a host of dignitaries and leaders from provincial and federal
political parties. Not one of them spoke against the separatist
chants or the endorsement of a controversial leader who many view
as a terrorist.

A week later, in mid-April, a former member of the
International Sikh Youth Federation visited a Punjabi radio station
in Surrey to relay information to its owner about a new hit list
having been drawn up to get people back for pursuing the Air-
India case. My name was supposedly on it, as was that of
Sukhminder Cheema, the journalist who backed out of being a
witness. The man who passed on the information, Jaspal Atwal, was
the same man who was convicted in the 1986 assassination attempt
of the visiting Punjabi cabinet minister. He was also the man
charged and acquitted in the 1985 beating of Ujjal Dosanjh. He
warned that the information he was providing about the hit list
should not be provided to police. But it was, even though earlier
reports of threats to the police had never lead to a conviction.

On May 3, 2005, World Press Freedom Day, Crown prosecutors
announced they would not appeal Josephson's ruling despite dis-
agreeing with several conclusions the judge had reached. In the
Canadian system, as the prosecutors made clear, there is no avenue
for appeal against findings of fact. If Josephson said the Crown's
witnesses were liars, appeal court judges, who never saw or heard
those witnesses, simply had no right to reverse his judgment. If
Josephson said the Ross Street temple plaza did not exist in 1984,
then it did not – even if there are pictures and videotape to prove
that it did. And, if Josephson said that Hayer did not expose
Bagri when he actually did, the truth would not matter. The

prosecutors could appeal against faulty interpretations of the law, but not against errors of fact. They had no choice. Ironically, the Crown's decision came as the Canadian Newspaper Association called for a public inquiry into the Air-India bombing and justice in the Hayer murder.

It was a final blow to victims' families, who have lost so much faith in their country and its institutions. It was also a final blow to the Sikh community, which fears a return to the violence of the 1980s, where police do not have the ability to prosecute killers even when they know who they are.

And it was also devastating to Rani, who will likely never resume the life she once had – full of family, friends, and joy. She had to stay away from her eldest son's university graduation. She doesn't know if she'll ever see him get married, or if she will ever be able to be together again with her whole family for a wedding or a funeral or another special occasion.

Rani was at work when she got the news about the not-guilty verdict. Doug Best had called and said Justice Josephson ruled that none of the Crown witnesses were credible. She was devastated. But she couldn't react. How can you explain to people who don't know who you really are why you are an emotional wreck?

She left work. She couldn't stand to be there pretending to be someone else.

The verdict was international news. At home, she turned on the television to watch the reaction. Hers was instant: she should never have gone to police.

"My whole life ruined, and on top of it, I am called a liar," she said in a telephone interview.

Then she watched the emotional news conference of the victims' families. One by one, they explained their loss, tears streaming down their faces. Some, like Rattan Kalsi, clutched photos of their murdered relatives. Their pain was palpable.

"When I was standing there watching each of them say their piece, I thought if I have to go through it again, give this testimony again, I would go for it. They lost everything. I lost everything."

Although the families' agony made Rani feel that she would do it all again, she felt she could never advise anyone else to take the same risk – to sacrifice everything to help the police, only to be vilified and to spend the rest of her life on the run.

"There is nothing there for me. I lost watching my oldest son grow up into a young man and my younger son lost being with his brother and his father. And that is something I will never have again. I don't know if I will ever have the whole family be together again with me. It will never happen.

"I am two different people now. If you look at it, it is very difficult to hide in this modern world unless you do what I have done: You don't go anywhere. You don't do anything."

It means a lot to her that the families of the victims believe her despite Josephson's judgment. But she is worried that she will never be safe, will never be able to stop looking over her shoulder.

If someone else were in her shoes today and asked her for advice, it would be simple and unambiguous: Don't do what she did.

"If they hadn't taken the decision – if they still had their family, they still had their life, I would never say to them to do it, never. Our justice system is not made for truth."

Ultimately, that loss of faith is the real legacy of the Air-India bombing. Canada failed to protect the innocent, to punish the guilty, and to bring out the truth.

Epilogue

O N JUNE 23, 2005, more than five hundred people stood around a sundial in the picturesque Irish hamlet of Ahakista, looking out over Dunmanus Bay and to the Atlantic Ocean beyond. It was a sombre gathering, which included the Canadian prime minister, the Irish president, an Indian cabinet minister, local townspeople, Canadian and Irish police officers, and almost two hundred relatives of the people who were killed aboard Air-India Flight 182 twenty years earlier.

Behind the sundial was a curved copper and stone wall that stands less than a metre tall and lists the name of every person who perished aboard the Air-India flight. You can see how many doctors, engineers, and priests were on board. You can count how many whole families were wiped out. You can see that some were Sikhs, some Hindus, some Muslims. There were also Christians, Buddhists, and Zoroastrians.

The beauty of the spot made the gathering all the sadder. Hills covered with green pastures rolled gently into the grey sea; the waves lapped against the rocky shore; the sky threatened overhead; a cold mist and drizzle was blowing in from the water.

On the twentieth anniversary, there was an overwhelming sense of despair. Not only were the mothers and fathers, sons and daughters, aunts and uncles and friends of those who died still grieving their terrible loss, they were feeling more hopeless than they had felt since that horrible day.

This was the first such gathering since a judge in Canada acquitted the two suspected terrorists many had hoped would be held accountable at last for the murders of 331 men, women, and children. They knew it was unlikely now that anyone will ever be convicted of plotting and executing the worst mass murder in Canadian history. They knew that they may never get answers to the difficult questions that still remain about how and why such an evil act could have been plotted and carried out under the nose of RCMP officers and CSIS agents.

Several senior RCMP officers were there, mourning alongside the victims' families. Gary Bass, the assistant commissioner for the B.C. region, had worked tirelessly for a decade to answer these questions. But it has not happened. Two Crown prosecutors – Bob Wright and Richard Cairns – who tried to convict Ripudaman Malik and Ajaib Bagri were also there. They have all become close to family members over the years. There is no personal animosity, despite the sense that justice has not been done.

The head of CSIS, Jim Judd, had wanted to come. But the families asked him not to. It was not that he had anything to do with two-decades-old mistakes that the families blame in part for the lack of convictions in the Air-India bombing. But he represents an agency that followed around the suspects as they plotted the murders of hundreds of Canadians; an agency that routinely erased critical taped phone calls among the suspects before and after the bombing without thinking of their prospective value in a criminal prosecution.

Dave Hayer was there too. He sees his father – Tara Hayer – as the 332nd victim of the terrorist plot that targeted Air-India in 1985. He hopes that the investigation into his father's 1998 murder will someday result in the conviction of the culprits.

Daniel Brown, the British seaman who was just twenty-three when he pulled the bodies of the Air-India victims from the sea near here, came to the service for a second time. He is still trying to come to terms with the horror he witnessed that awful day. He had arranged to meet his shipmate Mark Stagg at the memorial ceremony. They met in Ireland for the first time since the plane went down. It was very emotional for both of them.

Perviz Madon of North Vancouver was her usual dignified self as she stood through the emotional ceremony. It hit me that I have known this woman for twenty years. Her children, Natasha and Eddie, were just four and eight when Sam Madon was murdered. Now they are intelligent, successful adults. But they are also angry. Perviz told me she is tired of the fight. She said she would give up her quest for justice and move on with her life after this memorial service. She can't do it any more. But Eddie said he will continue for as long as he needs to get justice for his father.

Parkash Bedi and his second wife came all the way from Detroit. At a memorial service at the Cork hospital on June 22, 2005, Bedi – still hoping that his daughter, Anu, had somehow survived – asked the hospital administrator if, by chance, there were any unclaimed remains from the plane.

No, he was told. All the bodies had been taken by family members. Bedi was left unable to eat or sleep. His wife was worried about his health. It had been a difficult journey to Ireland.

As the clock struck at the exact moment when the plane disappeared from the radar screen, there was a minute of silence. It was followed by a melodic chant and desperate sobbing. The sobs brought more tears. Almost everyone cried or wanted to cry.

The Irish were there too. Agnes Hegarty, the innkeeper, is like a family member now to the Indo-Canadians who have stayed with her every June for nineteen years. She still charges them her mid-1980s rates, and she cares for their needs far beyond providing rooms and food. They consider her children their children. They bring gifts from Canada for her grandchildren.

Hegarty wore a gold cross around her neck. She bristled at the thought of someone justifying terrorism in God's name.

"My goodness – innocent children, innocent people. To take all those lives in one go – that was just horrific. They wiped out whole families. They don't know who God is if they do something like this," she once told me.

Nuela O'Donovan also came to the memorial service again this year to pray. And again this year, she spent days baking her famous pies for the roadside reception that followed. This year the simple tables usually placed along the narrow winding road were inside a giant white marquee, resembling a circus tent, brought in for the dignitaries.

Brenda O'Tighearnaigh drove five hours from Dublin to Ahakista for the service, as she has done every year to see the people with whom she now has a permanent bond. She still wears dozens of silver bangles on both arms, each one given to her by a victim's relative she met and mourned with so long ago.

"Everywhere I go, I get asked, 'What are these?' and I say they are a reminder of the fragility of life and they say, 'What's that?' and then I tell the story," O'Tighearnaigh told me.

Irish president Mary McAleese spoke eloquently on behalf of her people – the doctors, nurses, and priests who tended to the dead twenty years ago, many of whom came to the ceremony to remember. With 329 dead, there were probably more people killed in the bombing than live in the vicinity of the Air-India memorial. There is a school, a church, two pubs, and a collection of farmhouses. It is so remote that the nearest town – Bantry – is twenty kilometres away and there is no regular bus service. But the locals have not forgotten. They come every year to commemorate the lives of those who died because of a terrorist plot carried out by religious fanatics on the other side of the world.

At the memorial, schoolchildren played tin whistles and sang hymns. They have learned Indian songs over the years, as well. The Air-India families have tried to give back. They have organized cultural programs and given annual scholarships to local students.

For the first time since the plane went down, a Canadian prime minister saw fit to come here and grieve with the families of the dead. Prime Minister Paul Martin was joined by all three leaders of the opposition and by B.C. premier Gordon Campbell. But the presence of these high-ranking politicians caused some bitterness among family members, who know that militant Sikh separatists for years used the Liberals and other political parties.

Martin's speech did not come close to satisfying the families' search for justice. He committed to build a memorial for their loved ones; he said June 23 would be declared a "National Day of Remembrance for Victims of Terrorism," something the family members first proposed back in 1988. Martin noted that across Canada flags had been lowered to half-staff to say, "We are with you." He did not explain why it had taken two decades for Canadians to "be with" these victims.

Martin made no mention of the public inquiry being demanded by family members, nor did he promise to bring the perpetrators to justice. Strangely, he did not call the bombing an act of terrorism or even of murder. He didn't even call it a crime. He called it a "hateful deed," an "act of evil." He called it "a Canadian tragedy." His words seemed too carefully chosen.

In his speech, Indian cabinet minister Prithviraj Chavan did not hesitate to use the word *terrorism*. He referred to it over and over again: "While grieving these twenty years, all of us – particularly those directly affected – had hoped that the guilty would be brought to justice. Regrettably, we still await that closure and this makes each anniversary so much more difficult. The absence of justice makes it harder to come to terms with the consequences of this heinous crime." His speech struck a chord with families.

President McAleese also seemed to understand exactly how the victims' families were feeling, far better than the Canadian politicians did.

"This isn't how things were supposed to be, is it?" she said, the lovely lilt in her voice making it so comforting. "No one who got on that plane on that dreadful day had this destination in mind. This is not the place they were coming to. The tragic and the cruel end to those lives of so many lovely men, women, and children who left Toronto for Bombay with their hearts lifted and full of thoughts of tomorrow and the next day. It was, of course, to mark a journey that was to end their lives and the start of a journey of extraordinary grief for those they left behind."

She called the bombing "a dreadful event, a wicked and an evil event without parallel."

McAleese said the Indo-Canadians were like the Irish, seeking a better life in a land far away, coming home for that precious family visit. "We know how important such a visit home is, how long it's looked forward to. We know how long it is looked forward to in the hearts of the emigrants and how much it's looked forward to by those who await them in their homeland. And so many hearts full of loving anticipation were wiped out that day by hearts full of hatred."

Family members then took the microphone. They told their stories of what it was like on June 23, 1985, to get the awful news, to come to Ireland, to be the parent searching for the body of a son or daughter, to be the young child trying to make sense of what you were being told about never getting to see your mother or father again, to be left behind in your anguish. No faith allows for such terror to be inflicted upon innocents, they said.

This year, the speeches were tinged with anger and frustration.

Dr. Padmini Turlapati and her husband, Narayana, organized the service. They don't normally like politics. They have come every year to remember Sanjay and Deepak, their two wonderful sons. Padmini has told me many times that she only allows herself to be a mother once a year when she comes to Ireland for a few days. It is a part of her that is put away back home in Canada.

"This senseless mass murder – the worst air disaster in the entire history of the world – continues to rob us of our right to privacy, dignity, and justice," she said so eloquently. "The verdict appalled and decimated back to ground zero. All repressed memories of horror and terror returned. No one was accountable. . . . It seems to me an unpardonable insult to injury when the convoluted soap opera still continues and all those innocents sacrificed seem in vain. Is no one accountable except us who put them on a plane? Are we never destined to find closure?

"Do not trivialize the magnitude of this tragedy by saying nothing can be done or twenty years have gone by. History will never forgive the impotence of our inaction. It is our belief that not having a public inquiry will just do that."

Narayana, affectionately called Babu by all his Irish friends, also did not mince words. Think of all the children killed, the generation lost to Canada, he urged. "The mass murder was conspired, planned, and perpetrated by terrorists and criminals in

Canada, and . . . the killers are still loose and roaming free in our country, Canada."

The Turlapatis and a few other regulars have built a stunning garden around the memorial, and marigolds, lilies, roses, and snapdragons add punches of colour below the shrubs and trees planted in earlier years. Right under the names of the dead are the azaleas, which bloom pink just before the ceremony every year. Sticks of incense were stuck in the ground around the flowers, their pungent sweetness permeating the damp morning air.

The Indian government paid for the land where the memorial sits on this rocky shore. The Canadian government constructed the bronze wall that bears each victim's name. The Irish maintain the site. The flags of the three countries fly together beside the road.

At the end of the ceremony, 331 white balloons were let go – one for each person who died on June 23, 1985. The balloons floated slowly upwards, bobbing as the wind carried them closer to where Air-India Flight 182 once blew apart. Then lanterns were placed in the water and floated gently out to sea, where the remains of 197 victims are somewhere under the dark, cold water. Some of the relatives waded into the sea to be closer to them.

The victims' families spoke of the peace they feel when they come here. They said they feel connected to their dead, especially to those whose bodies weren't recovered. There is goodness here, they said. The Irish have taken on the grieving, as if the victims were their own kin. Strangers who see the relatives in town know why they are here and greet them. Locals still invite them into their homes for tea or a meal.

After the politicians departed, the families were alone again with their dead. They scoured the beach for oval-shaped black stones that are encircled with a ribbon of white, which are in abundance here. To Hindus, they are sacred. They represent

Vishnu – the Hindu God of destruction. It is a good sign that there are so many here. It makes the place holy, blessed.

After the service, Mark Stagg, one of the British seamen, was looking at the photographs stuck into the wreaths placed in front of the copper wall of names and saw the face that has haunted him for twenty years. It was the boy whose body was the first he pulled from the Atlantic that day. At last he knew the boy's name: Sanjay Turlapati.

Daniel Brown took him to meet Sanjay's parents, who were overwhelmed that this man recovered the body of their first-born. "We just put them on a helicopter and we never saw them again," Stagg explained. "We've never known who the people we recovered were. Today, for the first time, I have been able to know who at least one of the people was, and it was your son, Sanjay."

He told Padmini that Sanjay was beautifully intact, with all his clothes on. The only clue to his violent demise was a missing shoe. He told her he wished he could have saved Sanjay.

"It was not in your hands," she reassured him.

Padmini, a pediatrician, feels her sons' spirits here. They are ghosts who comfort her, who talk to her. She is not the only one who sees and feels the spirits on the rocky shore of west Cork.

Murthy Subramaniam, who lost his wife and only daughter, returns every June from Toronto because here he feels closer to Veena, his little girl. She was just eight when he lost her.

"When I come to this place, at least I could feel like I am talking to my daughter. She is here," he said.

When she is here, Padmini sometimes closes her eyes and sees Deepak, her youngest boy. When she came in 2004, he was holding a bowl and she asked him what it was for. "To catch your tears, Mom."

Twenty years since his death, she still felt his presence in the water that lapped the rocky beach beside the Air-India monument.

"Sometimes it comes very fast with the tide and I think he is running, he's walking, he's talking," she explained with a big grin on her face. "So I sit down and I talk to him. I tell him what I did in the last year. I ask him for advice and he tells me some things. I get peace here. I get comfort here."

Key Figures

Arora, Inderjit Singh (Khalsa School teacher, Malik defence witness)

Atwal, Harjit Singh (former International Sikh Youth Federation member)

Atwal, Jaspal Singh (former ISYF member convicted of assassination attempt on a Punjabi cabinet minister)

Babbar, Sukhdev Singh (Parmar associate, militant at Golden Temple, killed in 1992)

Bagga, Harkirat Singh (would-be Hayer assassin)

Bagri, Ajaib Singh (former number-two man, Babbar Khalsa. Tried and found not guilty in Air-India bombings)

Basran, Daljit Singh "Umboo" (gangster alleged to have murdered Hayer)

Bass, Gary (assistant commissioner of the RCMP who has overseen the Air-India Task Force since 1995)

Bellows, Joe (Crown prosecutor who led the evidence against Malik)

Bhandher, Balwant Singh (Akhand Kirtani Jatha member and Air-India suspect)

Bhandher, Raminder Singh "Mindy" (former Khalsa School student-turned criminal and Malik defence witness)

Bhindranwale, Jarnail Singh (Sikh separatist leader, slain at the Golden Temple)

Brown, Daniel (Merchant seaman, aided in the recovery of victims' bodies)

Cairns, Richard (Crown prosecutor who led the Bagri evidence and worked on the earlier Narita prosecution against Reyat)

Chaggar, Kuldip Singh (one-time Reyat lawyer later convicted in the United States of witness tampering)

Cheema, Sukhminder Singh (former ISYF member-turned journalist who was to be an Air-India witness)

Chohan, Dr. Jagjit Singh (original Sikh separatist leader)

Code, Michael (Bagri defence lawyer)

Crossin, David (Malik defence lawywer)

Dhillon, Kashmir Singh (Montreal Babbar Khalsa member who was convicted but successfully appealed a 1986 charge of conspiracy to bomb an Air-India jet out of New York)

Dosanjh, Ujjal (moderate Sikh Vancouver lawyer who went on to become B.C. premier and later a federal cabinet minister)

Doust, Len, (prominent lawyer hired to aid with the Crown's case against Inderjit Singh Reyat)

Dulai, Pary (Jaswinder Parmar's friend hired as an investigator by the Bagri defence team)

Gill, Gurmit Singh (Babbar Khalsa director from Kamloops)

Gill, Balwant Singh (moderate Sikh leader who received threats)

Gill, Gurdev Singh (Babbar Khalsa International leader in Canada and former Khalsa School director)

Gill, Joginder Singh (Nanaimo man who drove Parmar and Mr. X to see Reyat on June 4, 1985)

Gill, Karam Pal Singh (former Punjab police chief who eradicated the separatist movement there)

Narwal, Avtar Singh (Babbar Khalsa, Kamloops)

Narwal, Jethinder Singh "Roman" (alleged gangster, son of Avtar Narwal)

Parmar, Jaswinder (Talwinder's son)

Parmar, Kulwarn Singh (Talwinder's brother)

Parmar, Narinder (Talwinder's son)

Parmar, Rajinder (Talwinder's daughter)

Parmar, Surinder (Talwinder's wife)

Parmar, Talwinder Singh (founder, Babbar Khalsa and suspected Air-India mastermind)

Pawa, Amarjit Singh (former owner Friendly Travels agency, Air-India suspect who died in the mid-1990s)

Peck, Richard (Bagri defence lawyer)

Premika (alias for Vancouver single mother, Crown witness against Bagri)

Purewal, Tarsem Singh (publisher of *Des Pardes*, slain in 1995)

Rai, Amrit Singh (former national spokesman, ISYF)

Reyat, Inderjit Singh (convicted in the Narita bombing and pleaded guilty to manslaughter in the Air-India bombing)

Reyat, Satnam (wife)

Rowe, Nick (CSIS agent who met with Rani, Crown witness)

Sandhu, Daljit Singh (former Ross Street temple president and Malik defence witness)

Sandhu, Satwant Singh (electronics expert and former Khalsa School and credit union director who testified for Malik)

Schneider, John (former RCMP officer who headed the Air-India Task Force in the 1990s)

Sidhu, Malkiat Singh (Punjabi politician shot near Gold River, B.C.)

Singh, Bhai Jiwan (spiritual leader, AKJ)

Singh, Manmohan (former Vancouver restaurant owner and spokesperson for ISYF)

Singh, Ranjit (former *jathedar* of the Akal Takht, central ruling body of the Golden Temple)

Singh, Tejinder Pal (the convicted hijacker who was living in Khalsa School)

Sivia, Gurdeep Singh (former British Babbar Khalsa leader arrested in India in 1992)

Smart, Bill (Malik's lawyer)

Solvason, Bob (former RCMP sergeant, took Hayer's first formal statement)

Stagg, Mark (Daniel Brown's shipmate)

Tait, Mark (RAF winchman)

Tammen, Michael (Bagri defence team)

The farmer (former Malik associate, whose name is protected by court order, became a Crown witness at the Air-India trial)

The millworker (Crown witness, whose identity is also protected, who came forward only in late 2003 and said Malik asked him to carry bomb to airport)

Trimble, Dr. Edward (defence expert on aircraft accidents)

Uppal, Aniljit Singh (Malik's key ally, former Khalsa School director)

Wright, Bob (led the Air-India prosecution team)